A TENDER ROAD Home

A TENDER ROAD HOME

The Story of How God Healed a Marriage
Crippled by Anger and Abuse

PAUL & SUSIE LUCHSINGER

WITH KEN ABRAHAM

BROADMAN
&HOLMAN
PUBLISHERS

Nashville, Tennessee

© 1997
by Paul and Susie Luchsinger
All rights reserved
Printed in the United States of America

4260-82
0-8054-6082-9

Published by Broadman & Holman Publishers, Nashville, Tennessee
Acquisitions and Development Editor: Vicki Crumpton
Page Design: Anderson Thomas Design

Dewey Decimal Classification: 362.82
Subject Heading: FAMILY VIOLENCE
Library of Congress Card Catalog Number: 97-13819

Library of Congress Cataloging-in-Publication Data
Luchsinger, Paul, 1955-
    A tender road home : the story of how God healed a marriage crippled by anger and abuse / Paul and Susie Luchsinger.
        p.   cm.
    ISBN 0-8054-6082-9
    1. Marriage. 2. Communication in marriage. 3. Marriage—
Religious aspects. I. Luchsinger, Susie, 1957- . II. Title.
    HQ734.L7678   1997
    306.81—dc21
                                                                97-13819
                                                                CIP

1 2 3 4 5   01 00 99 98 97

CONTENTS

❦

♪ *written by Susie*
written by Paul 👢

ACKNOWLEDGMENTS

First of all, we would like to graciously thank you, the reader, for having enough faith in God and us to pick this book up, buy it, and finally, read it. We hope you enjoy our story and that you find a bit to chew on for awhile.

Thanks to all who have played a part in our lives—from minute to humongous—our parents, siblings, cousins, aunts and uncles, grandmas and grandpas.

To our buddies and friends from the past—thanks for helping God mold us!

To brothers big enuff (for you Hutch) and bold enough (for you Jimbo) to believe God's Word and get involved intimately with our lives, and especially mine (Paul)! Thanks!

To Vicki Crumpton of Broadman and Holman for believing enough in two Okies to listen to our story. To Charley Redmond who got the ball rolling.

To Ken Abraham who stuck with us through thick and thin to get this story together. We talk long, hard, and fast, but Ken is patient and enduring. Ken, it's been a hard eighteen months, but there's a light at the end of the tunnel. Hope it's not a train! Thank you!

Finally, to my (Susie's) first grade teacher, Mrs. Eula Kelly, who spanked me one day for being in the coat closet too long. If she'd never done that, I might still be hiding all these skeletons in the closet. Boy, it feels good to clean 'em out!

Chapter 1

THIS CAN'T BE
HAPPENING TO US!

$\mathcal{I}$ saw Paul's strong right hand coming in my direction and in an instant of time, a million things raced through my mind. I knew that if his fist was closed, I was a dead woman. My husband, Paul Luchsinger, had the strength of a steer—in fact more strength than most steers. Paul earned his living and reputation by wrestling steers to the ground with nothing more than his own brute strength. Not a big man by some standards, his five-foot, ten-inch frame was rock solid muscle, and the grip of his hand could crush another man's hand or my neck just as easily.

Ordinarily, Paul was a happy-go-lucky, congenial cowboy, smiling at everybody and waving or talking to everyone. Most of our friends or relatives would not even have imagined Paul rampaging through the house like a raging bull, spewing harsh, demeaning epithets, breaking up furniture and throwing it out into the yard. Few people were aware of the explosive power of Paul's temper, but I knew that if that seething volcano within him erupted in my direction, I could count on a steady flow of hot words, blows, and bruises.

I had noticed the tenseness beginning to build in Paul a few days earlier. As he often did before a violent blowout, he became somber and untalkative, clenching his jaw in anger. His eyes took on a dark, glassy look, darting back and forth like a wild animal. Both of us could tell that he was about to blow his stack, but neither of us knew what to do to prevent it.

The afternoon of the blowup started out quite pleasantly. It was 1988; Paul and I and our children—E. P., our five-year-old son, and Lucchese (pronounced Lu-cay'-see) our two-year-old daughter—were in our Allegro motor home, parked outside a church in Llano, Texas, where I was to do a concert that night and Paul was to give his testimony of how Jesus had changed his life. Since we had arrived early, we turned the afternoon into a picnic, grilling out on the Allegro's roll-out grill, playing ball with the kids on the church lawn, and having a great family day. Later that afternoon, I was teaching E. P. to read. Although E. P. had not yet started kindergarten, he was extremely bright and easily took to reading. Everything was going fine until Paul took over while I took a break to fix us something for supper.

Paul was on the couch with E. P. "What's that letter?" Paul asked loudly, pointing to an "A."

E. P. knew what the letter was, but Paul's intensity was a little more than E. P. could handle. The boy wanted to please his daddy, but he quickly became so nervous and flustered, he could not speak. As E. P. looked up into Paul's demanding eyes, our son's little hands began to sweat.

"Come on, E. P. " Paul chided him harshly. "You know what that letter is. What's that letter?" I knew that Paul was trying to encourage our son, but his manner was so forceful he frightened E. P. instead. I could see that E. P. was becoming more and more upset, and because his daddy was so emphatic, E. P. retreated into silence, like a turtle pulling back into its shell. His little hands, however, were shaking.

"Paul, I think you are making E. P. nervous," I said.

"What? I'm not making him nervous. Now, what is this letter E. P.?" Paul demanded, pointing again to the letter "A."

E. P. looked at the letter, yet no words came out of his mouth.

"You know what it is!" Paul bellowed at E. P. "What is it?"

"Paul!" I pleaded.

Paul was convinced that E. P. was simply being obstinate, that he knew the correct answer, but he would not say.

"Paul, you are scaring him," I spoke in E. P.'s defense.

"You just stay out of this. I'll deal with my boy my own way."

"Paul, the boy is scared!"

"I told you to stay out of this!" In what seemed a single motion, Paul leaped up from the motor home couch and in one powerful burst shoved me at the same time. I felt my feet leave the floor as I flew through the air, slamming into the side wall of the motor home, my head bouncing off the wall like a basketball off a back board. I crumpled in a heap on the floor, pain throbbing through my entire body. I just wanted to lie there and die, but Paul was already hovering over me. He was not done yet.

"I told you to mind your own business!" Paul roared. His eyes darted back and forth in uncontrolled rage.

"E. P. is my business!" I said through my tears. "He's my son, too, you know."

"Don't tell me whose son he is. I know whose son he is!" With that, Paul began kicking me in my behind with the edge of his cowboy boot. Each blast from his boot jolted me a few feet across the floor. Like a body receiving electrical shocks, I jerked spasmodically with each blow, and then curled into a fetal position on the floor once again, trying to protect my myself from the next kick that was sure to come. Paul kicked me inch by inch, all the way to the back of the motor home, where he turned around and started kicking me back toward the front of the vehicle.

"Leave me alone!" I finally screamed at the top of my lungs.

Two-year-old Lucchese was terrified and crying along with E. P. They were both cowering in a corner, behind the driver's seat of the motor home.

Satisfied that I was not going anywhere, Paul turned his anger toward little E. P. Paul picked the child up by the arm, dangling him in the air, and began to boot the boy in the behind. Each kick from the side of Paul's boot contorted E. P.'s body like a rag-doll. E. P. screamed and screamed.

"Next time you tell me the answer when I ask you a question, ya hear?" Paul yelled into E. P.'s ear.

Still dangling between heaven and earth, sobbing violently, E. P. was in no condition to answer.

"Do you hear me?" Paul bellowed again.

Miraculously, E. P. mustered enough courage to blurt, "Yes, sir" through his convulsive gasps for air.

Paul flipped E. P. back onto the couch and went over and slumped into a chair on the other side of the motor home. E. P. and Lucchese continued bawling loudly, but I remained motionless on the floor, my head down on my forearms with just enough space between my arms that my eyes could keep a wary watch on Paul, should he decide to initiate another attack. For the longest time, I simply laid on the floor and wept, too traumatized to move. I tried to make sense of it, but for the life of me, I couldn't understand what had caused Paul to become so angry. I knew that Paul wanted to control every part of our lives; he always wanted to do things his way. But what caused him to become so violent? It must be my fault, I thought, but what did I do?

For the moment, he seemed calm enough; with his head leaning back on the chair, his eyes closed, looking similar to a spent prizefighter. The storm having subsided for the moment, it seemed safe to take stock of what had just happened.

It wasn't the first time I had experienced an outburst of Paul's violent temper. Domestic violence had been a part of our relationship since the early days of our marriage. Paul and I married on November 27, 1981, and at first our marriage was one of absolute newlywedded bliss. Paul was rodeoing on the professional circuit and I was singing country music on the road professionally with my sister, Reba McEntire. Paul and I would sometimes go for several weeks without seeing each other. When we reunited on the road somewhere or at home in Chockie, Oklahoma, we were like two teenagers who were madly in love with one another.

But by early 1984, through a series of events we will be telling you about in the pages ahead, Paul began venting his anger violently. At first Paul took out his frustrations by simply smashing things around the house, but before long, he moved to grabbing me and shoving me to the floor, kicking me in the rear, and utterly humiliating me by his demeaning words and actions.

One of the reasons I put up with Paul's temper was that he apologized immediately after each incident, always asking for my forgiveness and promising not to let his temper get the best of him again. He felt so ashamed for what he had done. That strong, tough rodeo cowboy would cry like a baby. "I am so sorry, Susie," he'd say. "Please forgive me." His apologies were always so heartfelt that when he asked me to forgive him, I always did. "It will never happen again," Paul promised, and I believed he was sincere.

Paul wasn't putting on an act. He truly was sorry. He wasn't just apologizing to get me to stay with him. He was extremely remorseful for what he had done.

Nevertheless, despite Paul's profuse apologies, we had opened the proverbial "Pandora's box." Paul had discovered that he could control me by not controlling his temper. It was only a matter of time before we experienced another eruption. The violence continued, escalating in frequency and intensity. So did the emotional stress with which we were living. I found myself becoming more guarded in my conversations with Paul because I constantly feared that I might say something wrong. Mistrust and jealousy came to characterize Paul's attitude toward me.

Not that our relationship was totally bad; oh, no; just the opposite. Ironically, when things were good in our relationship, they were very good! We enjoyed many elements of an extremely well-balanced, loving marriage. We talked and laughed, worked and played together like any other happily married couple. I rejoiced at Paul's rodeo victories, and Paul listened proudly when he heard me singing in Reba's shows. But when Paul's temper exploded, our dream marriage quickly turned into a nightmare.

After more than seven years of verbal and physical abuse, I was nearing the end of my rope. I had thought that the problem would be solved when in late 1984 Paul and I had genuinely committed our lives to Jesus Christ. We had been casual, compromising, convenient Christians before that time, but after our "recommitment," we were sold out. I decided to quit singing country music, start singing Christian music, and join Paul on the rodeo circuit.

God blessed our efforts and many people received spiritual help as a result of Paul's and my presentation of the gospel—but the abuse never stopped. I kept asking myself, How can we be ministering to other people while this is going on in our lives?

After the 1988 incident in Llano, that night, as he had done on so many other occasions, Paul wanted to apologize and make up before going into the church service.

"I am so sorry, Susie. I just don't know why I do these things. I'm sorry for hitting you and I am really sorry for kicking E. P. I know he was trying to read for me, and I probably scared him. I guess maybe I was just jealous of all the attention you have been giving him. I'm sorry, really I am. Please forgive me, Susie."

My back got stiff. I didn't want to have any part of that. Of course, we needed to make up, but I didn't want to make up just so we could go minister at the church. I wanted Paul's apology to be a first step to a new quality of relationship, not simply another Band-Aid to cover the most recent emotional, spiritual, and physical bruises.

Nevertheless, we had to go inside the church and sing and talk about God's power to heal hurting relationships, and I knew I could not do that very well if I was harboring unforgiveness in my heart toward Paul. Gradually, I warmed up to him, and allowed him to wrap me in his arms. Paul pulled me close to him and hugged me for a long time. "I love you, Susie. I'm sorry. Please, please forgive me," Paul sobbed into my shoulder.

"I forgive you, Paul," I answered as I had so many times before. The words had grown almost insignificant to me.

I closed my eyes and thought, *How did we ever come to this point in our relationship?* And more importantly, *Where are we going from here?*

Chapter 2

BORN
COUNTRY

$\mathcal{B}$eing "country" has never been an act for the McEntire family. We were born and raised as country folks. Along with three siblings, I grew up on a ranch in southeastern Oklahoma, thirty miles south of McAlester and fifteen miles north of Atoka. I am the "baby," the youngest of the four McEntire kids. Our oldest sister, Alice Lynn, is the "stable" one, our security blanket. "Pake," our one brother, is two years younger than Alice. "Pake" is a shortened version of Pecos Pete, the nickname Mama and Daddy gave to him while he was still in Mama's womb. Pake's real name is Del Stanley, but I could probably count on one hand how many times I've heard him called that. Next in line, and two years older than me, is my sister Reba. You may have heard of her since she's done all right for herself singing country music, but she's still just Reba to me. But more about that later.

My ancestors, especially my great-grandparents on the McEntire side of the family, were mostly backwoods people. My grandpap, John Wesley McEntire, was born in a wagon at Lula, Indian Territory, in February 1897. He was raised with five brothers and three sisters. He didn't have much of anything to speak of materially, and after the Great Depression hit, he had even less. But he still had his dignity. He became one of the original rodeo cowboys—and a good one too—helping to establish the Cowboys' Turtle Association, one of the first organizations of cowboys to be formed when rodeo was evolving out of ranch work and becoming a professional sport in the 1920s and 1930s. In 1934, he established himself as a champion steer-roper when he won the steer-roping event at the Cheyenne Frontier Days Rodeo in Cheyenne, Wyoming, one of the premier rodeos in the world then and today. Unfortunately, most of Grandpap's winnings never made it home. When he won money on the rodeo circuit, he usually "hooped it off," which means he would squander it away before he got home. It was Grandpap's reputation as a prankster and character, as well as a champion rodeo cowboy, that the rest of the McEntires inherited as their legacy.

Fortunately, his wife, Alice Kate Hayhurst McEntire, was a school teacher during the post-Depression years. Grandma Alice's meager salary was often all she and Grandpap had to live on during those days. They moved onto some land that they did not own just down the hill from the Limestone Gap School, about three miles north of where Paul and I and our children still live today. They made their home in "the cake house," a small tin shack that had been used to store cattle feed. The shack was never intended to house a family, but after many improvements and additions, my daddy grew up in the cake house and still speaks fondly of playing on sacks of feed Grandpap used to store there.

Grandpap was a happy-go-lucky man with little concern for the niceties of life. Grandma Alice thought differently. She liked pretty things such as china and silver and nice furniture. She died before I was born, so I never got to know her. But when I was little, Mama allowed me to hunt through Grandma McEntire's old tin trunk, filled with fancy hats, her best china, silver, and other priceless treasures. Grandma Alice must have been quite a woman. I've been told that she was a Christian and that she read Bible stories to her students in school.

My daddy, Clark Vincent McEntire, was born November 30, 1927, and weighed twelve pounds (Daddy says he was weighed on a cotton scale). He was an only child and the apple of Grandma and Grandpap's eye. Daddy quickly adopted the value system: "You better keep everything you got, save it, and make it good." At least part of the reason he developed that mind-set about work and money was because what Grandpap didn't squander he gave away, nearly everything he ever earned. He'd literally give someone the shirt off his back. Consequently, as my daddy was growing up, if he wanted anything, he learned how to work hard and to give generously, but also how to save and invest his money wisely.

Daddy learned to rope steers when he was just a boy. He entered his first amateur roping contest in 1939 when he was twelve years old. By nineteen, Daddy had won the Pendleton Round-Up All-Around Cowboy title in Pendleton, Oregon, winning the most money in two events. By 1949, he was the fifth-highest-paid steer-roper in the Rodeo Cowboy Association, earning $1,222. He won the world championship for tie-down steer-roping in 1957, 1958, and 1961. The best year of Daddy's rodeo career, 1957, he earned $5,184, a sizeable sum in those days. Daddy once won a horse trailer; another time he won a car at a calf-roping competition in Carrollton, Texas. Mama took the car and traded it for eighty acres of land for a home. To say the least, rodeo has been good to Daddy! Once he commented, "Rodeo was better to me than most people." Daddy claims he learned to read by trying to figure out the road signs on the way to rodeos.

Today, Daddy still looks the part of a rough-and-tough steer-roper and rancher. He acts serious, kinda quiet at first, but his personality will fool you; he is really quite an entertainer. Daddy likes to tell jokes and stories. He can talk to anybody; never meets a stranger, and will strike up conversation with passersby at bus stations, airports, anywhere. I'm convinced that we McEntires inherited a lot of our "entertainment gifts" from Daddy.

They're not making many like him anymore.

Growing up, Daddy wasn't too interested in dating, but one day he happened by Elvin and Reba Smith's farm. There he saw their daughter, Jacqueline, a redheaded, freckle-faced girl carrying two five-gallon buckets of water and slop to feed her daddy's hogs. *That girl might just fit into my business*, Daddy thought. Obviously, young Jacqueline knew how to work and how to get by with very little. In those parts, those were two good qualifications for marriage.

In 1946, Daddy went to New York City to compete in a thirty-day rodeo at the Madison Square Garden. Jacqueline Smith had already made an impression on Daddy's practical side, but while he was in New York, he realized that he missed that redhead more than he ever dreamed possible, especially when he heard Gene Autry sing "Sioux City Sue" at every performance throughout the thirty days. Every time Daddy heard the lyric, "Your hair is red, your eyes are blue; I'd swap my horse and dog for you," he longed to return to Oklahoma and see his favorite redhead. She had to be a special woman for Daddy to even consider trading his horse or dog!

Clark McEntire married Jacqueline Smith on March 17, 1950. Daddy was twenty-two and Mama was twenty-three. To this day neither of them will admit to asking the other to get married. Daddy didn't have much money in those days, so Mama bought her own wedding ring for twenty-seven dollars on credit.

Mama was teaching school at the time, while Daddy continued rodeoing, trying to win enough money to get a better start in the cattle business. Daddy enjoyed rodeoing and the fame and money it brought him, but he looked at it as a means to an end. His winnings paid their grocery bill, but his real goal was to own a big cattle ranch. Mama continued teaching school until my oldest sister, Alice, was born in 1951. Mama and Daddy named Alice after Grandma Alice, who had died the year before.

Because all our grandparents, aunts, uncles, and cousins lived within ten miles of us, I grew up surrounded by relatives. My cousins were like my brothers and sisters. We were a big, happy family, working and playing together.

Grandpap McEntire was around the house a lot as I was growing up, helping Daddy on the ranch, rounding up the cattle, and sometimes us kids too, with his famous "McEntire Yell." The yell was a sort of whoop and a holler mixed together and the sound carried far across the acres. If one of us kids ever got lost, we'd just let out a holler something like Grandpap's. He'd holler back, and eventually we'd find each other. Grandpap was a one-of-a-kind individual. When he walked, his feet sort of slapped the ground as a result of a knee injury when a horse flipped over backward with him.

And did Grandpap ever love to eat! Once when he and Daddy were gathering a stray steer off a neighbor's place, the family invited them in for a meal. Grandpap promptly set about eating all the woman's homemade butter, as Daddy kept trying to move it out of his reach.

Grandpap could never get enough of anything. For instance, no matter how much water Grandpap might have in his glass, he always raised it to get a little more any time it was offered.

One of his favorite things to do was to sit in front of our huge fireplace with his long legs crossed. Because he knew it rankled Mama, he liked to see how far away he could get from the flames and still spit accurately enough to make the fire hiss. Mama would fume, especially when Grandpap would spit and miss the fire. Grandpap would look at us kids and wink. Mama wouldn't say anything to him, but everyone could tell that she was furious.

Another family member who was around our house a lot as I was growing up was one of Grandpap's brothers, named Keener—we called him Uncle Keno. He was a bachelor, born in 1901, and was already moving kinda slow when I was just a kid. Uncle Keno never gave advance warning that he was coming to visit because he didn't have a phone. But we always had plenty of time to get things in order after he arrived. Uncle Keno had an old, green Chevrolet pickup truck. He would pull up to our house and park the pickup in the corner of the yard. He moved so slowly that we could sweep the floors in the time it would take him to get out of the truck. As I watched him, I'd call out to Reba, Alice, and Mama, "He's opened the door. He has one leg out. . . ." It was usually a long process.

When Uncle Keno finally managed to inch his way out of the truck, he'd stand up straight, pull up his britches almost as high as his armpits, and cinch up his belt. After what seemed like an eternity, he'd shuffle his way up to the house, where Reba and I were waiting for him. We were always excited to see Uncle Keno coming because he always brought us those peanut-shaped, marshmallow candies called "Circus Peanuts," as well as handfuls of candy corn. Life was slow and easy as far as Uncle Keno was concerned.

Grandpap was just the opposite; he was always in a hurry. His car—which he called his "hoopie"—was always banged up. With little wonder!

He rarely paid attention when he was driving. He'd come wheeling around our house, stirring up a cloud of Oklahoma dust.

"Watch out, kids!" Mama shouted. "Here comes Grandpap!" The action wasn't over when Grandpap somehow managed to come to a stop. That was the most dangerous time of all. Suddenly, he'd throw that car into reverse and back up, not looking all the while, until he banged into a tree. Then he'd hop out and greet everyone as though nothing had happened. He was totally oblivious to the fact that he had just wrecked his car.

Grandpap McEntire encouraged us kids to explore life. "Oh, you can drive," he'd tell us, with a wave of his hand. "Go ahead and drive the pickup. Better yet, take my hoopie." Of course, even Alice was several years away from having a legal driver's license, but that didn't matter to Grandpap. He always wanted us to live "the more exciting life."

He was the first one to give us chewing tobacco. Of course, at first it was strictly for medicinal purposes, using the tobacco juice to draw the inflammation from bee stings and other insect bites. But all of us kids were convinced by the way Grandpap chewed his tobacco that it had to be fun. He had a habit of spitting out the window of his truck, spattering the side of his vehicle with tobacco juice. In the wintertime, instead of rolling his window down, Grandpap simply spat in the opposite floorboard. When he turned on the heat in the truck, the air inside soon became almost unbearable from the smell of rancid tobacco juice.

Once we kids asked Grandpap for some tobacco as we were riding in the back of the pickup truck. Grandpap was happy to comply. I stuck it in my mouth and started chewing just like I had seen Grandpap do so many times. Before long, bouncing over the rough roads, I was sicker than a dog! I couldn't even stand up. I had to sit down quickly and take deep gulps of fresh air, trying all the while to make sure I didn't swallow any more of the tobacco juice. That about got me off tobacco forever.

Elvin and Reba Smith, my grandparents on my mama's side, were hardworking farmers. They weren't big-time farmers with their own combines and tractors. To make money they grew cotton and also sold cream. They had a garden in the backyard where they grew their own food to eat. The part of their yard that wasn't covered by the garden was covered by peach trees. Grandma didn't just preserve her food in pints or quarts; she canned in half gallons! Grandma and Grandpa were so self-sufficient they rarely went to town more than once a week. Everyone around knew that if they needed food, they could find some at Grandma and Grandpa Smith's house.

Grandma was a tall Native American-looking woman with long, dark hair and high cheekbones. She sang a lot around the house. Grandpa was shorter than she and could easily be located simply by listening for his whistling. Mama called him "Whistling Shorty." About the only time Grandpa wasn't whistling was when he was hunting for squirrels, which was one of his favorite things to do.

When I was five years old, Mama took a job working for the Superintendent of Schools at Kiowa, Oklahoma, where all us kids eventually graduated from high school. Since I was too young to go to school, I stayed with Grandma Smith during the day while Mama and Daddy worked. Grandma and Grandpa Smith lived about ten miles from us, so when Daddy couldn't watch me, Mama arranged for the school bus to stop at our house, and I rode the bus over to Grandma's house. It was like having my own chauffeur. The bus driver, Gene Wilson, lived up at Limestone Gap and was a friend of our family. He took extra special care of me and made sure I didn't get off the bus until he pulled in front of my appointed stop.

Grandma Smith was typical of rural Oklahoma homemakers in the 1950s. By the time I arrived each morning, she had already been up for hours, doing her daily chores, gathering eggs, and milking cows. She always had hot cocoa on the stove waiting for me.

Grandma's house was warm and inviting. It was not a large, fancy house, but she made it comfortable and cozy. And could Grandma ever cook! She cooked up the best batch of fried chicken, biscuits, and blackberry cobbler imaginable!

Grandma didn't have a television, and video cassette recorders hadn't yet been invented. She couldn't afford to buy me lots of toys, but she gave me something far more precious—her time. We'd spend long, lazy days together, whether sitting on the porch churning butter, or sharing bites of a pear, freshly picked off the tree. It was amazing how slow-paced Grandma Smith's life was, yet she was constantly busy, taking care of her household. I was content in those surroundings. We didn't have to do anything special. To Grandma, life itself was special; just being together was special. She talked with me, laughed with me, and told me fascinating stories from the Bible. Grandma had a way of making those old stories come to life.

Sometimes Mama and Daddy had to be away for several weeks at a time, either at rodeos or out scouting for new cattle to purchase. That meant I got to stay overnight with Grandma and Grandpa Smith. Their house was hot at night, if not from the sweltering Oklahoma summers, then from Grandma's cooking and baking, but I didn't care. Grandma and Grandpa Smith did not have an air conditioner, so Grandma opened the windows. With my nose pressed against the screen, I'd listen to the bobwhites and whippoorwills sing as I drifted off to sleep. It was a special time in my life.

Although Grandma Smith taught me many domestic skills, the most important things she taught me were about Jesus. I have many special pictures of Grandma Smith indelibly impressed in my mind, but one stands out more than all the others. It is an image of her kneeling by her bed, her long, black, gray-streaked hair flowing down her back. She and Grandpa had two double beds in their bedroom, so when I was visiting, Grandpa slept in one bed, snoring away, and Grandma and I slept in the other. Every night, before she climbed into bed, Grandma got down on her knees to pray and laid all of her cares and burdens at the feet of the Lord.

She prayed so lovingly and so sweetly, thanking God for our daily provisions, and bringing her special requests to Him. Sometimes I couldn't understand all she said, but I could tell by the peaceful expression on her face that she was in the presence of God.

Grandma introduced me to Jesus and taught me how to pray. She said, "When you pray, always thank Jesus. Thank Him for everything." Grandma was always looking for the signs of the times. She frequently reminded me that Jesus is coming soon. "The end is coming," Grandma warned. "Jesus is coming back to earth again. You need to be ready when He comes." I lived each day of my childhood wondering if that day might be the day of Christ's return. As I grew older I was less conscious of Jesus coming back, but occasionally, I'd look up at the sky and recall Grandma's words. I still do.

Grandpa was a believer too, but his faith was a bit different. He often seemed to have trouble living the way the Bible said. He especially battled impatience and anger, perhaps stemming back to the hurt he experienced when he had been orphaned as a little boy and shuffled from home to home. Grandpa sometimes lost his temper with Grandma and treated her cruelly. They loved one another immensely and had a tremendous respect for one another, yet every once in a while, Grandpa's temper would get the best of him and he would lash out at Grandma. Grandma never responded unkindly. She was very submissive and patient, and I carried memories of her example with me into adulthood. Years later, when my husband, Paul, would lose his temper with me, I drew strength from the example Grandma had set.

Grandma's good influence got me going to church as a child. I went to church with Grandma and Grandpa Sunday morning, Sunday evening, and Wednesday night. My parents didn't attend church regularly when I was little, at least not that I can remember. Mama and Daddy believed in God, but church-going wasn't a priority to them.

Grandma, Grandpa, and I went to the small, one-room country church at Chockie. Our congregation was so small—probably less than twenty people attended regularly—we couldn't even afford a pastor most of the time. In fact, when the choir got up to sing, there was nobody left in the pews to sing to! When the songleader asked for requests during the congregational singing, I always asked for "When the Roll Is Called Up Yonder." I still love to hear and sing that great old song.

One time the First Baptist Church in Kiowa was having a revival. Pake, Reba, and I decided to go—probably because most of our best friends were going to be there, and most certainly, Grandma's prayers influenced us. At the close of the service, during the invitation, all three of us—Pake, Reba, and I—went forward and received Christ as our Savior and were baptized. Shortly thereafter, we went to Grandma Smith's sickbed and told her that we had accepted Christ. I will never forget how brightly her face shined when she heard the news. My friend and mentor died in May 1970 when I was in the sixth grade. It was one of the saddest times of my life, but I know she's rejoicing at how my life has turned out to give glory to God.

Although I was surrounded by family as I grew up, in many ways I was very much a loner. I was content to play with my dolls by myself. Just as well, since nobody wanted to play dolls along with me. Alice was six years older than I, and was a typical tomboy. She would much rather be up in the hills chasing steers through the brush. She was not interested in playing with dolls. Neither was Reba, who said that she never had any interest in talking to anything that couldn't talk back. Pake was older, too, and was busy helping Daddy and doing other "boy" things.

I dressed my dolls up in hand-me-down outfits, including an old diaper with real diaper pins. I gave each of my dolls a personality and talked to them as though they were real live brothers and sisters. I always had a doll and a little suitcase to carry their various outfits with me. My dolls were my best friends.

My imagination could transform the most mundane situations into fascinating adventures. For instance, Daddy and Pake practiced roping at the "arena," which is what we called the roping pen. The fence posts of the arena were made out of *bois d'arc* wood. The wood lent itself to infestation by ants, which would bore holes into the wood and make their nests inside. One day, while Daddy and Pake were roping, I became fascinated watching those ants going up and down the posts and inside little tunnels.

Soon I began to imagine the ants having conversations with one another. I'd give some of them names and special assignments on the posts. "Come on, Artie. Let's go down to the tunnel and get that big knothole cleaned out. Then we can come back up and get a bite to eat." The ants were a flurry of activity, and I would amuse myself for hours by watching them, amazed at the weight they carried and their incessant work.

Another day, I went up on the hill with Daddy and stayed with him all day while he built a fence across a pond. I was sitting in the truck, watching him, when I noticed that there were bunches of horseflies buzzing around the windows. Soon I began imagining various games with the horseflies. I had conversations with them and, like my dolls and the ants, the horseflies soon took on personalities of their own. Because my imagination was always active, I was never bored playing by myself.

Mama says that Reba and I were really different in that respect. Reba was a spark plug, a bundle of energy, someone who had to be going strong, doing something all the time. Reba conversed readily with almost anyone. Me? I didn't talk much—nobody knew what I was thinking. I was just as happy to go off by myself and let my imagination run free.

Because I was quieter and more introspective than my brother and sisters, I was a prime target for their teasing. Pake and Reba especially loved to pick on me. Reba loved to dish it out, because as the next youngest, she was the object of a lot of teasing and jokes herself. Sometimes Reba left herself wide open. For instance, one time on the way home from a rodeo we stopped to eat at a new place that we had heard about called Pizza Hut. After we were all seated, Reba excused herself to go to the bathroom and came back just in time to hear Mama tell the waitress, "We'll have hamburger," ordering the topping for the pizza.

"Hamburger?" Reba cried. "I thought we're gonna have pizza!"

Pake loves to remind Reba of her naiveté to this day!

Alice was not exactly innocent either. Because she was the oldest, Mama and Daddy often put Alice in charge of keeping order while they were working. When Alice had had her fill of Reba and me, she'd push us outside and lock us out of the house. Eventually, Reba and I wised up and unlocked the window screen to the bedroom we shared. When Alice locked us out, we'd moan, groan, and cry; but as soon as Alice thought she had won, Reba and I would climb through the bedroom window and surprise her.

One time when I was about seven years old, Reba and Pake conspired to convince me that I was an adopted child. "Why, look at yourself in a mirror, girl," Reba said with a straight face. "You don't even look like the rest of us. We all have red hair and freckles. You don't!"

I looked in a mirror, and sure enough, Reba was right. My hair was a sandy color at that time, nowhere near the reddish orange of Reba's or Pake's. And there wasn't a freckle on my face.

"That's right," Pake agreed. "If you don't have red hair and freckles, you ain't no real McEntire."

I was getting upset, so as I usually did, I sought solace in the company of my dolls. I was pouring out my heart to one of my favorites as I pulled another doll outfit from my suitcase and started to change the doll's dress.

That's when I saw it.

As I lifted my doll's dress to take it off, I let out a wail. Pake had painted my favorite doll's navel bright green!

That did it! First I started bawling, then slowly my hurt turned to anger. Finally, I got so mad, I told Reba and Pake that I was leaving. I was going to run away from home. I packed my doll and some of my clothes, slammed my doll's suitcase shut, and stormed out of the house and down the hill. Reba and Pake made no effort to stop me.

Down the hill I went, all the way to the "cattle guard," a grated bridge used to keep the cattle from going out the gate.

There, I stopped cold. I stood crying my eyes out. I knew I could go no further, and so did Reba and Pake. Any time one of us kids would threaten to run away, Mama said, "Go ahead and run. But if you ever go beyond that cattle guard, and cross those tracks, don't bother to come back."

So much for running away. I tearfully trudged back up toward our house, where Reba and Pake were rolling on the porch, howling with laughter.

Reba and Pake were just having fun with me, but as a child I had extreme feelings of insecurity, and their teasing didn't help. I sucked my thumb until I was in the third grade. I had a lisp when I spoke, and stuttered too. My insecurities accompanied me all through elementary school, high school, college, and into my marriage. Along the way, insecurity picked up a partner—fear of failure. This fear prevented me from accomplishing everyday tasks such as learning the multiplication tables and telling time, and later, from pressing on to more difficult college subjects such as accounting and statistics. It also caused me to shy away from many fun activities such as swimming in the deeper water, riding horses, and even singing in front of people.

Chapter 3 ♪   # LOVING WITHOUT SAYING SO

$\mathcal{I}$ rarely heard Mama and Daddy say the words "I love you" to each other. Until recent years, I cannot recall my Daddy telling me that he loved me. Nor did he ever say "I love you" to Alice, Pake, or Reba, for that matter. I thank God that on Daddy's birthday recently, I had the courage to tell him thanks for being my daddy, that I loved him, and I knew it wasn't easy raising us kids.

He replied, "Oh, it wasn't hard."

Daddy's mellowed over the years, and today he is better at expressing affection toward family members. But as I was growing up, he just didn't do that. Mama made up for Daddy's lack of verbal expressions of love. She lavished her love upon us.

I knew that Mama and Daddy loved each other. They just didn't say it out loud. On the other hand, they hardly ever had major disagreements. In fact, it was so rare that my parents had a fight, that one day, when they did have an argument before I went to school, I was afraid they would be divorced by the time I got home. It was just a little argument, but because I didn't see them arguing very often, I thought for certain our world was going to fall apart.

Daddy felt that he showed his love to his family by working hard to provide for us, which he did. He couldn't be bothered by saying the words "I love you."

"Mushy words turn my stomach," he'd say. He once told one of our friends, "I would just as soon someone tell me where to go as to say, 'I love you.' " Concerning some of our relatives, Daddy said, "They tell Grandma, 'I luuuuuve youuuuu, Grandma,' and it just makes me sick." Daddy lived by the adage, "Sure I love you. I take care of you, don't I?"

Daddy started ranching with just a few head of cattle, but by the time I was old enough to help, Daddy was buying a hundred head of cattle at a time and having them trucked in from Texas, Florida, or Mississippi. Each animal weighed about four hundred pounds, considered relatively small yearlings, but bigger than calves. Daddy grazed the cattle up in the hills, letting them grow to seven hundred to eight hundred pounds, at which point they would go to a feed lot, where they would be fattened still further and then sold to meat packers. Usually, Daddy made just enough money to buy more cattle and start all over again.

Taking care of the cattle was a family affair. Daddy expected all of us to be involved. He once said Reba and I could help him better than some boys. When we got a new load of cattle in, the work day started before day-break and ended after nightfall. Daddy's day began around 4:00 A.M., when he started planning the work he wanted to get done that day. Then he would wake us for breakfast. Mama would be getting ready to go to her job as the secretary to the school superintendent, so Daddy did the cooking— plenty of eggs fried in bacon grease and his special homemade bread that he called his "bachelor's bread."

Before the sun was even close to coming up, we were already on our horses, heading out to herd cattle. I didn't care much for those early morn-ing expeditions, not because I minded the work, but because Daddy was often curt and short-tempered early in the morning.

Daddy wasn't much on explaining things. As we mounted our horses, he'd say something such as, "Go up to the gap, and I will meet you on the flat," or "Go up on the hill about five hundred yards, and I will meet you at the gate." And all the while he was saying this, he was riding off and looking in the other direction.

Alice, Pake, Reba, and I would look at each other dumbfoundedly and ask, "What'd he say? Did you hear him?"

Daddy wasn't being mean; he just wasn't a communicator. To him, his instructions were perfectly clear. You could learn more by watching him because he's a doer, not a talker. He is more "at one" with the land and animals than any man I know. You don't get that out of a book. You don't get that unless you have lived that way, and Daddy has. To Daddy, telling us to "Go meet me at the gate," or "Meet me by the big rock" was just as plain as telling us to go down to the corner house and turn right. I understand that now, but I didn't when I was growing up.

We didn't dare ask Daddy what he meant. On those few times when one of us did hint that we didn't understand Daddy's instructions, he would become visibly irritated.

"Uh-oh!" one of us would say. "We shouldn't have said that."

I will always wonder how much easier our work would have been if we would have learned to communicate better. Today, I tell my kids, "If you don't understand what your daddy means when he gives you something to do, talk to him. Ask questions." Questions are for learning. How can a child learn without asking questions? That's something I was always too afraid to do with my own father.

Daddy's communication was no better when we were processing the cattle (vaccinating, castrating, and branding them). The cattle were used to the open country and were not accustomed to being herded into a narrow alley that forced them to walk single file into a "squeeze chute" to hold them still. Once we got an animal into the squeeze chute, we could brand it, vaccinate it, give it worm medicine to keep it free from parasites, eartag it, and if the animal was a bull, castrate it.

My job was to check to see whether they were bulls. At first I thought Daddy was just giving me a job to keep me busy, but I later realized the significance of my responsibilities. The animals' testicles have to be removed if the meat you purchase in the grocery store is to be tender. A steer—a castrated bull—grows fatter than one that is not castrated. A bull that is not castrated will grow muscle, which will cause the meat to be poor quality and tough. That is the meat they make bologna, hot dogs, and other junk food out of.

Also, if there is a female in the herd, the bull will try to mate with the female, which creates all sorts of problems for the rancher. Bulls will literally tear through a fence and fight with one another to get to the female. On the other hand, after a bull is castrated, he becomes easier to work with. All they do is eat and get fat, which makes them better for the marketplace.

My job put me right where the action was. As the animals were being moved toward the chute, I'd peer at the one about to go into the chute, check its anatomy, and call out, "D-D-Daddy, it's a b-b-bull." (I stuttered when I was a kid.)

In what seemed like one continuous action, Reba would then grab the animal's tail, pull it out of the way, and Daddy would step around the bull and whack off its testicles. Alice or Reba would then stick it with one needle to vaccinate it and another to inject some penicillin to keep it from getting infected. Needless to say, the newly castrated animal was not too thrilled with this entire procedure, so he would often react violently by kicking and bucking. It was not a safe place to be standing. The chute was often a hectic, noisy, tension-filled place. No wonder Daddy got so intense when one of us made a mistake.

There was little time for formal communication.

Daddy believed in corporal punishment too. He never debated whether to spank a child. He just did it. He used a buggy whip sometimes, cracking it across one of our behinds without a word of warning when we did something wrong. He also had a "quirt," a short, braided leather cord used by jockeys to whip horses, that he switched across the back of our legs. Yowee, that quirt got our attention. When he found himself without a whip or a switch, Daddy was not adverse to using his strong right leg and giving us a swift, hard boot in the rear. Daddy didn't put up with anyone questioning his authority, or any back talk from us kids. He may have been harsh, but when he disciplined us, we were quick to obey the next time. Years later, when my husband, Paul, wearing similar hard-edged cowboy boots, kicked me, it was not anything I had not felt before.

Nothing went to waste around our house, including the castrated bulls' testicles. They made good food, and we wintered well on them. As the bulls were castrated, we put the testicles in a bucket and took them to the house. We girls cleaned the testicles, then Mama sliced them up real thin, rolled them in flour, and fried them in hot grease. We called these delicious fried tidbits "mountain oysters." City slickers might not appreciate them, but around our parts, it was not unusual for people to pay four or five dollars a pound for mountain oysters.

In an interview on The Nashville Network, Reba jokingly told Ralph Emery that she didn't always admit to eating fried cattle testicles. When she was serving mountain oysters to out-of-state company for lunch, she'd tell the visitors they were having fish.

We always had plenty to eat as I was growing up, lots of meat and potatoes and vegetables, and "poke salad," made from poke weed that grew wild up in the hills. And Mama always had some mountain oysters ready to fry up in a hurry.

As I grew older, Daddy acquired more and more land. He paid about $5 to $11 an acre. It was mostly rocks and trees but Daddy saw more than that—he saw a cattle ranch. He bought the land and cleared it, little by little. He made cross fences and improved it, ran his cattle, and then would buy a little more land and add to what he had. Then the gas came in, and he was able to lease the mineral rights from the land. Later, he sold the timber from the land as well. With the profits he bought more land and more cattle. Daddy was fond of saying, "I hit a lick here and there," which is his way of saying that he made money sometimes and lost money others.

He would buy a poor yearling here, buy a poor piece of land there, and as Daddy once told Lorianne Crook and Charlie Chase on *Music City Tonight*, "Pretty soon land and cattle started sticking together like dough."

As of this writing, Mama is seventy years of age and Daddy is sixty-nine, and they still have seventeen thousand acres of ranch land. Daddy takes care of it with the help of a couple of hired hands. Mama is his chief bookkeeper and cook. They have no illusions about ever getting rich at ranching. Mama says, "Ranchers were never made to be rich anyway." But for them ranching remains the best lifestyle, because they are able to be their own bosses.

Daddy is the type of guy who won't take Social Security and doesn't want any handouts from the government. He says, "I'll pay my own way." Even when the government passes a bill to provide emergency aid to farmers and ranchers, Daddy won't take it. He says, "I don't need any help from the government. If I can't make it on my own, I'll quit!"

Daddy would go broke before he accepted a handout. He did just that two or three times while I was growing up, but he impressed me by being up-front and honest with his debtors. He simply went to the people to whom he owed money and told them, "I can't pay you right now, but I will get it to you as soon as I can." Then he'd go back to the ranch and start over. When he got some money, the first thing Daddy did was pay off the people he owed.

Daddy modeled honesty for us kids in other ways too. If one of the neighbors' head of cattle happened to get mixed in with ours, Daddy loaded it in his trailer and took it home. Then he'd call the neighbors and tell them, "I got your steer." It would have been easy for Daddy to simply ship the animal to market as his own, but he would not even consider doing such a thing. Everyone around Limestone Gap knows Clark McEntire is a man of integrity, a man who has a reputation of keeping his word.

Perhaps that explains why few people were surprised when in 1958 Daddy became a Christian. When he talks about things of the Lord, and about Christianity, he gets soft-hearted. Nevertheless, he doesn't have much time for the "organized church" or for "professional Christianity," including most preachers and all televangelists. He calls Christians "church people," and refers to preachers in less than complimentary terms as living on that "gimme money."

Part of Daddy's distrust of clergy may have come from his and Mama's wedding day. They set out to find a preacher who would perform the marriage ceremony for them. Someone suggested a certain preacher who had conducted weddings in the past, and told Daddy, "Oh, he'll charge you, maybe two or three dollars to marry you." Daddy didn't think that was too bad, so he and Mama contacted the preacher.

After the minister conducted the wedding, Daddy handed the preacher a twenty-dollar bill, expecting change. Twenty bucks was the sum of Daddy's savings at that point in his life. The preacher took the twenty, thanked Daddy, and walked away.

Daddy has been a little leery of most preachers ever since. Maybe that's why he was never bashful about raising his hand right in the middle of the preacher's sermon, especially when he didn't understand what the preacher meant by what he had said. One day in the middle of the preacher's sermon, Daddy raised his hand. "Now, hold on there," he said loudly. "What do I give ten percent of? You said I need to tithe to you before I pay my grocery bill?" Daddy wasn't being rude or belligerent. He just figured that if he was going to take time away from work to attend church, he wanted to get the most from the service. Although the preachers were cordial to Daddy, answering his questions succinctly but politely before continuing their remarks, I doubt that the various pastors who came our way were too disappointed when they looked out into our tiny congregation and didn't see Daddy's ruddy face staring back at them.

Mama was more subtle than Daddy, but she was just as cagey. She was a spunky redhead, but sometimes her bark was worse than her bite.

Our property was located just off the main highway that runs between Tulsa and Dallas. Often, people pulled off the road to rest or sleep, or simply to take a break. Mama wasn't too fond of that.

One evening, a car pulled off the road down near our cattle pens just as Mama and we kids were on our way to a basketball game. When Mama saw the uninvited visitors, she got riled. With a tough sounding voice, she said "I am not going to stand for that. I don't like people coming down on our property, throwing their old beer cans out on our ground and messing up everything." She said, "I am going to go down there and tell them what for."

As Mama drove down the hill, we just knew that she was going to tear into the folks in the car, and maybe even get into a fight. We remained still and quiet as she got out of our car and walked over to the driver's door of the parked vehicle. When the driver rolled down the window, to our surprise we heard Mama say in a sweet-as-sugar tone of voice, "May I help you?"

To this day, Mama insists that she told off the driver of the car, but we kids know better. The folks in that car explained to Mama that they had gotten tired and had pulled off to rest for a while. She said that's fine, but that she would appreciate it if they would go and leave our land, which they did.

Mama was always kind and considerate, but even Daddy knew to get out of the way when Mama was in a bad mood. On Reba's CBS television special, aired in 1995, Daddy joked, "My daddy always told me there are three things in life you don't need: a roguish sow, a fence-breaking cow, and a redheaded woman. And I wound up with all three!"

Although Daddy was the undisputed head of the McEntire clan, Mama was definitely the heart of our family. She wasn't able to go back to teaching school full time with four young ones, but when Alice was old enough to keep an eye on Pake, Reba, and me, Mama decided to take a job at a bait shop at Atoka Lake. Mama drove back and forth to work in a pickup truck with no starter and no brakes. She had to park on a hill to get the truck started. And once she got that pickup going, we weren't sure where or how she would get it stopped. She earned only $6 a day, but the extra income helped us get by.

Mama's heart, though, was in the school. She had started teaching at sixteen years of age. Back then, it wasn't necessary to have a certificate to teach, so she taught in a little, one-room schoolhouse at Tipperary, which eventually became the Chockie church. She traveled to and from school by horseback. Each morning, she started a fire in the potbelly stove before her students arrived. The students' ages and backgrounds spanned a wide gap. At one time Mama had thirty students, some of whom were older than she was. She would teach during the regular school term, and then catch the bus to go back to summer school during the week at Southeastern Oklahoma State College at Durant, about forty-five miles south, to get more hours toward her degree. Mama never got her teacher's degree, but I wouldn't count Mama out. She might get that teaching certificate yet!

One of the great things that Mama instilled within her children was a love for music, especially singing. We sang together all the time—around the supper table, in the car, traveling to a rodeo, just about anywhere. Mama taught us how to harmonize, and to this day, there is no music I enjoy more than that of close, family harmonies. Deep inside, I think Mama had an unfulfilled dream of being a professional singer; and although it seemed like a pipe dream, she believed that her kids would one day stand on a stage to live out her dreams.

Chapter 4 ♪ CHILDHOOD MEMORIES

$\mathscr{I}$n recent years an interviewer asked Daddy what he would do differently if he had the chance. Daddy didn't think long before he answered straightforwardly, "I wouldn't have any kids!"

Daddy kept up a rough, gruff exterior, but he also had a soft streak that he occasionally allowed us to see. For instance, when I was in the fourth grade, I won my school spelling bee. That day, I came home from school and, as usual, got right to work. The hours after school and before supper were always precarious around our house. We kids often avoided Daddy when we got home from school, because that was about the time he would put hay out for the cattle or doctor the sick ones.

Daddy put the hay out by standing in the bed of the pickup truck, scattering hay from side to side as one of us kids drove. I dreaded driving for Daddy when he was scattering hay because the ground was so rocky. If I wasn't careful, Daddy could easily get pitched right out of the back of the pickup. As a youngster barely able to tell my left from my right, let alone steer the truck in the proper direction, I'd hear him hollering, "Whoa! Whoa, I said!" in a tone of voice that said to me that Daddy was mad. Driving for Daddy was not my idea of fun. Consequently, I quickly learned that the best way to keep from having to help was to make myself scarce during the time between school and supper.

On the day I won the spelling bee, I heard Daddy coming up the hill in his pickup, so I went to the back porch and started gathering the laundry in preparation to wash it. *Keep busy. Avoid a confrontation,* I thought.

Suddenly I heard Daddy ask, "Where's Susie?"

Reba came in and whispered, "Susie, Daddy wants to talk to you."

"No! Tell him I'm busy," I implored my sister.

Reba shook her head. "No, Susie. He wants to talk to you right now."

I thought, *Oh, no! Daddy wants me to help him put out the hay for the cattle.* Reluctantly, I stopped sorting the clothes and resigned myself to hearing what I was certain would be, "Come drive for me." I could feel the fear of failure even before I attempted the task.

Slowly I walked back inside the house from the porch where I was working. I went in to where Daddy was and said, "Hi, Daddy. Did you need me?"

By Daddy's expression, I could tell he wasn't thinking about hay or cattle. "Now what's this I hear about you winning the spelling bee?" he asked.

I could feel my face blush with pride as I broke into a smile and said, "Yes, sir. I did win the spelling bee. I even beat Kelly Rhyne, an eighth-grader! And I get to go to Tulsa to the state competition."

"Well, that's good," Daddy replied. He reached into the pocket of his dirty Levis and pulled out two one-dollar bills. "You did good," he said with a smile.

Daddy didn't say much more, but I could tell he was proud of me. That was all that mattered to me. He and Mama and I made the trip to Tulsa and stayed overnight with Daddy's cousins the night before the state competition. I was thrilled that my parents took such an interest in what I was doing. I was eliminated in the second round on the word, "graphite," but I was proud to be there. (And I haven't misspelled that word since!)

It's a wonder any of us kids survived childhood, with runaway horses, rattlesnakes, and dangerous swimming holes part of our daily lives. One day, for instance, Daddy took Mama to the dentist and left Alice in charge. Now, there are three different views in our family as to how this happened, so here is mine. Alice, Pake, and I had been down at the roping pen and were on our way back to the house. Alice was riding a horse named Pelican, and Pake and I were on Ole Brownie. As we neared the gate at the bottom of the hill, Pake dismounted so he could open the gate. Alice rode right on through and straight toward the house. Apparently Brownie felt that he should do the same. He took off after Pelican—with me hanging on for dear life! Since I was young at the time, I didn't know how to get Brownie to stop. I was screaming at the top of my lungs as Brownie approached the house. Reba heard my screams and came running out the front door, but there was nothing she could do. Reba started screaming herself when she saw what was about to happen.

Just beyond our house was a double-line, wire clothesline. Brownie raced right under it with me still hanging on to the saddle. As the horse ran beneath the clothesline, both wires caught me full in the face, one about nose high and the other right in my mouth. I flew off the horse, flipped in the air, and landed hard on the ground. Blood was streaming down my face as Alice ran to my assistance. She took me inside and tried to clean me up. Then she held me up to the mirror and said, "Now, see here, Susie. You aren't hurt a bit." Not hurt? When I saw all the blood still dripping down my face, I thought I was dead!

Another time, I was riding behind Pake on his horse, when suddenly Pake shouted, "Duck!" I was pretty dense, to say the least, because instead of realizing we were going under the limbs of a pecan tree and I needed to protect my face, I raised higher, looked to the sky, and asked, "Where?"

Pake thought that was the funniest thing. The only time he'd laugh harder at me was when all of us kids were riding in the back of Daddy's pickup, and as the vehicle slowed down to stop, one of the kids would yell, "Last one out is a rotten egg!" Pake usually won. Thinking I had discovered a way to beat him, however, I'd sometimes jump out of the truck while it was still moving.

That was a mistake. *Splat!* I'd hit the ground like a sack of feed. I'd end up bawling while Pake, Alice, and Reba again howled with laughter at my expense. Worse yet, I repeated this mistake three times, once suffering a concussion from my tumble. Okay, so I don't give up easily. For years now, that story has been a favorite at all of our family gatherings.

Unquestionably, having four children within five years placed a strain on Mama and Daddy's budget as we were growing up. Daddy worked the ranch hard, but it seemed he could never get far enough ahead to be able to ease back and enjoy the fruits of his labor. When things got tight, as they usually did, Daddy turned to what he knew best to earn some quick money—the rodeo. He often was gone for weeks and sometimes months at a time on the rodeo circuit. It took Daddy's rodeoing, running cattle, and Mama's income from the school to make ends meet. We got along fine, but the rodeoing sometimes made Mama feel like a single parent.

Nevertheless, since Daddy was a rodeo champion, all of the McEntire kids grew up with a desire to rodeo. All, that is, except me. Because I got hurt on horses, I had no real desire to compete.

On the other hand, because Grandpap, Daddy, Alice, Reba, and Pake competed in rodeos over a span of fifty years, my family developed lots of lasting friendships at the rodeos. Rodeo folks are like one big, extended family. Later, when Paul and I began ministering in rodeo church services, we had invitations from all across the country, many as a result of the friends we had made in those early days at the rodeo.

A lot of people thought my family was wealthy because of the McEntire reputation in the rodeo world and the fact that we lived on a large ranch. Often when the activity bus from school would stop to pick us up along the road on the way to a ballgame, we'd hear the kids gush, "Man, they are rich!"

It wasn't that way. We didn't always have the newest clothes, and our supper was often a worn out roping steer that Daddy had butchered. We were not rich, but we worked and played hard. My siblings and I enjoyed a good life, playing outside and using our imaginations rather than just playing board games or sitting in front of a television for entertainment.

Rattlesnakes were a constant concern in our part of Oklahoma. They were always lurking nearby, even when we were unaware of their presence. Once, Alice, Pake, Reba, and I were walking across the railroad tracks on our way to the roping pens. We all stepped over the rail near the same spot, and then for some reason, one of us looked back. There, lying in the shade of the rail, only inches from where our ankles had been exposed only moments before, was one of the biggest rattlesnakes I have ever seen! That big rattler could have bitten any one of us as we stepped by it; but fortunately it stayed put, and none of us were bitten. We did, however, take a good look at each rail on our next trip to the roping pen.

Our favorite thing to do was to go swimming in Limestone Creek, which ran behind Grandpap's house. It felt especially good after a hard day's work. Limestone Creek flows between two craggy, steep ridges, probably 400 feet tall, creating a place known as Limestone Gap. As kids, that was one of our favorite places in the world. The creek was lined with big oak trees and large rocks, and there was a peace and "aloneness" there that was special.

The creek was only about fifteen to twenty feet across where the water slowed down and formed a little pool, our swimming hole. Pake, Alice, and Reba loved to run and jump off the banks into that little pool area, but not me. I'd ease my way in nice and slow. I had already had enough bumps and scrapes in my life; I didn't need any more. Back and forth we'd splash in the refreshing water, rarely taking time to rest or sunbathe. We could rest at home, and we weren't interested in getting a suntan. Redheads burn!

When Daddy or Mama was unavailable to take us swimming, we often turned our powers of persuasion toward Daddy's hired hand, Louie Sandmann. We'd say, "Aw, come on, Louie. Please take us swimming. *Please!*" Louie's response was classic. With a thick drawl, Louie replied, "Nah, you can't go swimming. You'll get your feet wet."

To me, that was valid reasoning. *Okay*, I thought. *I guess we won't go swimming today. After all, if we do, we'll get our feet wet.* I looked at Louie with awe, amazed at his profound logic.

Although my sisters, Pake, and I worked hard along with Daddy, we didn't get paid for doing what he figured we ought to do anyhow. The idea of an allowance was a foreign concept to Daddy. He did, however, encourage us to earn our own money, and he readily endorsed our entrepreneurial adventures. During deer season in November, Daddy let us charge the deer hunters one dollar each to come on his land to hunt. Any money we made was ours to do with as we pleased. During my early years, collecting from the hunters was the primary way we kids earned enough money to buy Christmas presents for each other.

Collecting payment from the hunters was not as easy as it sounds. It took a concerted effort on the part of our whole family to make it work. We made copies of our deer hunters' "permits," which looked like raffle tickets. Then Pake, Alice, Reba, and I would post ourselves at the cattle guard with a rope across it. When the hunters approached our land, they were met by one or all of the McEntire kids. We stepped right up with our permits and requested payment. Most of the hunters paid up good-naturedly, but there were always a few who squawked about the exorbitant charge.

"Why, I hunted here last year, and your daddy didn't charge me a penny," one fellow complained.

"Well, you are welcome to hunt here this year, too, but it'll cost you a dollar," one of us would reply.

The funniest thing was when one of Daddy's uncles came through. He said, "You can't charge me. Why, I'm your kinfolk!"

We said, "Yeah, sure you are. Everybody 'round here says that." We weren't about to let him through for free. "That'll be one dollar."

Despite our diligence, hunters sometimes slipped onto our land without contributing to the McEntire kids' Christmas fund. That's why most nights during deer season, Daddy piled us into the pickup and set out across the acres to spot the hunters' campfires. When we found a camp, we stopped to visit. Daddy greeted the hunters cheerfully without mentioning anything about money. Most of the hunters knew Daddy and always responded respectfully. Meanwhile Pake and we girls went around the group checking for permits. Some of the hunters, of course, were unaware of the fee we were charging, and they quickly paid when we told them.

Others were reluctant, and some made excuses. A few downright lied to us.

Daddy wasn't concerned about the money, since he never wanted to encourage us to focus on monetary things. But in helping us track down the hunting camps, he was teaching us a lesson—you can't always trust people to be true to their word. As McEntire kids, we were accustomed to being around men and women whose word was as good as gold. As I mentioned previously, Daddy was known as a man of his word, but he wanted to make us aware that not everyone operated by the same code of ethics.

I saved my portion of the deer hunters' money and wouldn't spend a dime of it thoughtlessly. After all the other kids had spent their money, they borrowed from me. Daddy had me write down their debts so I wouldn't get cheated. Come Christmas, I could walk into a store and browse with confidence, knowing that I had money in my bank. I was pretty good at managing my money, so nobody was surprised when years later I decided to study business in college.

In high school, all of us kids were involved in activities such as 4-H Club—which, because of its many programs, helped us develop our performing abilities—Future Farmers of America, Future Homemakers of America, basketball, track, and school plays. But along with Pake, a new interest had taken possession of most of Reba's and my spare time. We had developed a passion for music.

Chapter 5

THE SINGING
McENTIRES

*A*s far back as I can remember, the McEntires have been a musical family. Reba is fond of saying we got our lungs from Daddy and our harmony from Mama. She's right. Daddy taught us how to sing loud—he can get cattle to come from all around by just hollering, "Whoooah! Suuck, suuck!" (If you want to know how this sounds, just ask a rancher!) Mama taught us how to sing pretty, filling in the harmony notes that nobody else was singing. More often than not, Pake sang the melody, while Reba sang the high harmonies and Alice and I sang the lower parts. Eventually, Alice would become more interested in rodeo-ing than singing; but when she sang with us, she sure sang pretty.

We sang a lot around the McEntire home, while Mama fixed supper, around the supper table after the meal, in the car on the way to a rodeo, and before we went to bed at night. As young children, Alice, Pake, Reba, and I loved to strut down the hall in our pajamas, singing the theme song of the television show *77 Sunset Strip*. Reba and I, equipped with hairbrushes as "microphones," loved to lip sync songs in front of our folks' dresser mirror in their bedroom.

Pake learned to play guitar and, before long, he was accompanying Reba and me as we three sang. Pake's favorite music artist was Merle Haggard, so we learned every song on every Merle Haggard album Pake got his hands on. Reba loved to listen to Loretta Lynn and Dolly Parton albums. She and I would listen to the albums over and over until we knew every song by heart.

Although I sang with my family around the house, I didn't sing publicly until I was in seventh grade. I did, however, sing the lead part to "How Great Thou Art" in our second grade Thanksgiving program at school. (That was when it was still permissible to sing Christ-exalting songs in our public schools. My, how things have changed!)

Our school wasn't big enough to have a marching band. We had a number of students who were interested in music, however, so Mama felt that the school should offer some sort of music instruction. Since she worked for Mr. Toaz, the school superintendent, Mama was always planting ideas for a music curriculum in his mind. Most of her suggestions fell upon deaf ears, but when Clark Rhyne was hired to teach at Kiowa High School, Mama found the ally she needed. Although Clark had not been hired to teach music, he played guitar and sang at local clubs. He volunteered—with some help from Mama—to help form a school-sponsored country music band. The school established a one-hour class centering around country music. The initial members were Pake, Reba, our cousin Diannia, Clark Rhyne's younger brother, Kelly, David Jones, Gary Raiburn, Carol Johnston, and Roger Wills. Roger wanted to learn to play bass guitar, so Clark Rhyne taught him the rudiments of the instrument. Roger was a quick learner and was soon playing things on the bass most pickers only dream of. In the years to come, his music career would include five years in Reba's band before becoming the band leader for country superstar Alan Jackson.

I joined the Kiowa Cowboy Band when I entered junior high. We sang at fund-raising concerts, banquets, 4-H contests, dances, and before the kick-off and at halftime at high school football games.

As the band became more popular, we began receiving invitations to play in real, live, paying situations. Most of those were honkey-tonks and dance halls. We would not have dared to darken the doors of those places in the big city, but in the small, rural towns we could do it safely—well, relatively safely. Some of the places got pretty rowdy. It was not unusual for several fistfights to break out in the back of the club while we were singing on stage. Mama advised us to just keep on playing. Mama and Carol Johnston's parents always accompanied us, and I'm sure they would have packed up two carloads of kids and equipment and off we would have gone, had there been any serious danger.

Working those rowdy places, however, taught us at an early age how to handle a crowd. It also instilled in us the old show business adage: "The show must go on." After the show, our parents helped us pack up our equipment, take it back to the school, and then drove us all home. Often the members of the Kiowa Cowboy Band didn't get home till nearly dawn. It was a good glimpse into just how unglamorous a musician's life on the road could be.

The band played for three years, until Pake, our lead singer and band leader, graduated. After that, the Kiowa Cowboy Band dissolved. At least six of its members, however, went on to carve out productive careers in professional music—not bad for a school that didn't even have a music curriculum.

As a fringe benefit of our association with the Kiowa Cowboy Band, we took part in our first recording project. Clark Rhyne had written a ballad about our Grandpap, John McEntire. Grandpap was a legend around our part of the country, and Clark, being a history buff, wanted to do something to immortalize Grandpap. Clark wrote the song one day and sang it for my family. The day after we heard it, Mama, Pake, Reba, and I traveled to Oklahoma City to Benson Studio, owned and operated by Larry Benson, to record "The Ballad of John McEntire." Grandpap went along with us to enjoy his special honor and to add his "trademark" for all to hear for years to come.

We recorded the song on one side and an interview with Grandpap on the other side. While doing the interview with Grandpap, Pake said, "Well, Pap, everybody talks about your famous McEntire yell. Would you let us hear it one time?"

Grandpap was only too happy to oblige. He let out a yell that could have been heard in downtown Oklahoma City, even through the sound-proof studio walls. The needles on the control board peaked and then pegged way over in the red, as the sound engineer scrambled to turn down the sound and the recording levels.

When the recording was completed, Clark had some 45 rpm records pressed and distributed to local radio stations. The song got lots of attention and requests at a radio station in McAlester, a town about thirty miles north of our home. Everyone wanted a copy. Even today people still want copies of it, though it's hard to find.

After Pake's graduation, he, Reba, and I began singing under the name "The Singing McEntires." Actually, Pake was the lead singer, so we might have been more aptly called "Pake and the Girls," but we decided to use our family name instead. We performed at dances, banquets, bars, fairs, you name it. Our program included a wide variety of music—a little rock 'n' roll, country, some gospel, and some bluegrass.

One time Pake, Reba, and I entered an amateur singing contest, hoping to win a prize. As we were doing our precontest interview, a woman asked us our name, where we were from, and where we sang. She surprised us when she asked if we were professionals. We said no, we aren't professionals, we just sing.

"Well, have you ever been paid to sing?" she asked.

"Oh, sure, yeah," Pake told her, trying to sound like getting paid was old hat to us. We had been paid alright, but singing for four-hour-long dances and splitting the receipts from the door between seven people (a top job pulled in $30 each) sure didn't make us pros like Merle Haggard or Loretta Lynn.

The woman looked perplexed. "Well," she huffed. "You can't compete in this contest."

"Why not?" Pake asked.

"Why, you have been paid for your performances," she said. "You are *professionals.*"

We went away disappointed that we couldn't enter the contest, but our egos were soaring, nonetheless. "Oh, my. We are *professionals!*" we kept saying to one another.

Professional or not, usually our only musical accompaniment was provided by Pake on his acoustic guitar. But our family harmony was what stole the show. We performed together until Reba got her big break in the music business.

In December 1974, Reba was hired to sing the national anthem at the National Finals Rodeo in Oklahoma City. The NFR is the Super Bowl of rodeo; it is the best of the best, the top fifteen money winners of the year competing against one another. Nowadays, crowds of 20,000 people often show up to watch the rodeo finals. Reba figured that singing the national anthem was good for two reasons: to sing in front of such a throng was a pretty good showcase, and they paid her to sing it. After all, to sing for that size crowd was exciting enough, but to sing to a group that wasn't fighting and throwing things, and who might quiet down long enough to actually hear the performer, well, that was more than any singer could ask for. Of course, coming from a rodeo legacy such as ours, Reba was simply honored to sing for so many people who had been such an important part of our lives. Besides, Daddy had always told Reba to do something she was good at.

At the NFR, Reba met Red Steagall, a country singer who was a favorite with the rodeo crowd. Red had recorded several top ten hit songs of his own and had written a few hits for other artists as well. After the rodeo, Red and a number of the rodeo contestants and performers gathered for a party in a suite at the Hilton Hotel. Mama, Daddy, Pake, and Reba were invited and decided to attend. Several country singers were passing a guitar around and sharing songs, when one of the rodeo cowboys called out, "Hey, Reba, do 'Joshua.' " Reba sang the Dolly Parton song and blew the listeners away—including Red Steagall. Later that night, Mama asked Red if he might be able to help get The Singing McEntires a recording contract in Nashville. Red was kind and courteous, but not too encouraging. He said he didn't think there was much chance for a country trio act at that time; but he did, however, think that Reba had potential as a solo artist.

In March 1975, Reba and Mama traveled to Nashville so Reba could record a demonstration tape under Red Steagall's guidance. After a few rejections by recording company executives, Reba's tape was heard by Phonogram—which eventually became Mercury Records, then Polygram-Mercury. She signed a long-term recording deal with Phonogram on November 11, 1975, opening up a whole world of opportunity for Reba and, for all practical purposes, putting an end to The Singing McEntires.

I was genuinely happy for my sister when she achieved every singer's dream, a shot at becoming a recording star. I wasn't jealous or bitter. I didn't feel that Reba had deserted Pake and me. In truth, although I loved to sing and loved country music, I wasn't all that enamored with the idea of becoming a country music star. Besides, I was still in high school, and I was busy with that part of my life.

Pake was affected more by Reba's signing a recording contract than I was. After all, he was the lead singer of The Singing McEntires. He was the emcee and the leader of the group. Suddenly, it was all over. He knew, however, as I did, that the deal was best for Reba. And in the back of our minds, we both dreamed about getting back together someday.

In the first few years of Reba's career, I did indeed get back together with her on stage and in the studio. I enjoyed singing background vocals for Reba. I still remember what fun it was when Ricky Skaggs came to the recording studio to do harmony on "Small Two Bedroom Starter." Occasionally, Reba would call and invite Pake and me to come along to sing with her for special dates. Before I went on the road full time with Reba, we made road trips to Pendleton, Oregon; Mobridge, South Dakota; and San Angelo, Texas. The concerts with Reba were always fun, because Pake would be there and we were all together again. It kept our dreams alive that someday . . . maybe we'd all sing together again. . . .

Chapter 6

A FRESH ENCOUNTER

I still have my green checkered clipboard that I used in sixth grade. I have to smile when I read on it: Susie + Ronnie . . . Susie + Pete . . . Susie + Marc . . . and on and on! We were typical sixth-graders, passing notes asking the heartpounding question, "Do you love me? Check yes or no." Sounds like I missed a hit song, huh?

My first lesson in "what *not* to do with boys" happened at an afternoon basketball game where all the kids gathered at the gym to watch. Our gym was old, with bleachers made in two-foot tiers. My boyfriend (at the time) and I were seated on the very top row. At one point during the game, he made a big move to hold my hand. Lo and behold, Mama was directly across the gym! When I looked at her, she gave me the wave of her index finger, which meant, "No, no!"

I quickly unclasped my boyfriend's hand. I was so embarrassed! I had learned an important lesson, although, unfortunately, not well enough.

In junior high, I didn't know how to just be a friend to a boy. Instead, I quickly fell into the trap of going steady. Fortunately, those early relationships never got too serious. Usually the boy and I spent most of our time looking at each other with goo-goo eyes—until we found somebody else and began new relationships.

I didn't date a lot of guys in high school, but I did date steadily, staying in a relationship with one fellow exclusively through my last year of high school and my first few months of college. I thought I was in love. A few months later, he dumped me. He said that he wanted to go out with the guys more often and that he didn't want to be tied down to me. I didn't really want to break up with him. After all, although I did not realize it at the time, by being sexually intimate with him, I had given him a part of myself that I could not give to any other person. But, looking back, it is easy to see that breaking off that relationship was the best thing for me.

Still, the breakup was a blow to my self-esteem as well as to my sense of security. I had relied too much on that guy. I had followed him to Oklahoma State University, where I was majoring in business; and now, barely halfway through my freshman year, I was on my own.

I dated a couple of guys throughout college, but nobody quite as seriously as my first boyfriend. One thing I noticed was that I was drawn more to the kind of men I grew up around—ranchers, farmers, and rodeo cowboys.

I wasn't certain about many of the qualities I was looking for in a man, but I knew what sort of lifestyle I definitely did not want—that of a rodeo cowboy! I had even told Ruby Maxwell, a cook at my high school, "I'll never marry a rodeo cowboy." I had been on those long trips with hot days or cold nights, and I did not want to have to endure the traveling that goes with that lifestyle.

I knew, too, that I wanted a home. I didn't necessarily want someone with a nine-to-five job, but I wanted a man who had strong family ties. Strangely, although I had vowed that I would never allow myself to fall in love with a rodeo cowboy, I was rarely attracted to any of the "suit and tie" guys. Instead, I was drawn continually toward fellows who were farmers or whose families were ranchers.

In my last year of college, I dated a guy with whom I became serious and wanted to marry, but he remained noncommittal. Then one night I went out with friends and came home drunk. I called him up and with slightly slurred speech, asked, "What's in our relationship? I don't understand what we are doing. Is there any future in this?"

Thunderstruck by my bluntness, he stammered around, and finally replied, "Well, I don't know."

I said, "Well, when you figure it out, you call me," and hung up the phone.

I never heard from him again.

I graduated from college in 1980 with a degree in personnel management and a minor in accounting. I laugh now, when I think that I actually went to college with hopes of one day being an accountant. I just don't have a mathematical mind. In fact, nowadays, I balance our checkbook and five minutes later, Paul asks, "How much money do we have?"

I have to confess, "I don't know. I have to go look." Nevertheless, my accounting training has come in handy. When Paul and I married, someone needed to be the bookkeeper, and Paul hates dealing with receipts.

After graduation, I went to work in Oklahoma City at J. D. Simmons, Incorporated, an oil lease company that Reba and I had worked for during the summer of 1976, checking oil and gas records at the Coal County Courthouse. I didn't relish the idea of moving back to the big city by myself—I was born and raised in the country—but it was the only job offer I got, so I packed my bags and moved into a small one-bedroom apartment. To assuage my loneliness, I went out drinking after work. I knew better, but I just got caught up with the party crowd. I was all by myself, and I was lonely. I'd work all day, then after work, go shopping or to "Happy Hour," and drink, dance, and party the night away. If I didn't do that I'd stay home with my plants and spend the evening sewing.

About that time, Denna, my best friend from my school days, moved in with me. Together, we started hitting a lot of clubs, but the dancing and alcohol could not drive away the loneliness and gloom I felt on the interior of my life. I was growing increasingly depressed and disgusted with myself. Extremely weight conscious while in college, I had slimmed down to 108 pounds. Now I was eating and drinking too much, and my weight was beginning to balloon.

Perhaps because of a lack of intimacy in my personal relationships, about that same time I began yearning for intimacy with God. I had believed in Jesus since my childhood days when I received Christ at the age of twelve, but I had drifted further and further away from the Lord. Since I had not been greatly encouraged at home to develop my spiritual life, I didn't even know where to start to develop a closeness with God.

In high school, I had occasionally gone to church with my friend Denna, but it seemed pointless. Instead of talking about God and how to know Him better, most of my Sunday school class was consumed with talking about what everyone had done the night before. After a while, I just quit going to church.

Now, however, I felt that God was pulling me back. I met a man named Sam at the oil lease company where I was working. He was a Christian, and he was really concerned about me and my life with Christ. He recognized that I wasn't doing so well spiritually, so he offered to take me to church one night, and I accepted. Sam attempted to encourage me in the renewal of my spiritual life, and I will always be grateful to him. Throughout this time, God was trying to get my focus back on Him. One day I was alone in my apartment, ironing some britches. Not only was I all by myself, but I felt so lonely, so detached from my family, friends, and most of all, from God. I didn't know much about the Lord, but I knew that prayer was simply talking to God. I believed that He heard my prayers, so while I was ironing, I started talking aloud to Him.

I said, "Lord my life is so empty. I have so many good things—a job, a car, food to eat, and a place to sleep, and a bunch of stuff, but I feel so empty inside. If You are there, would You show me Your love?"

Instantly, I felt a warm sensation enveloping my body. It was as though someone were pouring warm oil on the top of my head and it was running all over me, from head to toe. I had never in my life experienced such a sensation. I was ecstatic, and I wanted to laugh, shout, and cry all at the same time. Most of all, I wanted to tell somebody—anybody, everybody!— that God is alive and that He had answered my prayer.

But there wasn't anybody for me to call, so I took a walk through the neighborhood. It was the same neighborhood that I had been living in for some time, but suddenly everything around me seemed fresh, clean, and new. I remember seeing a house with a green roof—just a normal house, with a normal roof, but for some reason that roof had never appeared as magnificent as it did that day. Slowly it began to dawn on me that it was not my world that had changed; it was my heart that had been changed. With one touch from God, everything looked brighter and better.

Since Reba had signed her record contract and was appearing as a solo act, I hadn't done much performing. Pake, however, was recording a project, so I helped by singing harmony with him. But I really wasn't inclined to pursue a singing career on my own. I was much more interested in settling down and becoming a homemaker.

In late 1980, the National Finals Rodeo was held in Oklahoma City. Reba was scheduled to sing the national anthem each night, and since I was living there in the city, I attended the rodeo with her. Reba had recorded several hit records and was well on her way to becoming a bona fide star. The NFR put her up at the Sheraton hotel, so I accompanied her from the hotel to the arena each evening. Because Reba was part of the show, we entered through the performers' entrance, where the cowboys were congregating, getting ready for the rodeo.

One night as we went in, I noticed a good-looking cowboy riding in our direction. I recognized him immediately. Reba and her friend Karen Duvall, wife of rodeo cowboy Roy Duvall, had pointed him out to me earlier in the week. They said he was single and available, but that it was doubtful that I could get a date with him. He was so dedicated to practicing his steer wrestling, he didn't take much time to socialize. Worse yet, Reba and Karen confided that one woman had circulated a rumor that the cowboy was a homosexual because he showed so little interest in sleeping with her. As I observed the cowboy riding his "bulldogging" horse, he sure didn't look gay to me. He was a hunk!

The cowboy passed by, and as he did, he looked down at me and smiled. I smiled back politely, trying to look calm and reserved, but my heart was all aflutter.

On Friday and Saturday night, after the rodeo, Reba and her band provided a dance at the Myriad Convention Center adjoining the Sheraton. Mama was selling the tickets, so I offered to help. My job was taking tickets at the door as the throng of cowboys, cowgirls, rodeo personnel, and friends and family members entered the dance hall. I was busy, taking tickets and greeting people, when suddenly I looked up and my heart took another little leap.

The handsome cowboy I had seen at the arena and some of his rodeo buddies were headed right toward my door! His friends handed me their tickets—or at least I think the pieces of paper they gave me were tickets. I wasn't paying much attention to them, but the rugged cowboy lagged slightly behind the group going through the door.

I looked him full in the face as he handed me a ticket and said, "Hi, I'm Paul Luchsinger."

Chapter 7

PAUL'S ROUGH AND TUMBLE EARLY DAYS

*M*y dad, Eldon Paul Luchsinger, is a huge, burly man. Dad says he weighs about 275 pounds, but he looks bigger than that to me. He wears a size sixteen ring that will no longer come off his finger. His arms are as big as my thighs.

Dad was the oldest in his family of six brothers and two sisters. He was raised on a farm outside the small town of Surrey, North Dakota. Life was tough, and he had to work hard. He left home and struck out on his own when he was only fourteen years of age. He worked on construction jobs and learned the trade so well that he eventually started his own company. He was a strong, self-made, seemingly self-sufficient man.

Dad met my mom, Beverly Monroe, in Helena, Montana. They were married in 1953 and in the first year, Mom gave birth to my sister, Cathy. Dad had received a scholarship to attend Washington State University at Pullman, where Cathy was born. A few years later, I was born at Columbia Hospital in Great Falls, Montana.

I have four sisters, three of whom are younger than I. During my childhood we moved over two dozen times. My dad was a good provider for our family, but to do so, we had to move where he was transferred. One year, we moved so frequently, my sister was unable to finish first grade.

As the only boy in the family, I was glad when Dad allowed me to go to the construction jobs along with him. Even as a toddler, I loved to watch him operate the heavy equipment. I was especially happy when Dad gave me simple chores to do. He was probably just trying to keep me busy, but I felt like one of the guys because I was working, too.

Dad didn't go easy on me, though. Once, when I was three years old, I messed my britches while "on the job" with Dad. My dad took me over to the fire hydrant, turned it on, and hosed me off with the high pressure water flow.

Dad rarely had time to play with me as I was growing up. He was always too busy working. One of the few times when my dad and I were playing ball in the back yard, he threw the ball so hard, it bounced back off my glove and hit my head. That was the last time I can remember playing catch with my dad. I was ten years old.

It wasn't that he didn't want to play with me; he just didn't know how to be easygoing. Years later, I would have the same problem being gentle with my kids. I really have to work at playing tenderly with them, trying to be kind, and patient. That's not something that came naturally to me or something I was used to doing. But it is something I continually work at now because I love my family.

Dad honestly tried to be involved in my life. He coached my Little League baseball team and tried as best he could to be patient with the other boys and me. But it was obvious that Dad was like a fish out of water. Putting Dad in charge of teaching eight- to twelve-year-olds was like putting a Marine drill sergeant in charge of a preschool. Dad really wanted to help people; he has always had a big heart. But he had trouble being an encourager. Somehow or other, the words he meant as encouragement tended to come across as criticism. I carried that trait into my own relationships later in life.

My dad drank a lot. Mom, too, drank heavily, either as an escape from reality, or from the pain in her life. Mom's parents also drank heavily, so as is often the case, my mom ended up marrying my dad who had a problem with alcohol, and then developed her own problem with alcohol as well.

Throughout my middle school years, my parents' relationship contin-ued to be volatile. Often, I'd hear Mom and Dad arguing, their voices esca-lating in volume and intensity, until there was some sort of explosion. At first I tried to ignore my feelings of hurt and insecurity over Mom and Dad's anger. I wanted to intervene, to say or do something to make them stop, but I didn't know how. Instead, I simply internalized their anger and made it my own.

I carried that anger with me throughout most of my life, establishing a pattern that later showed up in my relationship with my wife, Susie. When our marriage became strained, I responded similarly to the way I had as a child. I pretended that it wasn't happening. Then I began to steam, slow-ly at first, then hotter and hotter, until finally, the teapot boiled over and my anger exploded violently in our marriage and family. Looking back now, I can see how easily that became a pattern in my life, but at the time, I had no idea that I would one day carry such heavy baggage from my childhood into my own relationship with my spouse and children.

Mom stayed around the house during the daytime, but at night she worked as a bartender at a steakhouse in the small Montana town where we had moved. This was the first time she had worked outside the home. While Dad was drinking and Mom was bartending, my oldest sister, Cathy, who was about nine years old, babysat my younger sisters and me. Cathy also cooked and did most of the housework.

In Montana, family life revolved around the bar. That's where we spent most of our time. At least one of our parents was there most any time of the day. Either Mom was working or Dad was there drinking. Often, as a boy I hung out in the bars with my dad.

I actually had great fun at the bars. For instance, one of my favorite places to go with Mom or Dad when I was about six years old was Buckhorn bar in Fort Peck, Montana. It was one of those old taverns, with silver dollars imbedded in the bar, huge oversized railings, and pictures of cowboys all over the wall. The joint had a skeet-shooting range out back. (Nothing like semi-inebriated men with guns in their hands to liven up the evening!) The customers would fire away at clay pigeons. As soon as the customers were done shooting, my friends and I—other kids who were at the bar with their parents—all raced out into the fields to gather any of the clay pigeons that the drunken shooters had missed. The owner of the bar paid my friends and me a nickel for each clay pigeon we retrieved. The more the customers drank, the more clay pigeons they missed, and the more money my friends and I made. Of course, rather than saving our money, my friends and I bought candy and soda pop, so the bar owner had a built-in return on his money.

My family never stayed in one place very long, so we didn't put down any strong roots. Worse yet to me, because we moved so often, I was always the new kid in class. I hated that! As the new kid on the block, I always had to prove myself to my peers, usually in some physical way, either through sports or fighting or just being tougher than the other kids. In a way, I guess the training helped me, because later on I excelled in high school sports. But it also taught me that the way to make people like and respect me was to be stronger or tougher or better than they were.

We moved from Glasgow, Montana, to Albuquerque, New Mexico, in 1965 where Dad was transferred. One day, not long after I started the fifth grade, I got involved in a flag football game. As usual, I was giving it all I had, trying to make a strong first impression. I was playing quarterback, when suddenly I was hit hard by a boy with protruding buck teeth. As he slammed into me, his teeth caught right on my eyebrow and split it wide open. The school nurse was worried because his teeth had punctured my skin. I probably should have had a tetanus shot, but I didn't. It took a bunch of stitches to sew my skin shut, but I was marked as the new tough guy in school. I bear the scar from that boy's teeth to this day.

Although I quickly discovered that I could win the acceptance of my buddies by excelling in sports, I still had trouble establishing lasting friendships. The next January we moved to Deming, New Mexico. I didn't have a chance to make any friends during that school term, either. Eventually, I graduated from high school in Deming, but on my commencement day, I still had few close relationships with my peers.

The few buddies I had were probably not the best influence on me, but then I wasn't too good for them either. When I was twelve years old and in the seventh grade, Mom and Dad bought their own bar business. The first year, both of my parents worked in the business; Mom bartended and Dad did the cooking. By the second year, Dad couldn't stand working inside, so he went back to work with a construction company. As part of his compensation package, he was given a company pickup truck to drive.

About this time, my basic rebellious nature collided with my adolescent recklessness. I'd wait until Mom had drunk too much, then I'd sneak booze out of my mother's bar and give it to my buddies.

Sometimes, I'd sneak the alcohol out earlier in the evening and stash it somewhere until Mom and Dad were sound asleep. Then, I'd take my dad's truck out of gear, push it out of the driveway, real quiet like, so they wouldn't hear me starting it. As the truck, loaded with tools and fuel, picked up speed, I'd pop the clutch to catch the gear, and the engine started right up. Then I would sneak to town and go pick up my buddies in the middle of the night. We'd go drinking all night long, and then I would sneak back in around four or five o'clock in the morning.

Even as a child, I was better at establishing relationships with animals than with most people. I always liked horses, and I loved rodeos and cowboys. From the time I attended my first rodeo as a boy, I thought that was the greatest thing I'd ever seen! I thought, Man, *would I like to be a cowboy!* Not just in the way that most little boys dream about being cowboys; I was obsessed with it.

But I was raised in town. I didn't know anything about cowboy life. I had ridden a horse very little in my life, and one of those times, the horse ran off with me, the saddle slipped, and I fell smack on the ground, scraping my face all up. I was lucky; a fall such as that, I later learned, could have killed me. But I was not about to let that hold me back. *Someday, I thought, I am going to be a cowboy.*

At Deming, once again I established my reputation in a physical way, this time on the football field. I really wanted to play football, especially since my dad had been a football player. I had heard all the stories about my dad's football days, and I desperately wanted to be like Dad. I went out for football and earned a starting position on the team. Suddenly, all the cool guys in school wanted to be my friends.

One day when football season had been going on for about two weeks, I was walking around the campus and a big, tall kid came up to me. His name was Dick Pool, and he was one of the "in" guys at school. He said, "Hey, why don't you come and hang around with us?" That made me feel good, and before long, Dick became my best friend. He is still a faithful friend today.

I'm sure my parents loved each other, but I never heard them say so, nor did I see many expressions of affection between Mom and Dad. Throughout my early childhood, I was honestly confused about what love really was. Although I had four sisters, we never talked about love. Nor did I know how to legitimately express affection when I began dating as a teenager. Consequently, I had all sorts of questions when, as a teenager, I started becoming involved in relationships with the opposite sex.

Well, do I love or don't I love her? I wondered about any young woman for whom I felt a physical attraction. *I know I want to jump in the sack with her. Does that mean I love her or don't love her?*

Our family attended the Catholic church, so it wasn't as if I was totally devoid of moral instruction. Mom was adamant about us kids going to church. She even enrolled me in Catholic schools for the first four and a half years of my education. At home, we talked about God at times, and sometimes even talked to God, but never really considered that we could have a personal relationship with Him. Church was a social event to us. It didn't mean much to us; it was just church. My concept of God was that He was some far away being, waiting to catch me and punish me when I did something wrong. I rarely heard that God loves me and wants the best for me. It was more like, "You better be good, or God is gonna get ya!"

We did, however, learn some standards of morality from our association with the church. One of the statements my parents reiterated was, "Don't ever sleep with a woman that you're not going to marry."

Mom and Dad weren't really expecting or even encouraging sexual abstinence; they were simply implying that if I got a girl pregnant, I would be expected to marry her—therefore the adage, don't sleep with her if you aren't willing to marry her.

Most of Mom or Dad's questions or comments about my relationship with a young woman remained on a superficial level. Mom would ask, "Is she pretty?"

Dad asked, "Has she got money? Is she rich? If she's pretty and she's rich, then she's okay."

I assumed that Mom and Dad were joking—but I was never quite sure.

Regardless, I learned early on to evaluate women by external, superficial criteria, rather than looking for qualities of inner, true beauty. I never truly came to understand what love was until I became a Christian during my second year in college.

Meanwhile, sports became the center of my life. I tried to substitute the high school athletics program and the acceptance and attention I was receiving there for what I was missing at home. I went out for every sport the school offered—football, wrestling, track—I participated in them all.

During the summers, I worked with my dad, from 7 A.M. to 5 A.M. or later, and then he and I went to the bar for supper. To me that was normal; I didn't think anything was unusual about that lifestyle. Dad would not allow me to drink alcohol, but I was around it all the time. Often, we stayed in the bars until 11 P.M. or midnight. That was the way I spent most of my evenings from the time I turned twelve until my mid-teens.

Dad seemed angry a lot during my last few years of high school. Often, for no apparent reason, he'd fly off the handle at Mom, or my sisters, or me, or one of the guys at work. When Dad got mad, everyone knew the procedure: "Don't get in his way; don't confront him." Everybody was afraid of my dad. Because he was the superintendent on the job, he was accustomed to being the boss. Then, when he owned his own company, his bullheaded attitude intensified. His employees feared him. He didn't take any guff from anybody. He was a big, strong guy, and he wasn't afraid to let others know it.

As the boss's son, I always felt like I had to prove myself to the guys working on the job. I worked hard and I always felt like I outworked the other fellows. Even as a kid, in the eighth, ninth, and tenth grades, I was determined that no one was going to outwork me.

During my high school years, I ran a backhoe, a loader, the water truck, road-graders, big dumptrucks, bulldozers, and all sorts of other heavy construction equipment. I was just a kid!

After my high school graduation, I was selected to enroll in the Air Force Academy Preparatory School. I wanted to play college football, and hopefully, someday make it all the way to the National Football League.

My desire to play football set up a major conflict between my dad and me. It was the first time that I got mad at my dad for pressuring me to do what he wanted me to do, rather than what I wanted.

At the close of my senior year, I was selected to play in the South All Stars Game, which was a great honor, since it represented the best high school football players in New Mexico. To me, it was a big deal that I was picked to play offensive guard, on the first team, for the South All Stars.

Unfortunately, the game was to be played the same week that I was to report to the Air Force Academy for basic training. I tried to get out of basic, but there was no way. Dad, of course, sided with the Air Force. He said, "Your first week of basic training is a lot more important that any All Star game." It may have been more important to him, but not to me. As a teenager who had worked for three years, focused on the goal of making the high school All Stars, I felt I deserved a shot at it.

As it turned out, I got deathly sick, and couldn't play in the game or report to basic training. I went to the hospital. My head was pounding so badly, I couldn't even see. I had a bad case of diarrhea and was running a high fever. The doctors feared I had contracted spinal meningitis. They ran every test they had but couldn't find what was wrong with me.

Meanwhile, I started losing weight. I dropped from about 185 pounds to around 150 pounds before my body finally pulled out of its nosedive. This was the first of many bouts with an illness that has haunted me throughout my life, taking a heavy toll on my energy, patience, and attitude.

After a week in the hospital, I was released. The doctors still had not determined what had caused my sudden debilitation. Regardless, within days, I was at the Air Force Academy.

At the Academy, I played football, and I joined the wrestling team, but I hated being there the whole time. The focus at the Academy was on academics and military instruction. I was not interested in either one. I didn't mind all the studies, but the military lifestyle was not for me. I wanted to be a cowboy!

I wasn't fond of hearing the sound of reveille at 4:30 in the morning. Nor was I happy about the work duty, cleaning the latrines, hallways, and television rooms. Each dorm floor had a specific job to do, and it had to be done just right. It wasn't good enough for the floors to be clean; they had to shine like glass. Same with our shoes.

Of course, the Academy was excellent discipline for me, but before long, I became frustrated and wanted to quit. I knew Dad, however, would not hear of it. I decided I wouldn't even try, so I flunked out on purpose. That was the only way Dad would have accepted me leaving the Academy.

I attended the Academy only one semester, then I decided to go to New Mexico State University, which is sixty miles from Deming. I was still hoping to play college football, but New Mexico State is a big college, and I was a "walk-on," a nonscholarshiped player trying out for the squad. I didn't like the coach very well. He always seemed to find some reason for not playing me. He said, "You aren't tall enough; you aren't big enough, you aren't fast enough." I could have handled it if he had just told me I was not good enough, but because he kept coming up with new excuses, I became frustrated again, and eventually I quit.

I got to partying real hard, drinking and carrying on, doing crazy college capers. Country singer Ray Stevens had a hit song, "The Streak," on the radio about that time. "Streaking," peeling off our clothes, and running naked as jay birds through some public place, was a big thing on our campus in the spring of 1974. So a buddy of mine and I became known for our streaking. I started doing anything to get attention. If they were going to streak, well I could do it better, or longer, or in a more public place.

Eventually, goofing off began to grow old. Since I had been unable to secure a football scholarship at New Mexico State, I decided to drop out of school for a while and go to work full time for my Dad. That was a big mistake.

Dad had high hopes that one day I would take over his business, so in college I had enrolled in the engineering program. I worked for my dad from that spring until the following winter, but Dad and I just couldn't get along. Actually, I wouldn't submit to his authority. Beyond that, I hated being the boss's son. At the time, Dad employed a young foreman who I considered to be a smart-mouth, who didn't know much of anything about construction, but he thought he knew everything. We didn't get along at all. Seems he was always trying to tell me what to do. On the other hand, I was a nineteen-year-old with just enough college engineering courses in my brain to make me think I knew everything. Truth is, I didn't know much, and my rebellious, cut-corners attitude often got me in trouble.

Once, for example, I was running a big 966 Caterpillar loader, loading the dump trucks in a gravel pit. A problem developed with the loader's transmission. I called for a mechanic, who pulled his service truck next to me. In the meantime, I had already loaded a bucketfull of gravel and I had raised the bucket into the air, ready to load the next dump truck. When I told the mechanic about the problem I was having, he said, "Just let me check your fluid level real quick."

The loader's transmission fluid dip-stick was behind the loader's seat, which had to be raised for access to the motor. The mechanic and I set about the job of checking the fluid. In the meantime, unknown to me, another truck backed under the bucket of the loader. As I raised the seat, I accidentally hit the loader's DOWN lever. The heavy arm of that loader holding a full bucket of gravel went crashing down—right on top of the $50,000 dump truck that had pulled in to be loaded. A loud *Wham!* echoed around the gravel pit, as the loaded bucket of gravel smashed the truck and scared the driver inside nearly half to death. A few more inches closer and the heavy bucket could have killed him.

Of course, the safe way to have checked the transmission fluid would have been for me to have put down the bucket of gravel. But that would have been too much trouble. There was the right way of doing things, and then there was my way—the shortcut.

Most people would have learned a lesson from that near tragedy. Not me. Later in that same week, I was running a sheep's foot roller, a piece of heavy construction equipment that has teeth that stick out of the steel wheel rollers, with a blade on the front of them. In building a highway, the machine is used to push dirt, smooth it out, and then roll it to keep that dirt compacted. On this day, I was running the roller on the ground that would support an overpass. It was about twenty feet to the bottom of the fill. My job was to build up the fill on the edges. The rule of thumb when running a roller is: You never go back and forth perpendicular to the edge; instead you roll along the side horizontally so you don't accidently go too far and run the machine off the edge of the cliff.

I had run the roller all day long, and it was already past quitting time when I started to cut corners and run the roller back and forth, perpendicular to the edge. The ground seemed solid enough, and I was not having any trouble; I was rollin' along. I had just made a turn and was rolling toward the edge. I thought, *I shouldn't be rolling in this direction*, when all of a sudden, I realized that the throttle on the roller was stuck. I tried pulling up on the accelerator with all my might to get the roller to slow down, but it remained in gear, heading straight for the edge of the fill. Frantically, I pulled levers and pushed buttons, hoping that something would shut it down. Nothing did. The roller continued lumbering toward the edge.

At the bottom of the twenty-foot fill, part of the construction crew had been getting the iron cement forms ready so they could pour huge pillars to put the rest of the concrete beams on. The forms were about forty feet high. Fortunately, by this time of day, the workers had already clocked out, but the ironwork they had been grappling with for days remained.

As the roller approached the edge of the cliff, I could see the bottom, and the throttle was still stuck. I did what any college engineering student might do in such a crisis.

I bailed off the roller! I wasn't about to ride that thing to the bottom. Down it went, over the edge, right down the cliff into all that ironwork, smashing the forms below. A week's work by a professional construction crew was destroyed in a matter of seconds. Not only did the accident smash the machine, and destroy the forms, but my dad had to rent a big crane to pull the roller out of there. My dad said, "Jeez! It would be cheaper to pay you to stay at home!" Again, doing things my way had caused a major calamity.

About a week later, I was running the water truck for the construction crew, watering the ground to keep the dust down as the crew worked. Again, the rule was: don't water going into the steep work area, because the road will get muddy and you could slide off. I said, "Oh, it isn't that steep, so I'll just lay down some water on my way into the work area."

Do I need to tell you what happened next?

You guessed it. When I started to back out, sure enough, the heavy water truck started sliding down the hill. I hit the bank, and *Booom!* The entire truck rolled over with a thousand gallons of water, smashing the water truck and drenching the work area.

And that is the way my life has been ever since. "Oh, it will be all right." "We don't need to do that." "It will be all right." Then, *Boom!*

Once again, I felt like a total failure. My thoughts turned back to Montana and the cowboy way of life. I decided to get as far away from construction as possible. Dad was unhappy when I decided that the construction life was not for me, but I couldn't help it. I wanted to be a cowboy.

Before I continue my story, I want to let you know that as I write this, my mom has now been sober for fifteen years.. We kids celebrate each year by sending her a rose for each year of sobriety. She is one of the most respected bookkeepers in Deming, New Mexico.

My dad still does construction jobs around New Mexico and is very successful. He and Mom live outside Deming and their renewed relationship is a testimony to us kids. We're all proud of them.

Chapter 8

A CHRISTIAN
COWBOY

*A*fter my stint working for Dad on his construction crew, I decided I was going to get far away from New Mexico. I had always wanted to go back to Montana anyway, since, to me, that was my childhood home.

I enrolled in Montana State University, still hoping that I could play college football. Again, I was a "walk-on," a nonscholarship player going out for the team. Unfortunately, in transferring from one college to another, I lost a year of eligibility to play college sports, so Montana State did not offer me a football scholarship. They gave me a pat on the back and said thanks, but no thanks. My dreams of playing college and then professional football were dashed.

For a while I didn't know what to do, so I did what I knew how to do best—I drank and partied. I tried everything that came along. Marijuana, cocaine, speed, and all sorts of other drugs were available on campus, and I tried everything I could get my hands on. Fortunately, I never became seriously addicted, but I did smoke a lot of grass. My attitude was: it's here, so why not do it? Dad was still paying for my schooling, and he basically gave me a checkbook. Plus, I banked the money I had earned working for him, so I always had money for my "extra-curricular activities."

I dated a lot during my college years, but I had no idea what it meant to have a committed relationship with a woman. My only brush with love, or at least as much of love as I knew, had been while I was still in high school. At that time, I was going with a cheerleader who was a year older than I was. She was pretty, so that satisfied my mom's criteria. Her daddy owned one of the largest farms in the state. That satisfied my dad's requirements. I thought she was lovely. That satisfied my criteria.

Most of our friends and family members thought the young woman and I were going to get married. That's what worried her parents; they were not fond of the idea of their daughter marrying a wild-partying kid. They had little to worry about. Eventually, we broke off the relationship anyway.

After that, I soured on trying to establish anything like a serious relationship with a young woman. From then on, I just dated to see how far I could get a woman to go, the further the better in my estimation. I'm ashamed to admit it now, but back then, my goal in most of my dating relationships was simply to see how quickly I could get the young woman in bed. I was a user, using the young women for my own gratification. I was a worldly man, and proud of it.

Of course, to most folks who knew me, I was a good boy. I grew up with the double standard that said, "A teenage boy is going to have sex, but girls, by golly, you better keep yourself pure and clean." It was as ludicrous an idea then as it is today, but most of my friends and I readily accepted the message.

Today, Susie and I tell our three children, as well as the many teenagers to whom we speak around the country, that virginity is just as important for boys as it is for girls. We tell them that the sexual relationship is precious, that there's nothing dirty about it because it was designed by God, but it is meant to be kept exclusively in marriage, between a husband and a wife who are committed to each other. We shoot straight with the kids and tell them that they are sure to be tempted, but that true love waits until marriage to have sex. I wish I had.

As a young man, I had no real concept of true love. I had no clue what it meant to have a relationship based upon mutual trust or what it meant to be committed to a person. A sincere relationship to me was one that lasted through the night. I never saw uncompromising commitment modeled. Most of the adults in my life as I was growing up claimed to be men and women of integrity, and in some ways they were. Yet they had no qualms about lying to, verbally or physically abusing, or cheating on their spouses. Although they said that they didn't believe in doing those things, they certainly practiced them. In years to come, I would not believe in hitting a woman, either, but that would not deter me from doing it.

In 1976, my college roommate introduced me to a Native American named Bruce Contway. Bruce was a rodeo guy, so he and I hit it off right away. I especially loved to hear Bruce tell stories about rodeoing, and I was fascinated by his exciting tales.

Bruce's roommate owned some horses. By the winter of 1977, I had moved in with Bruce and his buddy at their house. There, Bruce taught me the basics of riding horses and rodeoing. He showed me how to rope calves and how to bulldog, the term cowboys use for the rodeo event known as steer-wrestling. As Bruce described and demonstrated how to bulldog, I could hardly believe that a grown man was going to slide off a running horse onto the back of a five-hundred-pound charging steer and wrestle it to the ground—all in less than five seconds. I had been told by my football coaches that I was too small to wrestle a two-hundred-pound man to the ground, and now Bruce wanted me to wrestle a running five-hundred pound steer! Besides, I was just learning to ride a horse, let alone jump off one that was moving. But I have always loved a challenge, so I said, "Let me at him!" Once I tried bulldogging, I was hooked.

By the following March, I decided to enroll in the Walt Linderman Bulldogging School, which was nearby in Gallatin Gateway, Montana. Walt had been a three-time runner-up champion bulldogger, and his love for the sport was contagious. I decided right then that this was something I really wanted to do.

Most bulldoggers are big, strong guys, weighing around 250 pounds, and I wasn't anywhere near that size. I weighed about 215 pounds, but I was in good physical shape, thanks to my football background and regular weight-training, so I felt that I was strong enough. In fact, I thought I was the toughest man on campus.

I had long, greasy hair, dressed wild, and thought I was "Mr. Bad" as I went to the bulldogging school with all those macho cowboy types. I was pretty much a loner, probably because the other guys didn't know what to think of me. Before long, however, despite my odd appearance, the bull-doggers took a liking to me. I was a party animal and a fighter, so they accepted me. They didn't like my long hair, but then I wasn't a cowboy. I wore an old, rolled-up, black hat, and it was ugly. But I wore it everywhere I went, sort of as a symbol that I wasn't your ordinary bulldogger.

About this time my dad caught on to some of my shenanigans, so he cut off my money supply. Dad was more than willing to pay for my college education, but he was not about to bankroll my partying and bulldogging. I didn't care at first. If I needed any money, I figured I'd earn it on my own. Nevertheless, money got tight quickly, and I started watching every penny.

Whenever Walt and some of the bulldoggers would ask me to go with them to eat lunch, I always refused. I had no money to spare for lunch.

"Oh, I don't want to eat lunch," I'd say.

Walt would not let me off that easily. He pressed, "Why aren't you going to eat?"

I said, "I'm not hungry."

"Well, I don't believe that. You can't be out here bulldogging like you do and not work up an appetite. Why aren't you eating?"

Finally, I admitted to Walt that I didn't have any money. "I can't afford it, Walt."

Walt rubbed his chin for a moment. Then he said, "All right; I have a deal for you. If you take care of my horses and help me to unsaddle them and feed them at night, I'll pay for your lunch."

Walt and I became buddies that day, and bulldogging became my life. I was consumed with it, and everything else took second place.

Although I had hardly ridden a horse prior to meeting Bruce Contway and attending bulldogging school, I caught on quickly. Few cowboys would have guessed that I would go from knowing virtually nothing about the sport in 1976 to making it to the top fifteen in the world and being a competitor at the National Finals Rodeo in 1979.

I had natural athletic ability, and was committed to becoming one of the best. I worked hard for two years, totally dedicated to my goal. I was also riding bulls. I was equally dedicated to learning that aspect of rodeoing, but those bulls were tough. It was a challenge. So I went to two schools—Gary Leffew's school and Jerome Robinson's school—hoping to learn how to better ride bulls. I injured my ribs in the process, so I decided to stick to bulldogging and calf roping instead. To this day, I have a tremendous admiration for the guys who ride bulls. Those bulls hurt you every time you get on them, whether you walk out of the arena or are carried out.

My dad was devastated when he discovered that I wanted to be a rodeo cowboy rather than an engineer who would one day take over his business. Dad had thought my rodeoing was just a passing thing. He didn't realize I was sold out to it, and nobody was going to take it away from me. I didn't care who said what or who got in my way, I had decided that rodeoing was what I wanted to do.

Rodeoing soon became my all-consuming passion. I could hardly wait for the whistle to blow on Friday afternoons, because, as soon as I was done working, I was on my way to enter two or three rodeos each weekend. I'd drive like a maniac to get to them. One rodeo might be halfway across New Mexico, and I'd have to drive two hundred miles in three hours. The next day I drove another couple hundred miles to get to the next rodeo. I spent all weekend at rodeos, often getting home just in time to make it to work on Monday mornings.

I did fairly well during my first summer of serious rodeoing. Then, in 1977, I got my Professional Rodeo Cowboy's permit, which is kind of an initiation, a rite of passage, for every rodeo cowboy. To receive a permit, a contestant must pay a fee plus entry fees for each rodeo he enters. A cowboy can enter rodeos on a permit until he wins a minimum of $1,000 in professional rodeos within a year, proving his ability to win. It is known as "filling your permit," after which he becomes known as a "professional rodeo cowboy."

It took seven rodeos to win $1,000, thus qualifying me to be a professional rodeo cowboy. Once I had obtained my professional card in 1978, my goal was to become Rookie of the Year. But by the time August rolled around, I had won little more than $1,200, and I was barely surviving the rodeo circuit. I was broke, and I had next to nothing as far as material possessions, savings, or any other source of income.

Rodeo cowboys are similar to professional golfers. If you don't win, you don't get paid. This is the way the system works. Every contestant pays to enter a rodeo. When I first started rodeoing, entry fees were usually $50 to $100 and $200 for the big rodeos. Today, entry fees can reach as high as $500. The top eight to ten finishers split the prize money in decreasing amounts, with the champion at each rodeo getting the most, and the eighth place guy getting the least. If a contestant fails to place in the top eight to ten, he gets nothing. In addition to that, each cowboy pays his own travel, food, and lodging expenses. So even though I had won some money on the circuit, I still was not making enough to pay my expenses. Nowadays, rodeos have gotten more popular, and big name rodeo cowboys can secure sponsors, similar to professional race car drivers. But when I started rodeoing, my only sponsor was me.

By August 1978, I began to question whether I could really make it in the rodeo business. There were, after all, easier ways to make a living, although none seemed nearly as exciting. I was scheduled to go back to college in a few weeks, so I figured I'd better get a "real job" to make some quick money. I worked for two weeks with a construction business in Helena, Montana.

When I got some money together, however, rather than saving it for school, I entered another rodeo in Great Falls, Montana. I lost again, but that did not discourage me. I entered rodeos in Sidney, Montana, and Deadwood, South Dakota. I didn't place again in Sidney, but at Deadwood, I split sixth place with Roy Duvall and earned about $150. The money was not impressive, but Roy Duvall had won the world championship three times and had made the national finals thirteen times. Roy was the epitome of what every professional rodeo cowboy wanted to be. Here I was, the new guy on the circuit, splitting a rodeo purse with him. There was no way I was giving up rodeo now!

I entered another rodeo in Big Timber, Montana. I needed a ride from Deadwood to Big Timber, a distance of about three hundred miles, so I started asking around the rodeo to see if anyone was going in that direction. Nobody was. Nobody, except Jim Bode Scott.

Looking back on it, I can see it was an important part of God's plan for my life that I ride back to Montana with Jim Bode, but at the time, I wasn't too excited about it. Frankly, Jim Bode wasn't my kind of guy. I knew Jim Bode from school at MSU, as well as a competitor on the rodeo circuit. His dad owned one of the biggest ranches in Montana and was the first man in Montana to sell a million-dollar calf crop. At one time, he had over ten thousand mama cows on a ranch that spread from Billings, Montana, to Miles City, Montana, covering more than one hundred forty miles.

Maybe because I knew Jim Bode came from money, I didn't care to have much to do with him. To me he always seemed a bit "uppitty." But he was the only driver going back to Big Timber from Deadwood that night.

I swallowed my pride and asked him for a ride.

"Why, sure, Paul," Jim Bode said with a broad smile.

Oh, great! Just what I wanted to do, I thought.

When Jim Bode stopped at a convenience store to get gas before leaving town, I said to myself, "Well, I don't want to waste this whole trip," so I went into the store and bought a six-pack of beer. Jim Bode eyed me curiously when I returned to his van with the beer, but he didn't say anything. We headed toward Montana, making small talk, and before long, Jim Bode started to talk to me about Jesus.

I wasn't totally surprised. I had heard on the circuit that he had "gotten religion," and I had noticed that he hadn't been around the party crowd for a while. Actually, I had heard that Jim Bode had been "born again," but I didn't know what that meant. I had only heard that term when the movie *The Exorcist* came out. I was attending New Mexico State in 1974, and the school paper ran a headline heralding, "Born Agains

Protest Movie, *The Exorcist*." I figured being born again must be like join-ing a cult.

That night in Jim Bode's van, however, he talked about Jesus, not just about religion, or joining a church. Amazingly, Jim Bode talked as if he knew Jesus—personally!

As we drove along, Jim Bode kept asking me questions. "What do you know about Jesus?" he asked. "Who is He, and what has He done for you?"

I wasn't afraid to talk about Jesus. After all, I went to Catholic catechism classes as a kid. I knew about Jesus. With a bit of smugness in my voice, I told Jim Bode, "He died on the cross. He died for the forgiveness of our sins. Just believe in Him and be good, and you might get to heaven."

Jim Bode threw his head back and said, "Oh, no! It's not a matter of whether you might get to heaven. You can be sure of that!"

I said, "How do you know? You can't be sure."

He replied, "Because the Scripture tells us that you can know so, not just think so."

"Where does it say that?" I asked belligerently.

To my surprise, Jim Bode started quoting the Scripture. He had a stack of plain white cards sitting on his dashboard. He pointed to the cards and said, "These Scriptures are on those cards. They are all in the Bible, and I have been memorizing them."

I looked at the cards on the dash; there must have been fifty of them, each one about the size of a standard business card with a verse of Scripture printed on it. I asked him, "Do you have all these memorized?" I knew Jim Bode had not been a good student in college. I couldn't imagine that he had memorized fifty verses of anything, much less fifty Scripture verses.

He said, "Yep."

I said, "Aw, baloney. Prove it."

I went through each of the cards, giving Jim Bode the reference, and he would quote the verse from memory. I thought, *Okay. This is some sort of a trick. He probably has the cards in a certain order so he can tell what the verse is.* So I reversed them and shuffled them. Jim Bode still correctly quoted the Scriptures. Then I said, "Okay, let's do this. I'll say the verse and you tell me what chapter and verse it is." Jim Bode agreed readily. And he never missed a verse. He had a phenomenal memory for Scriptures. Duly impressed, I was ready to listen as Jim Bode told me about the Lord Jesus.

We traveled about three hundred miles that night, and Jim Bode talked about Jesus almost every mile of the way. He spoke so convincingly about knowing Jesus that I was fascinated. So fascinated, in fact, I never drank a drop of my beer. We arrived at Jim Bode's home at about 1:30 A.M. After he showed me where I was to sleep, Jim Bode asked matter-of-factly, "Do you want to pray?"

I said, "Sure, yeah."

We knelt by the bed and prayed. And Jim Bode Scott introduced me to his best friend, Jesus Christ. We held hands as we prayed, yet for some reason, it seemed perfectly comfortable and normal. In retrospect, I can only imagine the picture we must have made—two big cowboys kneeling there, holding hands, and praying.

I prayed sincerely and asked Jesus Christ to come into my life. I didn't feel any different after the prayer, yet I recognized that something significant had happened. An eternal commitment had been transacted. I didn't change as far as my outward conduct—Jim Bode and I went to the rodeo the next day, and I consumed my usual quantity of beer—but I knew that by asking Jesus to become real to me, I had done something right for the first time in my life. There was something different in my heart. I just knew.

In the past, I believed God existed. But I didn't know if He really cared about me. I had never been assured of His presence. Now, even though my lifestyle hadn't changed as yet, the process had begun. It was like being, well . . . like being born all over again!

I went back to college, but by Christmastime I was bored with school once more. I decided to remain in Montana so I could keep rodeoing, but college ceased to interest me. I was riding the fence on a major decision: "Am I going to rodeo or not?" It was a turning point in my life when I talked to Chuck Karnoff, the trainer for the football team at Montana State University. He was a cowboy, and he and I had gotten to be friends.

I said, "Chuck, I just don't know what I should do."

He said, "Paul, what can you lose? You are twenty-one years old; you don't owe anybody nothing. So if you rodeo a couple years and you don't make it, so what? But if you don't try, all your life you'll be saying, 'I wish I would have gone after it.' "

You're right, Chuck, I thought. *I'm gonna go for it.*

I got on a plane along with a friend, Pat Nogel, flew to Omaha, Nebraska, and entered the rodeo there. There I met Dan Ackley and his wife, Dede, and we traveled together to the rodeos. The Ackleys owned a motor home and had a team of horses. Pat and I traveled with them all that fall. During that time I won about $5,000, which was enough for a single guy like me to live on.

At the rodeos, when I was not involved in the competition, I worked the "labor list." The labor list is a list of cowboys who want to earn extra money by doing the mundane, tedious tasks at the rodeo. For instance, at every rodeo somebody has to run the chute gates, untie the calves, and open the gates to let the animals out, including the bucking chutes, the gates from which the bucking bulls are released. In the late 1970s, rodeo contractors usually paid each of the labor list guys ten dollars per performance. Some of the more prestigious rodeo performers were too proud to work the labor list. Not me. I figured, *You work a couple hours, you make ten bucks. I am going to be there anyway, so I might as well be making a little money.* Ten to twenty dollars a day was enough to buy my food, and I was sleeping in the motor home, so my expenses were minimal.

During the state fair and rodeo in Oklahoma City, I was working the labor list and untying calves with a cowboy named Larry Smith. We were talking casually as we were working together when suddenly, Larry asked me if I was born again. At that time, I thought that I was probably the only born again cowboy at that rodeo. Few of the regulars knew me, and I was not about to tell anybody that I had become a Christian. I didn't realize that God has His representatives in all walks of life, even in the rodeo.

I said, "Do you mean a born again Christian?"

"That's exactly what I mean," Larry answered. "Ain't really any other kind."

"Yeah; yeah, I am," I replied. As Larry and I talked, he told me that he was a rodeo preacher. He did not pastor a church in the usual sense, but he conducted services at each rodeo and spent a lot of time one on one, talking and counseling with the guys.

Larry said, "We are having a fellowship meeting after the rodeo tonight. Why don't you come along?"

That night I could hardly wait for the final "go round" to be finished at the rodeo, because I was so excited about going with Larry. I knew something unusual was happening inside me. As much as I loved rodeoing, I had an insatiable desire to find out more about Jesus. Larry and I went to a room at the hotel where I met a bunch of Christian cowboys. I was amazed! I said, "This is neat. I didn't know there were so many cowboys who were Christians."

Dan and Dede Ackley decided to stay in Oklahoma City for a few days, so I stayed too. While there, we went to visit Willard Moody, another rodeo cowboy. Willard was one of the best calf ropers in the world. When we arrived at Willard's place, he and some other guys were practicing roping calves.

I jumped in and started helping. After a while, I thought that I heard the guys talking about spiritual subjects. I said to myself, *Are they talking about the Bible?* That was foreign to me because I couldn't figure out why anybody would be talking about the Bible unless they were in church. But there they were, a couple of rodeo cowboys, and it sounded as though they were talking about God and the Bible and how much Jesus had done for them. I didn't know much about the Bible, but I sure was interested.

I continued putting the calves in the chute, but at the same time, I edged closer to where the men were talking. Sure enough; they were talking about Jesus.

I said, "Hey, are you guys Christians?"

As it turned out, Willard Moody was a strong Christian, who eventually became a rodeo preacher. We got to be friends, and to this day, Willard is one of my best friends. He and his wife, Donna, have been very instrumental in helping Susie and me walk with the Lord. Not only have they been good friends, they have been great examples for us, and encouragers to us.

Once when Susie and I were at their home, Willard and Donna were trying to encourage me to be more affectionate to Susie. I was sitting on the couch, and Susie was standing in the middle of the room.

"Go ahead," Willard urged. "Just stand right up there and hug your wife."

"I can't," I replied.

"What do you mean you can't? You're married, aren't you? She's your wife, and she needs your affection. Now go hug her!"

"I can't hug her in front of you and Donna," I told Willard.

"Why not?" Donna asked, the surprise evident on her face.

"Because hugging is for the bedroom, not out in public."

"It is so. Now get up there and hug Susie," Willard told me.

Reluctantly, I rose to my feet. I walked over to Susie, approaching her warily as if I were sneaking up on a rabbit. My arms seemed to hang at my sides like detached limbs.

"Come on, now!" Willard encouraged.

"It's easy, Paul," laughed Donna. "Just pick up your arms and put them around her. She won't bite."

I stepped closer and reached out to my wife. I tentatively pulled her closer but not close enough to touch me, held her for a moment, patted her back, and quickly let go of her.

"No, no!" Willard cried. "That's not good enough. Give the woman a hug! Get a hold of her like you love her."

Once again I approached Susie, who was laughing at my hesitancy. I shuffled my feet, looked down at the floor, my face turning a deeper shade of red every moment. Finally, I reached out and wrapped my arms around my wife. Susie and I melted into each other in a long, closely knit hug, laughing all the time, and feeling wonderful.

"There now, see? That wasn't so bad, was it?" Donna asked with a smile, as though she were a nurse who had just given a little boy some medicine.

I smiled at Susie. Now that I was holding her, I didn't want to let go. We felt relief that we had overcome an obstacle in our relationship, where we could be truly friends, not just sexual partners.

In 1978, the National Finals Rodeo competition was also held in Oklahoma City. I got a job working the labor list, running the extra steers, and got a chance to see the national finals as a result. My goal was to become one of the best cowboys on the rodeo circuit, so I was excited to be able to see up close some of the top rodeo cowboys in the world.

The Fellowship of Christian Athletes Cowboy Chapter had a fellowship room every night where I would go to fellowship, and we had a great time. The Christian cowboys seemed to really love the Lord, and they had a strong influence on me. Being with them helped me to start out on the right foot in my walk with the Lord. During that period of time, I began to realize that God is real.

That week, the whole time I was working there, I was saying, "God, what do you want me to do? I don't know whether to rodeo or go back to school. What do you want me to do?"

One day as I was walking around the rodeo, I ran into none other than Sandy Gagnon, the rodeo coach at Montana State University. I was surprised to see him, but even more so, I regarded our chance meeting as nothing less than direction from God. I thought, *With more than nine thousand people in attendance at the National Finals Rodeo, what are my chances of running into a rodeo coach from Montana State University, fifteen hundred miles away? Surely, God must be trying to tell me something.*

As Coach Gagnon and I began to talk, I became even more convinced God was using the man to help redirect my course. Coach Gagnon said, "I have been looking all over for you. I was trying to get in touch with you. We would love to have you come back to MSU and rodeo. We might even be able to work out some sort of scholarship money for you."

By now, my reputation as a bulldogger and a first-rate rodeo cowboy was becoming established. In rodeo circles it was not uncommon to hear my name mentioned as one of the up-and-coming guys on the circuit. Still, I was still surprised when Coach Gagnon offered me a scholarship.

To me, the coach's invitation was a sign from God. I said, "Thank you, God. I'll go back to school and rodeo!"

Back at Montana State University, Jim Bode Scott and I became roommates. More than that, we became close, lifelong friends. We went to Bible studies together almost every day on campus. While I focused on my rodeoing, I was also growing stronger as a Christian.

When Jimbo and I rodeoed together, people started calling us "The God Squad," and the name stuck. A local newspaper did an interview with us that resulted in an article about the two rodeo cowboys who loved Jesus. Apparently, the article piqued the interest of quite a few people in the MSU area—especially those to whom I owed money.

During my earlier years at Montana State, prior to coming to know the Lord, I was a deluxe heathen. I used to go to bars, ring up a large tab, and then pay them with "hot" checks, knowing full well that I didn't have enough money in my account to cover the amount. Often, my friends and I went to restaurants and ordered the biggest steaks on the menu. After eating, we'd simply walk out the door without paying the bill. I was a master at such deceit.

Now, after becoming a Christian, I returned to MSU to go to school, and the article came out in the paper about Jim Bode Scott and Paul Luchsinger being known as The God Squad. The day after the article hit the paper, the rodeo coach called me into his office and said, "Say, we got a lot of calls."

I puffed up my chest, thinking that the calls were compliments in response to the article that had run in the paper.

The coach burst my bubble when he said, "Yeah, this collection agency, and this collection agency, they want you to come down and pay them a visit!"

I went to the collection agency that had a list of the places where I owed money. I walked in and said, "Hi, I'm Paul Luchsinger."

"Oh!" the woman at the counter said. "We've been looking for *you*."

"Yeah, I know," I replied as I pulled out my checkbook. I wrote out a check to pay off all of the debts I owed. Amazingly, they accepted my check! I apologized to the people I owed, and told them I was glad to make it right with them.

Clearly, God was working in my life.

But my commitment to God was still wishy-washy. I was being pulled between my old buddies whom I partied with when I had attended MSU in the previous years, and my new life as a Christian and the activities with which Jim Bode and I had become involved. I knew my relationship with God was real, but it was beginning to get stale, and I was getting bored.

When spring came, I decided to move out of my room with Jim Bode and move in with my old friends. I started drinking and went on terrible drunken sprees in which I stayed drunk for a week or more. I knew Jimbo was disappointed in me. He never said a word about my poor conduct; he just continued to love me and kept encouraging me to come back to the Bible studies. Eventually I did, but my walk with the Lord was still inconsistent.

Six months of the rodeo season were already over, so I knew my chances of making it to the National Rodeo finals were pretty slim. I wasn't worried about it, though. I was just having fun now. I just wanted to rodeo and love Jesus.

I qualified for the college national finals, held that year in Lake Charles, Louisiana. I rode in a van, along with four other guys, from Montana to Louisiana. Along the way, I entered rodeos at Belt, Montana; Branson, Missouri; and Gladewater, Texas.

I took third place at Belt and won first place at Branson. I went to Gladewater, Texas, home of the big Professional Rodeo Cowboy Association rodeo. The PRCA is the cream of the crop in rodeoing, comparable to the National Football League (NFL) in football, or the Professional Golf Association (PGA) in golf. Although there are numerous other rodeo associations around the world, winning in the PRCA was my goal. I wanted to be the best of the best.

Everybody who was anybody in rodeoing was at the PRCA rodeo in Gladewater. I entered and rode Roy Duvall's horse, "Whiskey," and to the surprise of many veteran rodeo participants, I won first place at

Gladewater, the first big PRCA rodeo I ever won. It was a two header, two go-rounds in which each contestant gets to run two head of stock.

I went on to the college finals at Lake Charles, and made it to the final rounds, but I failed to place. Afterward, I was angry, frustrated, and disappointed. Despite my newfound relationship with God, I got drunk and messed up real good down there.

One of the guys who saw my inconsistencies up close was my traveling companion and good friend Mark Muggli. Mark witnessed both sides of my extreme character—Christian on one hand, heathen on the other. We rodeoed together and partied together. Mark saw me smoking dope, drinking beer, chasing women—all after I had made a public commitment to Jesus Christ.

My life was inconsistent. When I would do well and win at my rodeoing, I'd often get away from God, get into my pride, and then crash. Then I would come crawling back to God and repent and do well for three or four months before slipping and going back on a bad binge of some sort. It was a pattern that would show up again and again in my life in the days ahead.

I was obsessed with trying to be the best, the toughest, the meanest, or the wildest. Often I did outlandish things simply to show other cowboys that I could do whatever they could do, only to the extreme. I'd say, "If you want to get drunk, I'll show you how to get drunk. If you want to be wild, I can be wilder than you!" Soon my reputation around campus and in rodeo circles was, "Yeah, he is a Christian, but when he gets to drinking, get out of his way, because he gets wild."

Sadly, none of my fellow Christians on the rodeo circuit ever confronted me about the inconsistencies in my life. Nobody ever called me on it, or said, "Paul, you need to straighten up. You know you really shouldn't be doing these things."

Jim Bode knew about my struggles and would tell me when he thought that I wasn't doing right, but Jim Bode wasn't around much. Besides, he didn't travel the rodeo circuit full time, and he was not always aware of what was going on in my life. I certainly can't blame him for not trying to keep me in line. He loved me and accepted me. He never criticized me or pointed his finger at me. Today, I can appreciate what Jim Bode was doing, expressing the unconditional love of Jesus Christ.

Nor do I blame anyone else for my personal failures. Nevertheless, in my life I needed someone to say to me, "Don't do that."

"Stop!"

"Don't cross that line!"

"One more mess up, and it's going to cost you big time."

I desperately needed someone to confront me and hold me accountable for my own actions. If someone I respected had said, "Paul, don't do that. You're making a mess of your life, and you are bringing the name of Jesus into disrepute," I probably would have responded positively.

But no such person was in my life at that time.

In July 1979, I met Charlie Battles. Charlie was a bulldogger who owned a bulldogging horse named Sleepy. Strange as it might seem, not everybody in rodeo owns a horse; I certainly didn't. Like many other guys, when I got to each rodeo, I'd enter and pay my fees, and then have to go asking everybody, "Who has a horse that I can use?" The rodeo is like a big family; all the regulars know each other and help each other, so it is not unusual for two competing cowboys to be riding the same horse.

Of course, the better a cowboy gets, the more likely it is that he might win. If you are a winner, then owners want you to ride their horses, because the owner then has a better chance of earning "mount money," 25 percent of all the rider wins.

That weekend in July, Charlie made $500 extra cash he could pocket simply because I had won while riding his horse. Not long after that, I entered a rodeo at Salt Lake, and again I rode Charlie's horse. I won the rodeo and $2,200.

About that time, I met Charlie's wife, a rather nondescript young singer named Reba. I didn't listen to much music, since all I was interested in was bulldogging. I didn't have any idea that Reba was just starting to break into the world of country music.

I saw Charlie again at Cheyenne, Wyoming, one of the most famous rodeos in the world, where I placed in the top ten and won about $5,000 that week. I was having a good time, earning some money doing something I loved and going to Christian fellowship meetings. Life was good.

I was a single man on a wild, raucous rodeo circuit, a slippery trail that could easily lead to a carousing downhill slide ending in quicksand. I wasn't too interested in settling down and getting married. I had my sights set on the world championship. I wasn't dating much, but I couldn't get one woman out of my mind. I had seen her at a rodeo in San Angelo, Texas, on stage singing with her sister Reba.

Chapter 9

BACK IN
THE HUNT

*D*uring the summer of 1979 I was traveling the rodeo circuit with Dan Ackley, "Punch" Hennigan, and John Boschi. All three guys had won sizable sums of money during the early part of the year and were well on their way to qualifying for the National Finals Rodeo. Punch had actually set a new record for the largest amount of money won at one rodeo by winning $12,500 at Fort Worth. By the time I teamed up with Punch and John, however, they had hit a dry spell, not even placing at many rodeos we entered.

On the other hand, about the time that they started cooling off, I got hot. I started winning at one rodeo after another. Nevertheless, I had no illusions of making the finals that year. The rodeo season officially ends on October 31 each year (although rodeos go on all year long), and I had gotten a late start. I had only been entering professional rodeos since June of that year.

But in October, at Billings, Montana, during the steer wrestling competition, as the announcer introduced me over the arena loudspeakers, he said, "This man has just entered into the top fifteen in the world."

I could hardly believe my ears! Even though I had been winning regularly, I hadn't been paying attention to my standings since I had little hope of being one of the top fifteen money winners of the year. I was amazed to find out that I had a chance to make the finals.

With my newly acquired status, I also inherited an increased amount of pressure. I felt I had to win in order to maintain my position in the top fifteen and to be able to compete in the finals in December. For the next few weeks, I gave it all I had and ended the season in fifteenth position, barely beating out Larry Ferguson by $300.

When the 1980 season rolled around, I started bulldogging really well, but I hadn't placed in any of the rodeos I entered. As sometimes happens in rodeo, you can do everything well and not win.

Previously I had won $2,500 at the 1979 finals, so I was able to cover my expenses and make a decent living . . . for a single guy. I wasn't planning on remaining single for the rest of my life, but I wasn't going to let a woman interfere with my bulldogging when my goal of being a champion rodeo cowboy was so close at hand. I dated a number of women, but I was too busy bulldogging to get serious with anyone. Besides, I was looking for a Christian woman.

Since committing my life to Jesus, I had learned that Christians are to marry only Christians; anything other than that according to the Bible is considered being "unequally yoked together" (2 Cor. 6:14, KJV). I had not only trusted my life to Christ, I had also learned that although I had been promiscuous in my past, those sins were forgiven. I did not want to repeat my mistakes. After all, Jesus told a woman caught in adultery that her sins were forgiven, but He also said, "Go, and sin no more" (John 8:11, KJV). Consequently, I committed myself to abstaining from sexual relationships.

That commitment was sorely tested on more than one occasion. For instance, in 1980, I was dating a young woman barrel racer named Sandy (not her real name). I had met her at the National Finals and had seen her off and on at other rodeos since then. I liked Sandy, but I had no plans to marry her.

Early in the season, I entered the rodeo at Denver. Denver is the first of the big winter rodeos; the indoor rodeos held in huge arenas often draw crowds of twenty thousand people or more per performance.

Before the rodeo, I could feel my strength ebbing, but I didn't know why. Then I got sick. It was the same sort of sickness that I had experienced just after I had graduated from high school and was about to enter the Air Force Academy. I had excruciating headaches, high fever, and chronic diarrhea. I lost thirty pounds in four days. One doctor diagnosed me as having intestinal flu; another said it was dysentery.

I stayed in bed in the motel right up until the time when I was scheduled to run my first steer at the rodeo; I was entered in the steer-wrestling competition for two runs, two opportunities to bring down a steer. I staggered to my feet and went out and tried to compete, but I was so weak, my performance was awful. I ran my second steer and did no better.

My traveling companions and I moved on from Denver to Fort Worth, where my performance was about the same. From there, we went to Deming, New Mexico, where I stayed with my parents for about a week and recuperated. My friends stayed at my folks' home and took a break too.

About that time, Sandy called and said, "I am coming through there on my way to Palm Springs. Why don't you travel with me?"

Although Sandy's offer sounded innocent enough, I knew exactly what could happen. I was trying to be a good Christian, but I compromised by thinking, *Okay, we'll travel together, and we can sleep in the same hotel room, but that's all we're going to do—sleep.*

Sandy and I headed for Palm Springs. Along the way, we stopped at a motel for the night, and I reiterated my conditions in my mind: *No sex; just sleep.* That night, I became terribly sick again. I got so bad, I finally told Sandy, "You gotta take me to the emergency room; I am going to die!" At the emergency room, the doctor concluded that I had amoebic dysentery and gave me a prescription for ampicillin. I was released from the hospital, and the next morning Sandy went her way and I got back in the rig with my traveling buddies. My determined mind against sex because of my Christian beliefs caused later false rumors that I was "gay."

I was still sick, so again, I laid in bed for two days, parked at the Palm Springs rodeo. I was nearly delirious when I heard someone say, "You have about fifteen minutes to get out there and run your steer." I was so sick that

I could hardly hold my head up, but I struggled to my feet, went into the arena, ran the steer . . . and won! I earned $900 at Palm Springs, which turned out to be the only money I won all winter long.

When I felt better, I decided to move on to Oklahoma and Texas that spring. There are a lot more rodeos in those states, and the distance between each of them is not nearly so far as the rodeos in Montana. It is seven hundred miles across the state of Montana, and there are approximately thirty rodeos. By contrast, it is easy to find nearly a hundred rodeos within a one-hundred-mile radius in Oklahoma. Every rodeo in Oklahoma and Texas paid a thousand dollars or more to the winners. During that spring, I traveled with Mark Muggli, the fellow who probably knew me better than anyone in the world at that time. A few years later, Mark would be standing next to me as my best man at Susie's and my wedding.

I moved to Stephenville, Texas, and lived with Lloyd Hodges and his wife, Kathy. I stayed there for several months, during which time Lloyd introduced me to the delights of southern cooking, including all sorts of fried foods, many of which I had never tasted before. The fried foods did wonders for my stomach! Once again, I became extremely sick.

Lloyd's brother was an internal medicine specialist. He set up an appointment with a doctor in Dallas, and that doctor diagnosed me with ulcerative colitis. I spent four days in the hospital, while the medical staff there ran all sorts of tests on me. They gave me some medicine, and I started improving immensely. Consequently, I was able to keep on rodeoing. The rodeo lifestyle, with little sleep, fast food, constant stress, and travel continued to drain my energy and my health remained shaky. I was determined to make the National Finals, and I had a long way to go.

Despite my physical problems, I soon began bulldogging again. I was doing well and had confidence that I could win. It seemed everyone else on the professional rodeo circuit recognized that I was going to be a champion. I just needed a good horse to ride in the competitions.

Throughout the spring of 1980, I didn't win a dime! That summer I began traveling with rodeo ace Roy Duvall. I had ridden Roy's horse, Whiskey, in Gladewater when I had won my first money as a professional rodeo cowboy. Now, I said, "I know in my heart, if I can compete on that horse, I can win."

A certain dynamic is required between a horse and rider to win at rodeoing, and I knew that Whiskey and I had that dynamic, which was missing with other horses I had been riding. I asked Roy if he would be willing to allow me to ride Whiskey, and Roy graciously agreed. The first night out, I won $900.

I rode Whiskey again in Ft. Smith, Arkansas, and won $3,500. In Gladewater I won $2,500, and in Clovis, New Mexico I won $1,800—all in a week's time! I catapulted from being at the bottom of the pile to being in the middle of the pack of contenders with a possibility of making the national finals. I was back in the hunt again!

By October, I qualified for the finals, ranking number eleven in the world. I was excited about competing at the National Finals Rodeo in Oklahoma City, but I had no idea that the week I spent there in December 1980 would change my life forever.

Early in the week at the NFR, I came out to warm up my horse. As I did, a pretty young woman caught my eye as she and another young woman walked in the back door of the arena. I figured that since she was entering through the performers' door, she must have something to do with the rodeo, yet she didn't look like the typical women I had grown accustomed to seeing perform at rodeos. She didn't dress in western garb, and she wasn't wearing a hat. I wondered what this woman's connection was to the rodeo. I decided to get a closer look.

When my horse spooked a bit, I had the perfect opportunity to ride by the young woman. I had little trouble getting my horse under control, but I allowed him to carry me in the woman's direction anyhow.

She was incredible. Her soft-looking, clear complexion was like that of an angel, and her trim figure was highlighted by sandy-red hair that enhanced her bright blue eyes, making them seem to dance. As I drew closer to the woman, I recalled seeing her somewhere before . . . *San Angelo*, I thought. *I remember seeing her at the rodeo at San Angelo.* She was related somehow to one of my bulldogging buddies, Charlie Battles, and his wife, that singer, Reba.

My horse swept by the young woman and her companion, and as it did, I looked down at her, nodded my best cowboy nod and smiled. It was not an unusual thing for me to do. I smiled at everybody, especially the pretty women who showed up at the rodeos. But as I smiled at this lady, her response puzzled me. At first, she looked back at me as though I had lassoed her and jerked her toward me. Then suddenly her lips opened to a bright smile, making her look even more radiant.

I was intrigued and thought, *As soon as this rodeo is over, I want to find out more about this woman.*

Mama & Daddy
in their early years

Elvin & Reba Smith

Paul at graduation
1973
Deming High School

Martha Susan McEntire
5 yrs old 1964

Our cousins were just like our brothers & sisters.
back-(L-R) Alice, Don Wayne Smith
middle-(L-R) Patricia Smith, Pake, Reba
front-(L-R) Me & Diannia Smith

Paul celebrating 8th birthday

"I sure like this ring."
Our wedding–November 27, 1981

Farewell kiss from
Mama to "her baby"

The weaning Shack & our Buick. If this
house could talk, it could write a Bestseller!

Shortly after our wedding Reba sang at the Orange
Festival in Florida. We got to honeymoon there, too.

samuel, Lucchese & E.P.

E.P., Daddy (Clark),
samuel, Mama (Jac), & Lucchese

My daddy, Clark McEntire

Life was exciting singing with Reba.
The Grand Ole Opry – Nashville, TN 1982

This was a normal sight in the
recording studio. Paul had to take
care of the kids while I sang & sang
& sang. Lucchese, Paul & E.P.

Here we are in Topeka, KS in
1989 in front of our motorhome.
We got out on the road as soon as
Samuel was born.

Here we are ready to take off in our bus!

Paul at 1985 NFR

Paul giving E.P. a "swig" on a hot Rodeo day in Oklahoma.

Susie's grandpap John McEntire Roping a steer in the 1920's.

Paul with our good friend Jim Bode Scott. Jim Bode led Paul to Christ, discipled him, and has been a great friend.

Paul Schultz baptizing Paul in the Holiday Inn swimming pool, August, 1980

I love to sing "Amazing Grace."
It's my favorite!

Paul & I at the Sweetheart Banquet,
Phoenix, Arizona

Our relationship with Roper Western
Apparel has been a good one! Here's the
first promotional picture they did.

I was honored to work with Mr. Ben Johnson
to benefit the Oklahoma City Children's
Hospital with a Celebrity Rodeo

Fan Fair

At our "listening party" for the album "Real Love." Daddy, Mama, Susie & Paul

Paul Overstreet, Glenn Wagner, Paul & Susie. Glenn Wagner was very much responsible for getting us together with Integrity Music.

Paul & I

Reba, Mama & I taped a "Mother's Day Special." We had a great time.

We had a great time filming Reba's special commemorating 20 years in the music business.

Here's all the family at the Induction (L-R) Pake, Calamity, Reba, Susie, E.P., Alice, Garrett, Daddy & Mama.

We encourage people to help one another ease a hard day by massaging their neighbors neck. I get in on the act, too!

It's hard to imagine my little boy is growing up. E.P. & I went to Reba's induction into the National Cowboy Hall of Fame.

Here we are after the Dove Awards in Nashville.

Here we with Paul's Mom & Dad. Beverly & Paul Luchsinger

Samuel, Paul, Lucchese, Susie & E.P.

Chapter 10

A DIVINE
ENCOUNTER

I could hardly take my eyes off Paul Luchsinger as he went through the door to the dance after the 1980 National Finals Rodeo. I wanted to see who he was with and whether he had a girlfriend. My heart sank a bit when I saw him dancing with a young woman, but I noticed that he didn't seem to be dancing with any one woman exclusively. When my ticket-taking duties at the front entrance were done, I hurried inside the dance hall to get a better look.

Music and people filled the large room, so for a while I lost sight of Paul in the din. My eyes were searching the banquet-turned-dance-hall looking for him. Suddenly, I felt a tap on my shoulder and turned to see Paul Luchsinger looking into my eyes. "Would you care to dance?" Paul asked politely. I hesitated for a moment, not wanting to seem overly anxious, but inside I wanted to shout, "Yes! Yes, I would love to dance with you!" Instead, I replied simply, "Why, yes, thank you."

My sister Reba was singing as Paul and I danced together for the first time. I liked him immediately. He was so friendly, easy to talk to, always laughing, joking, telling stories; it was almost impossible to dislike him. We danced a full set, then Paul thanked me and disappeared. The next time I saw him, he was dancing with another girl . . . and then another!

Later that night, Paul asked me to dance again. We didn't talk much, but we sure grinned at each other a lot. We got along like two old friends. At the close of the set, Paul asked if I would be willing to go out with him some time during the next week at the rodeo. I readily accepted his offer.

Thinking that perhaps Paul might want to walk me back to Reba's room or to my car, I began looking for him as the dance drew to a close. But by the time the lights came up, indicating it was time for the last dance of the evening, Paul had once again disappeared. Years later I discovered that he and one of his buddies had taken off with two attractive young women.

It was my first encounter with what I eventually learned was a pattern for Paul. He tended to have a double standard—he could act and talk a strong spiritual spiel, but he could also conveniently set aside his faith when circumstances or people pressured him into compromising situations. Paul's faith, at that time, depended more upon his mood than upon the Word of God.

True to his word, though, Paul asked me out later in the week, but not just once. On our first date, Paul took me to Applewoods, which was at that time one of the nicer restaurants in the Oklahoma City area. Our relationship took off surprisingly fast and after our first date, we were a couple. We went dancing, to movies, or out to dinner. And everywhere we went, we always had a hi-ho time. I had not been in a serious relationship for a while prior to the time Paul and I began dating, but before long, I began to settle into the idea that Paul might just be the guy for me. Along the way, I did something I vowed I would never do—I fell in love with a rodeo cowboy—a Christian rodeo cowboy, Paul Luchsinger!

We actually saw each other only eleven or twelve times over the next eleven months. Paul was on the road, going from rodeo to rodeo, so we maintained a long-distance relationship as best we could. Whenever possible, Paul visited me in Oklahoma City. He was always a perfect gentleman and was so much fun to be with, I could feel myself falling in love.

Looking back, it is easy to see how artificial our courtship was. We didn't become friends by sharing ideas, thoughts, feelings, and emotions. Instead, we instantly fell into a "boyfriend-girlfriend" type of relationship. We moved quickly from there to a "semi-married" mode, thinking, talking, and planning to get married, without really taking time to get to know each other on a deeper level. In the long run, this stifled our relationship. Although Paul and I got caught up in all the excitement of being in love, the lack of depth in our relationship would come back to haunt us in the years to come.Paul continued to visit me off and on when I was home and whenever he was passing anywhere nearby. One day he asked me directly, "Are you a Christian?"

I knew that I did not always live the way the Bible said, but I also was convinced the commitment that I had made to the Lord as a child was still intact. I answered, "Why, sure, I'm a Christian."

I knew there was something different about Paul, and I wanted desperately to please him. I asked Paul, "Are you a Christian?"

"Yeah! I'm a Christian," Paul answered excitedly.

"Uh-huh, I thought so," I replied, looking at him sideways, trying to figure this guy out. Actually, by this time, Paul was becoming a radical Christian, and he wanted desperately for me to be the same. I was certain of the Lord's love, which He had recently confirmed to me, deepening my awareness of God, but I was still timid and lukewarm about my faith. Paul, on the other hand, seemed as though he was on fire.

Often when Paul was visiting, he would arrive at my apartment before I got home from work. I showed him where I kept an extra key so he could come inside and wait comfortably for me. When I arrived at my apartment, I'd find Paul with his Bible open, Christian music in my tape deck, and the television tuned in to some sort of Christian program. One time, he rummaged all through my music collection looking for some albums by Christian artists. He was disappointed because I didn't own any overtly Christian music. I had been listening to country music all my life, so most of my music was by country performers, some of whom were Christians, but that wasn't good enough for Paul. He had to have *Christian* music performed by Christian artists.

One day, while Paul was waiting for me at my apartment, he ran across a tape labeled "Pake's project." It was a cassette with a rough mix (not the finished product) of four songs Pake and I had recorded as part of Pake's efforts to strike a recording deal of his own or as a duet with me.

Paul had never really heard me sing solo. Besides, by this point in our relationship I had shared with Paul some of my deep-seated insecurities about singing. I had told him about growing up with a lisp, stammering a lot when I spoke, and not being willing to sing by myself in public.

Imagine Paul's surprise then when he put the tape in the deck and heard me singing a solo on a song called "I Want to Ride in Your Rodeo." As Paul listened to the song, it touched his heart (even though it was not a Christian song), and he felt certain at that moment that I was the woman God intended for him to marry.

To Paul, the lyrics of the song sounded almost like wedding vows:

> I want to ride in your rodeo;
> I want to be the star in your show.
> I want to go wherever you go;
> I want to ride in your rodeo.

When I got home from work, Paul met me at the door with the tape in his hand. "Susie, the song on this tape is great!"

"What song?" I asked, not aware of what he had been listening to.

"This rodeo song. 'I Want to Ride in Your Rodeo.' Come on, sing it for me, will you?'"

I playfully pushed Paul away and said, "No, I'm not singing alone for you."

Paul persisted, but I kept refusing to sing. I wasn't trying to tease him; I was simply that insecure about singing solos. Paul has always encouraged me to sing. If it weren't for him, I probably wouldn't be singing today.

Paul continued to visit often, and our relationship deepened. Soon, we began to consider marriage. I knew we were getting serious when one night as we talked about the possibility of getting married, Paul and I started looking over my savings account to see how much money I had. I had earned fairly good money while working for the oil lease company, but I had spent a lot too. Despite my wasteful spending, Paul and I figured that we could make it financially with his income and mine. We were talking all around the issue of marriage, yet Paul did not ask me to marry him.

Chapter 11

LUCKY
IN LOVE

*A*bout the same time Reba called one day and asked, "Susie, how would you like to go to work for me? I could use someone to sing backup with me in my band, and to be my traveling companion. You are the perfect choice. I'm not asking you to come on the road with me for free. I'll pay you just like I pay the other members of my band."

I was bored working for the oil lease company, and I was definitely tired of living in the city, so I said, "You bet! When can I start?"

"How about right now?" Reba replied. "And you can live with me and Charlie."

Paul, Reba, and Charlie helped me load all my earthly belongings in a horse trailer, and we hauled everything down to their home in Stringtown. The price was right, and it was convenient to live with Reba and Charlie.

The first time that I can remember singing on stage with Reba in a concert setting was in June 1980, at an auditorium in Roosevelt, Utah. Before the show, Reba tried to set my mind at ease, but I was excited and terribly nervous. She sang several of her early hits that night, so at least I was familiar with the material. We performed "I Don't Want to Be a One Night Stand," which was Reba's first single; "Nothin' Like the Love Between a Woman and a Man,"

"Glad I Waited Just for You," "Invitation to the Blues," and "You Lift Me Up to Heaven," the song that really set Reba's career skyrocketing as it soared all the way to number eight on the *Billboard* charts. I loved "You Lift Me Up To Heaven," but I was always in horror that I couldn't sing high enough to reach the notes at certain points in the song where Reba lilted into falsetto voice and I was supposed to echo her. Fear gripped me, the same sort of fear that kept me from trying so many exciting things in life, fear of failure and rejection. Not just fear that I couldn't hit those notes, but fear that I might embarrass my sister. The part was not difficult, but I was psyching myself out by thinking that I could not do it.

Sure enough, when it came time to echo Reba's part, I missed the note. I knew I had missed it, and I knew that Reba knew that I had missed it, but nobody in the audience realized that I had done anything wrong. I just sort of looked off stage and pretended that it was all part of the song. Reba glanced across the stage at me, and I could see a hint of a smile. She wasn't angry or embarrassed at all. But that didn't mean she was going to let me get by missing notes. Later she said, "Susie, you did a terrific job out there tonight. Now, let's you and me work on that echo part of 'You Lift Me Up to Heaven.' " Even way back then, Reba was a perfectionist when it came to her on-stage presentation.

Besides the performances, I accompanied Reba on many of her promotional trips to radio stations or wherever her record company was promoting her latest single or album. It was great fun, and I learned a lot about the music business. Looking back now, I can see how even during those days, God was preparing me for the day when I would be going into those radio stations to promote my own albums. Years later, many of the older DJs recalled meeting me. They'd say, "I remember you. You were with Reba, way back when she was just getting started." Because of my association with Reba, a lot of the DJs were willing to give my music a spin, even though they had not yet heard me sing.

I performed on stage with Reba for nearly two years. It was a tremendous time for me in almost every respect. I loved being with my sister, and I enjoyed doing the shows and meeting all the great people. At some point in every show, Reba had me step to center stage with her as she introduced me as her little sister. She always treated me with love, dignity, and respect.

During the time I traveled with Reba, we served as the opening act for the Statler Brothers. The Statlers are a classy bunch of fellows and were extremely kind to us. After our stint with the Statlers, we fronted such outstanding artists as Ronnie Milsap, Mickey Gilley, B. J. Thomas, Merle Haggard, and T. G. Shepherd. Every night was an education working with those superstars. It was like going through a master's program for the performing arts, and I learned much about stage presence and showmanship from each one of them.

I also learned to be on time for sound check, to be friendly and helpful, and not to take too long once it was our turn to get set up. Another important lesson I learned during those days was to have respect for the other bands performing on the same program as we were. As the old saying goes, "Be nice to the people on your way up, because you will meet them again on your way down."

Not only was I on the road with Reba as a background singer; I was her traveling companion wherever she went. Since I was living with Reba and Charlie rent-free, to reciprocate their kindness, I did much of their housework and washed and ironed their clothes. I also took care of Reba's stage wardrobe, which in those days was not nearly as extensive or as extravagant as her stage clothes are today. Nevertheless, I made sure Reba's outfits were washed and ironed and on the bus before every show. After the shows, I was responsible for the product tables, where fans could purchase Reba's music, pictures, posters, and other items. Long after the concert was over and the hall was empty except for a custodian, I'd still be there packing up records and tapes in road cases and dragging the boxes to the bus.

Musically, my horizons were expanding. Spiritually, however, I wasn't doing as well. The traveling performer's lifestyle is not conducive to spiritual growth. I was still a "baby Christian," a new believer, and I failed to "feed" myself spiritually by studying the Bible; nor did I seek out any Christian fellowship. I started drinking again, mostly at parties and dinners, and I might have slid completely downhill had it not been for that rodeo cowboy keeping tabs on me.

Paul visited me at Reba and Charlie's whenever he could. On one visit, he was spending the night there with us, and after Reba and Charlie had gone to bed, Paul and I were talking. Suddenly he said, "Let's get married!"

He took me so off guard, I wasn't sure if he was serious or not, so I said, "Well, I don't know about that."

Paul spent the next hour or so listing for me all the pros and cons of our potential marriage. I later learned that Paul is a listmaker—he makes a list of reasons why we should do certain things or not do them. He simply applied the same analytical approach to our marriage.

He rubbed his chin as he thought aloud, "Well, our incomes together would be wonderful, and.. . ." He went down the list of the reasons why we should get married. Somewhere near the bottom of the list was: "Oh, yeah. Because we love each other!"

Paul's and my attitude toward marriage was basically, "You can do your thing, and I will do mine." We figured that I would continue on the road singing with Reba, while Paul would continue traveling the rodeo circuit.

Shortly after that, Reba and I went to Ada, Oklahoma, where we stopped at a jewelry store to look at wedding rings. Paul and I had discussed the kind of rings we should get, and Paul had said, "Oh, you know, just a band will be all right."

But Paul wasn't there that day in Ada.

I was twenty-four years of age, and I had been on my own for seven years. I had graduated from college and had been working, making my own money. Then I had been singing with Reba. I was comfortable earning and spending my own money.

As I looked in the jewelry cases that day, I thought, *Paul is just talking about a plain band, but I want a diamond!*

Nell Shaw, a long-time friend who worked in the jewelry store, showed me a ring that had been made for a bride-to-be, but then for some reason, the woman wanted a larger stone, so the original ring was for sale. It was fabulous! It was also $1,700. The jeweler agreed to let me pay for the ring over time, since I was working with Reba. So what's a girl to do?

I bought the ring for myself.

Looking back, I can see that the purchase of my wedding ring was part of a pattern in my relationship with Paul. I had a strong tendency to do what I wanted to do, without consulting him. It wasn't that Paul wanted me to ask him for permission on every little thing, but he felt that if we were going to be husband and wife, we ought to make most major decisions together. Years later, many people looked at Paul as the "bad dog" in our marriage, but I can now see that my independent streak was more belligerent and contentious than I would have believed at that time.

When Paul found out that I had gone ahead and purchased the expensive diamond ring without consulting him, he looked hurt, but he didn't respond angrily. He simply said, "Well, you can pay for it!"

Paul never felt like he gave me that wedding ring, since, in actuality, I bought it for myself. A few years ago, for our twelfth wedding anniversary, Paul bought me another ring. The one Paul bought and the one I bought go well together, but Paul was still somewhat perplexed when he saw me wearing them side by side. "Why do you want to put the new ring next to that big one?"

"Because you gave it to me," I replied. I put it on that day, and I have been wearing it ever since.

Paul and I attended some premarital counseling sessions with the pastor who had agreed to marry us. He didn't know us well, but he tried to stress the importance of building our marriage around Christ. We talked a bit about Christianity, but we didn't really deal with the fabric of our relationship. Had he asked us if we were sure we understood the realities of marriage, and the type of relationship we were about to enter into, we would have had to answer no.

The truth is that Paul and I didn't really know much about each other. We had a long-distance relationship, with brief interludes of time spent together. In the eleven months between the time we met and the day we married, I had never seen Paul angry. I had never seen a down side of him. I saw a happy-go-lucky guy who was always up and ready to have fun. At that time, we had not even had a major argument in our relationship. Nowadays, Paul and I advise dating couples not to get married until they have had at least a few major disagreements in their relationship. It is important for a couple to see how well they can resolve problems *before* they say "I do." Usually when we suggest something such as that, the couple looks at us blankly, as if to say, "What in the world are you talking about? We're in love. We're never going to have arguments. Just because you had troubles in your marriage doesn't mean we will have problems in ours."

How naive. Every couple should learn before the wedding how they are going to deal with conflicts when they come . . . because they *will* come. Now, I tell young women thinking about marriage, "See your man under pressure. Watch how he reacts. How does he treat you? Notice how he treats his mama, because that's probably how he is going to treat you. Look, too, at how his daddy treats his mama, because that is how the man has learned to regard a woman."

I had met Paul's family only twice before our wedding date and my first impression was very favorable. Twenty days before our wedding, I traveled to Deming, New Mexico, to attend the wedding of Paul's younger sister, Patty. I was glad to meet Paul's family, but still it was a very artificial get-together since everybody was in a festive wedding mood.

Because of Paul's mom's bout with alcohol, I didn't pay much attention when I noticed Paul's mom tiptoeing around Paul's dad. I should have. Paul's mom was always trying to wait on everybody, making sure everyone was happy or pacified, hardly ever sitting down at her dinner table. She hovered over the table, like a hen over her chicks, saying, "You need some of this," or, "Don't you want some of this?" or, "Have some of this." She especially seemed to be trying to placate Paul's dad, doing anything to keep him happy.

In the years to come, I would find that I was prone to that same sort of activity. When Paul became angry at me, he wouldn't say anything to anybody else, but he seemed aggravated with me. In an effort to compensate and diffuse the situation, I would do what Paul's mother did, tiptoeing around him, doting on him, trying to pacify him, and making his life easier. I didn't know it at the time, but I was attempting to do the impossible. It would be a long time before I would learn that it was not my role in our marriage to keep Paul happy any more than it was his to maintain my happiness. It is impossible to make someone happy who is not happy within him- or herself.

We planned the wedding for November 27, 1981, the Saturday after Thanksgiving. We figured that would make it easier on our families, since everyone would be getting together for Thanksgiving anyhow. We decided to be married at the First Baptist Church in Stringtown. Alice was my matron of honor, and Reba was one of my bridesmaids, along with two college friends, Beverly Yenzer and Sissy Worrell.

Paul and I both are extremely practical people, so we didn't spend a lot of money on the wedding. Nevertheless, our wedding was the first big, formal church wedding in our family. Like Alice and Robert, Reba and Charlie had gotten married in the Baptist church, and both weddings had been rather informal. Pake and his wife, Katy, were married by a justice of the peace.

In contrast, Paul's and my wedding was a fairly large wedding for our part of the country; the church was nearly full. I wore a gorgeous white wedding gown that I had paid $700 for. Lionel Ritchie sang at our wedding—well, at least we played a tape of Lionel singing. For the reception, we had a big dance. All my life I had dreamed of a southern plantation style, romantic dance at my wedding. Nearby Atoka didn't really have many southern plantations, but we did have a good size Veterans of Foreign Wars hall. It was formerly an old grocery store. It wasn't very nice, but Narvel Blackstock, Reba's steel guitar player at the time, rounded up some musicians including Pake and Roger Wills and my favorite fiddle player, J. V. Newberry. My! What a dance they put on for us. Of course, before the night was over, the dance got a little rowdy, but that was to be expected in our neck of the woods.

For our honeymoon we went to Fountainhead Resort, about sixty miles north of Chockie. We were so tired from the stress of Thanksgiving, decorating for the wedding, and the actual ceremony and reception, I was asleep before we got there. We stayed in the resort lodge only one night and then went back home. We said, "Why spend the money when we can go home?"

Paul and I had decided to set up housekeeping in the old Chockie Shack, the tiny house that had once been a schoolhouse for black children. We had ten acres of land, but no water. It was across the highway from Mama and Daddy's property, and all my siblings had lived there, so we called it the "Weaning Shack." Whatever the place was called, it was a mess.

We spent the weeks before our wedding fixing up the house. It had not been in great shape in the first place. One time when Reba and Charlie lived there, they went over to Mama and Daddy's for supper and when they came back, the entire ceiling in one of the rooms had caved in. Reba and Charlie had insulated the drafty building by using blown-in insulation above the ceiling. Apparently, the roof leaked, causing the insulation to hold water until the weight of the insulation had finally become more than the shack's ceiling could stand. What a mess!

After Reba and Charlie moved out, some of her band members lived there for a while. Single, young musicians are not known as great housekeepers, and Reba's band members were no exceptions. Our first job was to chop down weeds almost as high as the house. Paul went over there with a weed whacker and cut all those weeds down. Inside the house was just as bad. After the musicians moved out, the rats moved in. Rats were everywhere in that shack, in the drawers, in the cupboards, and hiding behind holes in the walls.

Paul had an idea. "I know how to get rid of those mice," he said. "I'll get two tomcats and put them in the house. The rats will be gone in no time at all."

Paul was right about the cats taking care of the rats. The one thing he hadn't figured on was that the cats would leave their mark upon the Weaning Shack as well. Scrub as we might, we never did totally get rid of the awful smell of cat urine that permeated the place.

But, we did our best in the weeks before our wedding to clean and fix up the house. Like most young couples, we were thrilled to have a place to live, even though the school district doubled our rent—from $10 a month that Reba and Charlie had paid, to $20 a month for Paul and me.

At any rate, we hit the ground running and immediately got into the groove of our everyday life. In the years to come, I would sometimes regret not having an extended honeymoon, but at that time, Paul and I had little money and we let our practical sides dictate our actions. Besides, we were sort of struck with the whole romantic idea of getting married. We never truly discussed our expectations of each other or what we considered to be "normal" in a relationship. We were just in a hurry to get married and start living together. Although I had vowed never to marry a rodeo cowboy, everyone around us seemed in favor of our marriage, including Reba. She thought Paul was a nice guy, and looked at the fact that he was a rodeo cowboy as a plus. After all, she had married a rodeo cowboy, and her and Charlie's marriage was okay. Wasn't it?

Paul and I were so caught up in preparing for the wedding—"Oh, it is so romantic!" and "This is a new adventure!"—we really didn't think about the commitment we were making. Paul continued to say, "You go ahead and sing with Reba, and I will rodeo. Then we will meet when we are not working."

It wouldn't be long before that tune would change.

Chapter 12

FIRST SIGNS OF
VIOLENCE

*F*or the first few months of our marriage, Paul and I basked in our newlywed bliss. We were head over heels in love, and that was all we needed. I was working on the road with Reba, and Paul was rodeoing and doing well too. When we both got home, we fell into each other's arms and relished our time together. It was a strange relationship in some ways, because we were apart so much, but when we were together, we were like two teenagers who couldn't stay away from each other.

Often while we were still lying in bed in the morning, enjoying our closeness, we'd hear a truck rattling up the road. Sure enough, it was Daddy, wanting Paul to help him with something, or just wanting to visit. It was barely seven or eight o'clock, but to Daddy, half the day was gone. Paul and I hurriedly threw on our clothes and acted as though we had been up for hours. After Daddy left, we'd tumble back into bed.

During those early months, Paul and I had fun, especially when we were off the road, because we were relatively footloose and fancy free. We did all sorts of simple things together. We worked on the house together. We made cinnamon rolls and sour dough bread together. Paul even washed the dishes for me, something Charlie and

Paul's rodeo buddies made fun of him for doing, but Paul did it anyhow. We didn't have a schedule to keep when we were home, so our time was our own, except for Daddy's frequent visits. Paul and I may not have had a lot of material possessions, but we had each other, and we were happy and content. Life was easy.

Wanting to please Paul and be the best wife I could be, I was a classic picture of "Susie Homemaker." I spent my days at home cooking giant meals for Paul, sewing his shirts, and doing all the other things that went along with being a housewife. And I loved it!

We had very few responsibilities at that time since we had no children. Then Paul started talking about having kids right away. Although I wanted children, I didn't think that was such a good idea just yet.

Several months into our marriage, I began to notice a change in Paul's attitude toward my being on the road with Reba. Actually, he didn't mind me singing with Reba; he just didn't like it when we played honkey-tonks and the guys made passes at me. I didn't appreciate that either, and usually when the guys realized that I was not encouraging them, they left me alone. What made Paul even more uneasy was the fact that I was traveling for days at a time in a tour bus with six male band members and Reba. When Paul and I had first met, Reba and I were traveling together in an old Lincoln, and the band traveled in a separate vehicle. Now, the entire troupe was traveling together in the bus.

Like most tour buses, Reba's bus had separate sleeping compartments, so everyone had some measure of privacy. Beyond that, when we were traveling at night, Reba and I slept in the back of the bus in her bed. Whenever possible, we stayed the night at motels. Nevertheless, Paul's imagination ran wild as he allowed himself to get worked up about what might be going on between six guys and two women who spent that much time together. Before long, Paul started showing up at Reba's jobs, jealous and mad and screaming at me.

Paul now admits, "I got to thinking about Susie and Reba on the road with six guys, and I talked myself into believing that they were having wild orgies and drinking parties in that bus. I know it sounds ridiculous, but because of my background, I didn't trust anybody. My attitude was: 'Always expect the worse, be critical and skeptical.' It was terrible. As I was rodeo-ing, I'd work myself into a frenzy, thinking about Susie, and what she might be doing. So I'd jump in the truck and start driving to wherever I thought she was, fully expecting that I would show up and catch her with some other man. I would be so mad by the time I got there, it didn't matter what Susie said, I was convinced she was fooling around on me."

I wasn't.

In March, Paul and I went to Mexico with our friends Dick and Melanie Pool, who invited us to go along with them as sort of a special wedding present. For us, it was going to be like a "second" honeymoon. We looked forward to the warm, sultry Mexican nights. Instead, the second honeymoon turned cold in a hurry. Paul and I had been in a few arguments with each other before this time, usually because of his jealousies, but this time I was in for a shock.

For some reason we always seemed to get into arguments right before we went to bed. We argued over anything, silly things, nothing. Yet we somehow seemed to become embroiled in a war of words at the end of the day—even on our second honeymoon.

To this day, neither Paul nor I can remember what we argued about that night in Mexico, but it changed the entire tenor of our relationship. Paul says I initiated the argument. I may have; I really don't remember. All I know is that he became enraged. Finally, I gave up trying to communicate and rolled over with my back to Paul. If I thought that would end the episode, I was sorely wrong. Paul began flouncing around on the bed and yelling, "If I am not going to be able to sleep, you sure aren't going to sleep, either!"

Paul later said that he thought I was trying to win the fight by becoming a sweet little angel who would go off to sleep rather than argue anymore. I was trembling and scared to death. I wasn't trying to be an angel; I was hoping and praying that if I refused to respond to his outbursts, he would calm down and go to sleep. In the past, that had worked at times when Paul was upset about something.

But not this night.

Paul was fuming. His face was red, and his eyes were darting back and forth in his head. He roared, "You are going to sit up and talk about this. I don't care if it takes all night."

What did I do? I wondered. *Did I say something to make him mad? Whatever it was, surely it wasn't a big enough deal for him to be this mad.* I ignored him and pulled the covers up over my head.

That was a mistake.

Paul grabbed the covers with me in them and started jerking them all around the bed, tossing me back and forth, rolling me over and over like a mummy wrapped in grave clothes. Finally in a fit of rage, he pulled the covers and the sheets—and me in them—right off the bed.

Lying in a heap on the floor of the condominium where we were staying, I could not believe my eyes. My easy-going husband was picking up the mattresses and pulling them off the bed, making it impossible to lie back down on the bed, not that I had any illusions about sleeping just then anyhow.

I was terror-struck. I was afraid to move for fear that Paul would pick me up and throw me across the room or through the window or something! I sat motionless, waiting for the storm to pass. I couldn't understand how Paul could be so nice and yet be so angry. It just wasn't like Paul. He was a happy-go-lucky guy. What was happening to us?

Later, after Paul had calmed down, he apologized profusely, but I was still terrified. I had never before seen this side of Paul, but it would not be the last time I'd see it. By the time we had been married a year, Paul was knocking doors off their hinges in his anger. Shortly after that, his anger and verbal abuse included physical abuse as well. It would not stop for more than twelve years.

Throughout the spring of 1982, Paul continued to pop up at Reba's shows, usually unannounced and right before we were to go on stage. Reba began to notice how distracted I was by Paul's arrival, and she began to suspect that something was haywire. Paul never lost his temper or made a scene in front of Reba or the other band members. He had a way of wait-ing until we were alone, and then tearing into me. He showed up one time in Jackson, Mississippi. After greeting all the other members of the group cordially, Paul got me aside backstage for a private conversation. He hurled one accusation after another at me, accusing me of sleeping with every guy from the concert promoter to our bus driver. Before long, he was in a blind rage, quietly but menacingly making his points. I couldn't reason with him. Anger blurred Paul's usual logical reasoning powers.

Paul's comments were totally irrational, but just before a show, or when we were on break, there was no way I could make him see that. He said, "I don't like this. You are up there on stage, and all these men are around you; I know what they want. I can see what's going on here. You're sleeping with that guy over there, aren't you?"

"No, Paul. You are wrong. I didn't do that. I wouldn't do that. I can't even believe that you are saying things like that."

"Well, you sure don't seem very glad to see me—"

"I am glad to see you, but you are ruining our relationship, coming here and accusing me of all these things that I haven't done."

"Yeah, sure. You're just like all the rest."

Paul's words sliced into my heart, hurting me deeply. I could feel the emotion building within me, and when I couldn't contain it any longer, I burst into tears. When I got up on stage again, it was obvious that I was cry-ing. Sometimes, Paul would upset me so much that I couldn't sing. It made Reba really mad. She glowered at Paul off stage; if she could have gotten her hands on him, who knows what she might have done. She had no idea what was really going on, but she knew that Paul was not only hurting her little sister, but he was disturbing our performance. Reba couldn't work well when she got upset like that, and the show was our job.

Usually when Paul came to the shows, he stayed around backstage until the show was over, just waiting for me. In most cases, he calmed down and was his normal self by the time the last song was sung. If he didn't have to travel on to another rodeo, Paul sometimes stayed overnight with me in the motel where Reba and the band were staying. Occasionally that was great; more often than not, however, when we were away from the other people and behind closed doors, Paul's anger and accusations reignited.

Now that I did not have to worry about going on stage, I was much more vocal about defending my honor, which frequently led to another incident of Paul's pulling the sheets off the bed and tearing up the motel room. When the maids cleaned our room the following day, they probably thought that a rock 'n' roll show had stayed there the night before rather than a country music act.

All I could say was, "Paul, why are you doing this to me? Why do you come here and say these awful things to me, when I'm innocent?" I just couldn't understand it. My mama and daddy were totally trusting of each other. Nothing in my family background prepared me for Paul's unwarranted mistrust of me. I said, "Paul, you are accusing me of stuff that I haven't even thought of doing!"

I reached the point where I *almost* entertained the thought, *Well, if he's going to keep accusing me of this sort of stuff, I may as well go ahead and do it.* But I never did. I can understand how that happens in some relationships, though. When one partner keeps accusing the other of misdeeds or impure motives, and keeps seeing things that aren't really there, soon there is so much distrust that your life becomes a self-fulfilling prophecy. You think, *Why don't I go ahead and do it, if you think I'm doing it anyway?* An otherwise good relationship can fall apart when there is a lack of trust between the partners.

Fortunately, I knew better than to allow that to happen to me. Paul probably would have killed me.

Throughout the spring and into the month of June, we continued that way. The tension was almost palpable. But things were about to get worse before they got better. In June 1982, married only six months, I found out that I was pregnant.

Chapter 13

GOOD DAYS
AND BAD

$\mathcal{G}$etting pregnant so soon was a mixed blessing to Paul and me. In one way, I was delighted to discover that I was pregnant. After all, I loved kids and had always looked forward to the day when I would have some "real, live dolls" of my own to care for, teach, and love. I enjoyed babysitting for Alice or my cousins Doris, Paula, and Rickie any time they needed someone to watch their kids. Being a mom was an adventure to me.

On the other hand, I was still getting used to being a wife. Paul and I had been married only six months, and the largest part of that time we had spent away from each other, Paul on the rodeo circuit and me on the road with Reba. We were still getting to know each other and learning how to live with each other. It didn't seem fair to bring a child into our situation yet. Besides, why did we need to be in such a hurry? I was only twenty-four, and Paul was only two years older.

Looking back, it is easy to see that consciously or subconsciously, one of the reasons Paul wanted to start a family right away was to pull me off the road with Reba. Had Paul asked me to come off the road, I feel sure that I would have agreed, especially if I felt that our marriage was suffering as a result of my travels. But Paul didn't approach me from that standpoint. He said that he wanted to have children while we were young.

We never sat down and talked about our goals or expectations. We merely lived from day to day. We didn't think of the consequences of our actions, or how that decision would impact our finances, careers, travel, housing, or the overall tenor of our relationship. When you are young and newly married, it's more like, "Yippee! We're going to have a baby!" We really wanted children, but we didn't realize how much having children would add pressure to our lives.

Worse yet, Paul didn't really believe that having children would change his life drastically. He felt that he would simply carry on rodeoing as he had been doing before, and the changes—if there were any—would be on my part. The adjustments would be in my career, my priorities. Now, in addition to the mistrust issue, which had already reared its ugly head, we began to experience tension concerning the issues of whose job was more important, whose income mattered more, and who would have to sacrifice the most to make things work. Since Paul was rapidly becoming one of the best steer wrestlers in the world, he felt that his success in rodeoing justified any accommodations on my part to enable him to keep making a living at his chosen profession. On the other hand, although I was not hung up on the idea of becoming a music star, I felt I had achieved some measure of success in my chosen field too. It didn't seem fair to me that I should be the one to have to make all the changes because we were going to have a baby.

Paul and I didn't know the first thing about problem-solving techniques in marriage. Frankly, we didn't know much about male-female relationships at all! And we certainly had little concept of how a marriage was meant to function. He didn't understand that I needed to spend time with other women—whether friends, sisters, or my mother—to have those special "girl" times. Nor could Paul figure out why it was important for me to go shopping or to get my hair done. On the other hand, I didn't support Paul's rodeoing as I should have. I didn't go to his practices or get involved in many other aspects of the rodeo life.

Even more important, Paul and I had little understanding of how to meet each other's emotional needs. Like many married couples, we assumed our list of priorities were similar. We didn't realize that the important things to most women are romance (not necessarily leading to sex), security (both monetary and physical), female companionship, and sexual intimacy. A man has similar needs, but his priorities might be radically different. For most men, sex is at the top of their list of needs, then respect and admiration, followed by companionship.

Nevertheless, despite our naive notions about marriage and family, Paul and I maintained a sincere happiness during those days—superficial happiness, maybe, but nonetheless sincere. We continued to work together to fix up the Weaning Shack, and were even more motivated now that we anticipated a baby. About that time, the school district to whom we paid our $20-a-month rent decided to put our house up for sale. Because we didn't want to lose it, Paul and I bought it at a sealed-bid auction for $5,500, which included ten acres of land on which the house was located. We later learned that we were the only bidders.

Getting water to the house was still a bit of an ordeal. Our neighbors had brought water up from Stringtown, running lines close to our property, but it would have cost us another $2,500 to hook up to the rural water system, and we didn't have the money. Instead, we kept hauling water from Reba and Charlie's place in a five-hundred-gallon trailered tank. It took about three hours just to fill that old tank. The tank was so rusty that the water was a reddish color, so we didn't dare drink it. We used it in the commode, for showers, and for cleaning, but for drinking and cooking, we hauled separate water in five-gallon containers we filled from a spring. We took our clothes to Mama's to wash. We hauled water for the first three or four years of our marriage.

For the first three months of my pregnancy I continued to perform with Reba on the road. By August, however, I started getting sick on the bus. Few things in life are worse than morning sickness on a swaying bus! Finally, I decided that I couldn't travel on the bus anymore. In many ways, it was perfect timing for Reba too. Although she and I loved each other dearly, we had a hard time working together, especially when Reba was the boss and I was the employee. We loved singing together, but everything that went along with the business of singing was a source of contention for us. When I began waking up sick every morning, Reba saw a chance to solve both problems. She offered me a job in her office.

The job was a blessing in several ways; I stayed on the payroll, but I didn't have to ride on the bus anymore. Paul was less suspicious—at least less suspicious of the band members—and I could remain at home and work as Reba's secretary and help organize her financial books. (I knew my college accounting classes would come in handy someday.) My top priority when I first went to work at the office was to straighten out Reba's checkbook. That was a full-time job in itself. At that time, Reba's idea of balancing the checkbook was to call the bank and ask, "How much do I have in my account?"

Eventually we got all the income and expenses categorized and set up a workable system for keeping track of everything. When I left Reba's employ two years later, though, she still had no idea how much money she was making or where the money was going. Her husband, Charlie, took care of all that. In recent years, Reba has become much more involved with the business aspects of her career. Reba is the consummate performer; the fact that she makes money doing what she enjoys is simply icing on the cake to her.

Paul rodeoed all summer long, and was doing well, earning a good living for us. In Gladewater, Texas, he attended a Christian Cowboys' Fellowship meeting. It wasn't a fancy meeting, just a rodeo preacher giving a little talk and a fellow named Dean Winborn singing some songs. But that singer caught Paul's attention. It wasn't so much what the singer sang, but how he sang that intrigued Paul. The vocalist was singing to background tapes, and Paul had never before heard anything like that. As he sat listening to the fellow sing with a full accompaniment behind his voice, Paul thought, *Susie could do that. In fact, that's exactly what Susie needs to do! If we could get her some tapes, Susie could sing by herself, and who knows? Maybe she could come along with me to the rodeos, and she could sing at our fellowship meetings.*

A few weeks later, in Cheyenne, Paul heard another singer using accompaniment tapes. Wanda Jackson, a famous 1960s "rockabilly" star, sang for the cowboy fellowship meeting there. Afterward, Paul approached her and asked, "How did you get started in this?" Wanda explained to Paul that she sang for a lot of Christian functions that couldn't afford to hire a full band. Because her only need was a tape player and a sound system, she was free to accept invitations in a wide variety of places, including Rodeo Cowboy Fellowship meetings.

Paul came away more convinced than ever that I should start singing to accompaniment tapes. He came home all excited and shared what he had seen and heard. His enthusiasm was contagious, but when he told me about his idea of me singing with background tapes, I was underwhelmed. I thought of the musicians with whom I had been working on stage with Reba. I said, "Why, I ain't going to sing to a tape. I sing with a band!" I thought singing to an accompaniment tape was just about the hokiest thing in the world. I have since gained a great appreciation for accompaniment tapes—I didn't have to feed those great musicians or pay them a salary! After working with tapes for nearly ten years, it was almost difficult to go back to working with a live band. But in the summer of 1982, I was not about to sing to a cassette tape.

While Paul was home, we continued renovating the Weaning Shack, getting it all cleaned up for our baby. One of the rooms that needed desperate attention was the bathroom. The bathroom extended out from the back wall of the house. It was really not much more than a lean-to type of construction, stuck onto the rear of the house and propped up by piles of rocks. Since Reba and Charlie had moved out, the rocks had shifted and the bathroom wall had pulled away from the house, creating a wide crack, almost big enough for a small animal to crawl through.

One day when Alice and her husband, Robert, were visiting us, Paul was working at propping up the bathroom and Robert offered to help. The two of them set about the task of jacking up the entire bathroom so they could put more rock around the base, which would cause the wall to push back flush with the house.

Robert and Paul were outside jacking up the wall while Alice and I were inside, yelling directions to the guys, telling them when the walls were closest together. Finally, when they had the walls almost right, Robert and Paul gave one final pump on the jack. They must have pumped too hard because the entire ceiling cracked, buckled, then unloaded an avalanche of blown-in insulation—right on top of the couch where Alice was sitting. Alice and I let out a yell that probably scared the bears in the hills. I was across the room and the mess missed me, but Alice was covered with small pieces of sheet rock and insulation.

Paul and Robert came running in when they heard us holler. They had no sooner gotten inside the room than we heard another loud noise from the ceiling. *Boom!* The remainder of the ceiling caved in on top of Robert. He just stood there, dumbstruck, with little pyramids of insulation stacked on his shoulders. When Paul saw Robert and Alice both standing there with piles of insulation on their heads and shoulders, he convulsed in laughter. We all laughed until we almost cried. The Weaning Shack was now air conditioned.

Despite such setbacks, by the eighth month of our pregnancy the old house was starting to look like a home. Paul decided that he wanted to put up some sheet rock on the inside of the shack to fix the ceiling that had collapsed. Since we did everything together, I felt it was my wifely duty to help Paul with the job of repairing the ceiling. Little matter that I was pregnant, the two of us lifted and handled the four-by-eight-foot panels. Once Paul got the panel maneuvered into position, my job was to hold the eight-foot panel while he tried to quickly nail it to the ceiling.

"Hold it up there, will you?" he'd call from his ladder as he tried to get the edges straight.

"Paul, are you sure it's okay for an eight-months pregnant woman to be putting her hands over her head like this?" I asked.

"I don't know," he gasped.

"Paul, I don't think pregnant women are supposed to lift anything above their heads."

"I don't know, just hold it up," he'd implore. Eventually we got that ceiling done, but it's a wonder I didn't have that baby right there on the ladder.

It looked as though Paul was going to make the National Finals Rodeo again in 1982. He had a great winter, winning $15,000 and the possibility of even more if he made the finals. Money was no problem early in our relationship. We didn't have much, but we didn't need much.

That's when Paul decided to buy a horse. A horse was not simply a perk. In Paul's line of work, a good horse was an essential element to success, but it was no small investment. A cowboy must count the cost of feeding, caring for, and hauling his horse versus someone else absorbing this cost. Up to this point, Paul had been able to use horses belonging to other rodeo cowboys, but he wanted to ride a horse of his own.

Paul found a horse that he really liked. We had nearly $10,000 in our savings account, from which we agreed to take $6,000 to pay for the horse. Then Paul bought another horse for $2,500. Next, he figured he needed a horse trailer to cart the animals from rodeo to rodeo, so he paid $3,500 for that, which decimated our savings, in addition to his borrowing about $2,500.

By some standards, we didn't owe much, but it was the first time Paul and I were in debt, something that went against both of our natures. Worse yet, Paul suddenly stopped placing in the rodeos he was entering. The horse he bought wasn't as good as those he had ridden before, and Paul was not yet confident in his horse-training ability. Without any winnings, and without any money coming in from my singing, we soon found ourselves sinking deeper and deeper into debt. The pressure built quickly.

Paul wasn't quite the shoe-in to make the finals that he thought he was. He dropped lower in the money standings, and we knew that he was going to have to work like mad now if he had any hope of making the finals. Cowboys depend on those finals to make their big money of the year and to catch up and cover the year-end expenses. To make matters worse, Paul missed making the finals by a margin of $300. He came in sixteenth and only the top fifteen rodeo cowboy money winners compete in the National Finals Rodeo. Paul was extremely frustrated by now.

About that same time, we borrowed $90,000 to get into the cattle business. Paul bought around three hundred head of cattle and paid rent to have them graze across the hill on Oklahoma City lake property. Growing up as a "city-slicker," Paul didn't know much about cattle, but he had learned a lot from being around my family and his rodeo friends. He figured raising cattle was worth the gamble.

Unfortunately, Paul was also doing some gambling of another sort at the same time. In hopes of winning a big bundle of money to pay off our debts, Paul began making wagers on just about anything. He bet on football games, on himself in the rodeos, and bet on other cowboys. Paul loved to gamble. Like most gamblers, he lost more often than he won, but he won enough to keep him coming back in hope of winning the big one. Meanwhile, we were accumulating a massive debt and kept sinking further into the hole Paul had dug for us and our as-yet-unborn baby.

Paul bet $100 on every professional football game, every week, all season long, which at that time amounted to about $2,600 each week. Toward the end of the year, Paul was $1,500 ahead on his betting—always a dangerous situation with a compulsive gambler. Then came the NFL play-offs. Paul thought for certain that he was going to clean up during the play-offs. Instead, he lost $6,000. We had to scramble again to pay off Paul's gambling debts. It was a downhill slide, and we were slipping fast.

I knew Paul's gambling was risking our future and that of our baby. But Paul had a way of making everything seem okay. He didn't simply talk me into believing that everything was fine; he'd lay it all out on paper, very convincingly assuring me that we'd be okay in the end. "Oh, it's gonna work out," he'd always say. And usually he was right.

But this time was different. Throughout this entire period, Paul's anger was always seething just below the surface. Like hot water in the teakettle, again, the steam was beginning to build.

Chapter 14

NASHVILLE
BLOWUP

*E*ldon Paul Luchsinger, our first baby, was born on March 4, 1983. From the beginning we called him "E. P.," and to this day, even many people who know our family well have never heard E. P.'s full name. He was a big boy at eight pounds, four and a half ounces, and he was a joy right from the start.

Paul was ecstatic to be a daddy, and he was a good one. He was always ready to help with the baby any way he could, whether it meant changing E. P.'s diaper or walking and rocking him when he fussed. Paul spent every day that he was home watching E. P., sitting with him for hours on end, using his best "training" techniques to teach our baby to hold his head up, to roll over, and eventually to crawl. By the time E. P. was two months of age, Paul had the baby literally standing in the palm of his hand, looking at his daddy in delight, his face beaming with an expression of pure trust in his father. Paul sure loved our baby boy, and E. P. loved Paul.

Paul did not anticipate, however, just how much time E. P. was going to require and how much our beautiful baby boy would monopolize my attention. As much as he loved our child, Paul soon became jealous of the time and affection that I was giving to E. P. rather than to him. On more than a few occasions Paul's attitude came across as, "You've been doting over and coddling this baby twenty-four hours a day. Leave the baby alone, and come spend some time with me."

Nevertheless, he was always excellent at caring for E. P. (as he was later with Lucchese and Samuel). Paul was especially helpful with our baby when we were in public. For some reason, it seemed that every time Paul and I sat down to eat in a restaurant, E. P. suddenly became hungry too. Being rather modest, I was uncomfortable about breastfeeding in public, and as a result I'd become very nervous. Although Paul supported my decision to breastfeed our children, he too was uncomfortable with the whole idea of breasts being used as "feed bags" in public. He was always quick to help me cover up and constantly stressed my need to be discreet.

My own nervousness coupled with Paul's concerns transferred to E. P. as I was trying to feed him. He must have sensed my discomfort, because he started fussing any time I tried to feed him in public. The more he fussed, the more nervous I became and the more embarrassed Paul became. Finally, he would take E. P. out of the restaurant while I finished my meal.

Nursing also interfered with our normal sleep patterns, since E. P. woke up frequently in the night, crying for nourishment. At other times he woke up crying because of colic. E. P.'s crying would upset me, but Paul took it in stride, calmly picking up the baby and bouncing him gently, trying to get him back to sleep. I greatly appreciated Paul's efforts, but being a mom, I felt that I could do a better job than Paul when it came to caring for E. P. during those stressful times. When Paul had to step in to help during the night, I felt like a failure in one of my most important roles as a woman— mothering my child. Paul didn't do much to ease my insecurities. Instead of consoling me, or making a plan such as, "Honey, you get some rest, and if I can't handle it, I'll come and get you," Paul simply ignored me and went about the business of rocking the baby.

Both Paul and I were constantly tired due to lack of sleep during those early days of parenting. I was often irritated with Paul, and he grew increasingly aggravated at both E. P. and me. The enormous responsibilities of raising a family began sinking in on us.

Meanwhile Pake was getting his music together, working on an album, and singing in bars and clubs on the weekends. He invited me to join him, and since I was no longer singing professionally, and Paul and I were financially strapped due to the cattle investments and Paul's gambling, I decided to accept Pake's offer. At first, Pake and I took only occasional bookings, but before long the job with Pake became more regular and began to consume my weekends. When I had to be away, Paul watched the baby; and when we both had to be away from home, I'd take E. P. with me.

Paul was still rodeoing and trying to make a go of the cattle we had purchased. I was still working in Reba's office during the week, singing on the weekends with Pake, and trying to take care of a baby in between. It was crazy! We were running every which way—every which way except toward each other.

I continued working in Reba's office until E. P. was almost six months old. Trying to be a working mom, at first I took E. P. with me to the office, but soon he was getting into everything. Also, my attention was divided, and Charlie thought that I wasn't getting enough work done trying to take care of E. P. and work at the same time. At first, he and Reba encouraged me to get a babysitter for E. P. Eventually, though, Charlie put pressure on Reba to let me go. Rather than cause problems between Reba and her husband, who was also her manager at that time, I decided to go quietly. I cleaned out my desk at Reba's office and walked out the door.

In addition to the tension in Paul's and my relationship caused by our work schedules, I was also being pulled in the direction of my family. My family members were probably not even aware of what they were doing, but to Paul, it looked as though every time he turned around, someone in my family was telling me what to do. And more often than not, what my family wanted me to do was the opposite of what Paul wanted me to do. Not surprisingly, Paul felt it more acutely than I did, and made much of the pull between my loyalty to my family and my loyalty to him.

Paul's grievances were not unfounded. As the baby of our family, I was easily influenced by the opinions of my family members. It made sense to me, though, that I should consider their advice since they had known me a lot longer than Paul had. Nevertheless, Paul had a legitimate gripe when it came to some of my family's ways. For instance, because Mama is proud of her children, she always includes our maiden names. To this day, she doesn't refer to me as Susie Luchsinger. She calls me Martha Susan McEntire Luchsinger. Similarly, she does not refer to Paul's and my children as Luchsingers; she refers to them as McEntires. or a "Smith," her maiden name.

To me, Mama's attitude could be written off as typical parental possessiveness—I was her baby and I'd *always* be her baby. To some it might even appear to be cute, but not to Paul. From his viewpoint, it was an unwillingness to accept the fact that I had chosen to enter into a relationship with him that demanded first place in my life, after the Lord. Consequently, the power struggle and contention did not disappear but was merely covered over until the next potential conflict.

Just such a situation arose in November 1983. Paul had not made the National Finals Rodeo for the second year straight, and he was extremely depressed. He had gone to the finals three times in a row in the years prior to 1982, and he had been sitting on top of the rodeo world. Now, he was angry at himself, and no doubt smoldering at me since the pressures at home had taken a toll on his performance in the rodeos. Not only was his ego bruised, but our bank account suffered by Paul's lackluster performance as well. He had traveled thousands of miles and spent thousands of dollars in his attempt to get a shot at the big money in the finals. Now he had little to show for it.

Once again, he threw himself into running cattle, trying to make a go of that. He had sold our first herd of cattle, but didn't make enough profit to pay off the $90,000 we owed on them. With both the cattle and the money gone, we still owed about $14,000. Then in the fall of that year, Paul borrowed another $90,000 to purchase more cattle.

Paul was pasturing the cattle on a wheat pasture in Bonham, Texas, to precondition the animals and get them ready for winter. Since Bonham was about ninety miles from our home in Chockie, Paul was staying with the cattle for a week at a time, coming home on the weekends only. By the middle of November, the cattle were coming along well, and it looked like we might be able to recoup some of our losses with this herd. But then the weather turned cold. All the forecasters were calling for the worst winter Texas and Oklahoma had seen in years. Their predictions proved to be accurate. It snowed early, and the water lines froze. The cattle had no water, and with snow on the ground, they had nothing to eat. Paul knew he was racing against time, trying to get the cattle preconditioned and settled onto a leased pasture for the winter. He was out there every day in the bitter cold, doctoring sick cattle and getting the others ready for winter. The physical, emotional, and financial pressure continued to mount as Paul worked long hours in the cold, coming back to his motel room at night nearly exhausted and frozen.

One Friday morning, back in Chockie, Pake showed up at my door and said, "Come on, Susie. We're going to Nashville to record some songs."

"We're going to do what?" I asked. I knew that Pake had hopes that the two of us might become a Nashville recording duet, but I was still surprised that he had sprung a recording session on me with no warning, no practice, no chance to prepare, no time to arrange babysitting for E. P., and most important, no opportunity to discuss what we were doing with Paul. Pake explained that he wanted to record a song called "Goody Two Shoes" and several others. He had enlisted the help of Glenn Keener, a Nashville producer who was living in Texas at the time. Glenn had produced Reba's first album back in 1976, so Pake felt that he would have a heart for what we wanted to do. But time was of the essence. Glenn said that if we could get to Nashville that week, he could get us a good rate on studio time.

Without thinking about the ramifications of what I was doing, I simply began packing my bags to go to Nashville. Then, as it began to sink in, I realized that I better let Paul know what was going on. There was no way to call him out on the cattle ranch, and he was staying at a cheap motel with no telephone in the room. I decided that I would drive down to Bonham, try to find him, and tell him that I was going to Nashville with Pake to record a few songs. Pake called Glenn Keener and told him we'd meet him at his place since he lived about thirty miles from Bonham. Then we'd all load into one vehicle and head for Nashville.

Pake was rearing to go, but I was torn between wanting to do what my brother wanted me to do and my loyalty to Paul. Finally, I figured that if I could just wait until the last minute to spring the news on Paul, everything would be all right. That way, he wouldn't have much time to get mad. I had already made up my mind to take the baby with me, so Paul wouldn't have to worry about taking care of a herd of cattle and a child too. I put E. P. into our Buick Century, hopped behind the wheel of the car, and pointed it toward Texas.

Meanwhile, little did I know that Paul was on his way back home to Chockie!

When I arrived in Bonham, I drove all over the area looking for Paul, but I couldn't find him. I must have been working the old Buick too hard because the engine overheated and the engine block cracked. Fortunately, Pake was driving behind me, or I would have been stranded along the road with a blown engine.

Not knowing where to find Paul, there was not much more I could do but leave the broken-down vehicle and go on with Pake. I never even thought about writing Paul a note and leaving it in the car. Pake was in a hurry to get going, so I simply followed the leader. We drove on to Glenn's place, packed our things in his car, and headed to Nashville.

When Paul arrived home on Friday afternoon, our house was empty. He had no idea that I had gone to Nashville to record, so he assumed that I had gone to the store or to Mama's, and that I would be right back. He had purchased a beautiful porch swing as an anniversary present for me, so he unloaded that and put it together. Still I was nowhere in sight.

Oh, she'll be back in a few minutes, Paul thought. He had also purchased a new seat cover for our pickup truck, so Paul figured that instead of sitting around waiting for me, he'd go ahead and get started replacing the seat cover. He had no sooner begun when he heard Mama's car driving up to the front of our house. "Hey, Jac," Paul called amiably to Mama. "Where are Susie and E. P.?"

Paul says he can always tell when Mama has some information that she knows he doesn't want to hear. That day, Paul noticed right off that Mama was fidgety. She got out of the car and began trying to explain, "Well, ah . . . Pake and Susie, they are going to . . . you have to understand this is something I have always dreamed of for these kids. . . ."

"Jac, just tell me!" Paul interrupted, his patience running out. "Where are Susie and E. P.?"

Paul recalls:

Jac was hem-hawing around, trying to tell me all the reasons why Susie was not home. Finally, she just blurted, "She's gone with Pake to Nashville to make a record."

My blood started to boil. I could not believe that my wife would go to Nashville, seven hundred miles away, without telling me or making any plans, and lugging a baby along with her at that! I made no attempt to hide my anger from my mother-in-law.

Jac gave me the hotel information, where Pake and Susie would be staying in Nashville. She told me the general time that they had started out, so I knew they would not be arriving in Music City until late that night. Tired, hungry, angry, and disgusted, I said, "Well, if they aren't going to be back home for four or five days, I may as well go back to Bonham and take care of our cattle."

I got back in the pickup, slammed the door as hard as I could, started it up, and stomped down on the gas pedal, leaving a cloud of dust that looked like an Oklahoma dust storm.

I was so incensed that I could barely see the road. I kept banging on the steering wheel all the way to Texas. When I got back to my motel room, I paced the floor, angrily rehearsing what I was going to say to Susie the moment I could get her on the telephone. The motel where I was staying had a pay phone out in the hallway. As soon as I thought that Pake and Susie might have crossed the Tennessee line, I started calling the hotel where they were to stay.

" I'm sorry, sir," a polite voice on the other end of the line said each time I called. "Nobody by that name has checked in yet."

It was late at night when I finally reached Susie at the hotel. Standing out in the hallway at the pay phone, I started literally screaming into the mouthpiece. I cussed her out one way and then another. I called Susie every foul name in the book. I was loud, mad, and totally out of control.

Finally the owner of the motel came out of his office and hollered, "Hey! You quit talking like that around here."

I didn't care what the guy said. I wanted my wife to get out of that hotel in Nashville and come home. Now!

In Nashville, I was shaking as I listened to Paul's tirade. Tears streamed down my face as I tried to get a word in edgewise, but it was useless. After a while, as Paul continued to curse at me, I said, "I am not going to be talked to like this!" and I slammed down the receiver.

At first I couldn't understand why Paul was so upset. There was no question in my mind or heart that I loved my husband, but I was so immature, naive, and easily influenced by my family members that I could not bring myself to choose Paul over my family at that time. That was a serious mistake and, as we learned in our marriage counseling years later, one that many young married partners make.

Paul soon called back, more furious than before. He ranted and raved and continued to curse me. I tried to explain to him that I had made an attempt to find him in Bonham to tell him what I was going to do. "I tried to find you, Paul. I drove all over Bonham looking for you. I even cracked the engine block on our car trying to track you down."

The news that I had destroyed our car's motor in my sincere search for him did nothing to soothe the angry beast in Paul. Not only were his wife and baby several states away, but now he knew that his car was broken down alongside the road somewhere in Texas. Regardless, Paul was not nearly as angry about the car as he was about me being gone.

I knew that I had messed up badly. To Paul, it was a matter of allegiance. Once again, I had demonstrated that I was more closely aligned with my family than I was with him. I had done what my family wanted me to do rather than what Paul wanted me to do. The issue was not so much going to Nashville but that I had not even bothered to discuss it with Paul. Quite possibly, had I talked it over with Paul, he might have responded positively to me going to Nashville and recording with Pake. Paul loved to hear me sing and was supportive when opportunities arose. But going to Nashville on the spur of the moment was not something he and I had planned. My family had planned it without any consideration of Paul's responsibilities, needs, feelings, or input; therefore, Paul felt left out of the loop.

I tried to apologize to Paul on the phone that night, but he was so overcome with rage that I doubt my words even registered. In a way, I was thankful that we were separated by the miles, because I'm sure he would have responded physically had I been anywhere near him and he could have gotten hold of me. Paul had been angry at me a few times before, but never anything like this.

Paul's cursing continued. I was hurt by his words, especially by all the names he was calling me. I had certainly never been called such names before, much less by a Christian man who claimed to love me!

I sat on the hotel bed and cried and cried.

Pake saw me being verbally abused on the telephone by my husband, and he became angry at Paul. Pake didn't see anything wrong with what we had done, and he especially did not accept any blame for his role in the fiasco. I felt as though I was caught in the middle of two tornadoes, Paul and Pake, two strong-willed, controlling men. I wanted to please both my husband and my brother, and I ended up pleasing neither.

Pake and I recorded the song, "Love Lift Us Up Where We Belong" that week in Nashville. The song eventually became part of an album titled "Back to Back," my first professionally done album. Despite my excitement about being involved with Pake's project, it was difficult to keep my mind on the recording process. I knew that when we were done, I'd be heading home to face an angry husband.

By the time we got home the following week, Paul was still mad, but his rage had subsided. He apologized for the nasty things he had said to me on the phone, and I apologized to him for running off to Nashville without telling him. We talked about the conflict, but we really didn't resolve anything. We desperately needed help in our marriage—we needed to learn how to communicate. We needed to deal with some of the difficult issues: Where are we going in our lives? What are our goals? Are we happy going separate directions? What's important to God in our relationship? Unfortunately, we didn't deal with any of those things. We simply swept the Nashville blow-up under the carpet, where we were beginning to accumulate a large pile of unresolved conflicts. Things were still tense around our house, and I felt as though I was walking on egg shells. But at least I was no longer afraid that there might be a more physical reprisal on Paul's part. Part of the reason Paul was slow to reignite his anger was due to his sheer exhaustion. While I had been in Nashville, Paul had been at Bonham trying to keep the cattle alive. The bitter cold weather was taking a severe toll on our cattle, and despite Paul's best efforts, it seemed almost certain that we were going to lose another big batch of money.

With his spirit broken, Paul decided to go back to the rodeo. Before he did, though, he prayed, "Lord, I don't know what you want me to do. I don't know if I should run cattle, or rodeo, but whatever it is, if you will just let me know, I'll do it as best I can."

Paul entered a "jackpot" on New Year's Eve. A jackpot is a competition that is not sanctioned by the Professional Rodeo Cowboy Association and usually has only two or three events, such as calf-roping or steer-wrestling, rather than the full, standard five events of the PRCA rodeos. Sometimes forty or fifty bulldoggers get together and say, "Let's all put $50 in the pot. We will have two go-rounds, with the first through fourth place winners getting paid."

On that New Year's Eve, Paul entered the jackpot and won $600. Immediately, he hitched a ride with Roy Duvall and his friends and they were off to Odessa, Texas, where he entered a regular PRCA rodeo. At Odessa, Paul won $1,450 in the first go-round. At that point, he had won over $2,000 in a week, so Paul interpreted that as God's way of saying, "This is what I want you to do. I want you to rodeo." Paul ended up that winter with almost $14,000 from rodeoing. We still had the major cattle debt, so $14,000 didn't seem like a lot of money considering that we owed over $100,000 by then.

To make matters worse, we lost more than thirty head of cattle, over 10 percent of our stock, due to the inclement weather. When Paul sold the remaining cattle, we made enough to pay for them, but not enough to make a profit. To Paul, it was further confirmation that God wanted him to rodeo. To me, it just meant that I needed to sing more dates with Pake.

Chapter 15

MORE BUMPS
AND BRUISES

*Th*ings remained tense between Paul and me as we began 1984. Although we had lots of good times, the hurt in our relationship was like a festering sore, never bleeding profusely but never quite healing either. Beyond that, the least friction caused the sore to become raw and irritated once again.

After we sold the cattle at the end of 1983, Paul went back to rodeoing full time, and I continued singing with Pake. It wasn't long before the steam in Paul's emotional teakettle began to build again. One morning in late January, Paul was scheduled to leave for Fort Worth, about a three hour drive from our home. He was supposed to arrive at the rodeo by 7:00 A.M. We planned to get up around 3:00 A.M. so he could have plenty of time to get ready.

We got to bed too late the night before and, as a result, we were late getting up. That put Paul in a bad mood right off the bat. We got into a terrible argument over which of us hadn't gotten out of bed on time. (Actually, neither of us had, but that was irrelevant.)

Paul hurried to get his things together. He thrashed around our bedroom like a bear that had forgotten where he had hidden his honey. After a few minutes, he realized that there was no way he could avoid being late, no matter how fast he raced to Fort Worth. He went into the kitchen to get something, and when he came back into the bedroom, he boomed, "Well, I just won't go to the rodeo then." He slammed the bedroom door so hard that it went past the door jam, got stuck, and wouldn't open. Paul flopped onto the bed in disgust.

He laid there for awhile, fully clothed, just seething, like a locomotive building up enough pressure to pull out from the train station. Suddenly I heard him say aloud, "Aw, I gotta go to the rodeo."

He bounded off the bed and went to open the door, but it was still jammed. At that, Paul went totally out of control. Since he couldn't get the door to open, he reared back and kicked the door down. The door flew open, bending all the hinges right out of the door jam, and causing the door to twist precariously in the door frame. Infuriated, Paul continued kicking the door until it came all the way off the hinges. Then he started jumping on it, beating it with his fists and kicking it with his feet, in what looked almost like simultaneous motions. It was an old-fashioned, sturdy, wooden door, made of solid oak, with inset panels and heavy round door knobs, yet Paul smashed it to bits.

An AM-FM stereo "boom box" was sitting nearby on the floor. Besides being a handy piece of electronic equipment, the boom box had been a special gift from one of Paul's groomsmen at our wedding. But as Paul turned his attention away from the door, he spied the boom box. Without missing a step, he whipped his leg toward that radio and kicked it all the way across the room. The boom box hit the wall and fell to the floor.

Meanwhile, I was sitting in a corner of the room, still dressed in my nightgown, and wondering, *What are you doing, Paul?* I had never before seen this kind of rage in Paul. Granted, he had shaken me around on the bed in a hotel room. He had spewed a litany of obscene names at me over the phone when I had gone to Nashville without telling him. But he hadn't smashed anything. This was the first time I truly saw such an extremely violent side to Paul's anger. I was too frightened to move, so I simply huddled in the corner, pulling my knees up under my nightgown as if that would somehow protect me from the flood of Paul's wrath.

Paul kicked his way out the door and went into the next room. He started out the door and pulled it open so hard it banged against the gas hot water heater, which was in the corner, behind the door. The door bounced off the hot water heater and ricocheted back at Paul, nearly hitting him in the nose. That made Paul even madder, so he grabbed that door and banged it a couple more times against the hot water heater, until both the door and the hot water heater were dented and damaged.

Paul stormed out of our house and eventually made it to the Fort Worth rodeo, driving the little Chevrolet Chevette we had bought after the Buick blew up. As soon as he arrived in Fort Worth, he stopped and called me. He said, "God has been dealing with me all the way down here, and reminding me of a lot of things, including how ignorant I was to be doing all those things this morning. I want to apologize to you, Susie, for losing my temper this morning. I don't know what caused me to have such a fit, but I'm sorry. That was stupid and childish. Please forgive me. I won't do it again. I promise."

Of course, I forgave Paul. I didn't have any reason not to forgive him. Nor did I have any reason to think that the violence I had witnessed that morning would happen again and again. I loved Paul, and I was sorry that I caused him to be upset—though I wasn't exactly sure how I had done so.

I felt better after Paul's telephone call, and Paul felt refreshed and inspired, as well. He went out and won the go-round, pocketing over $4,000.

Thinking back on the events of that morning, Paul says, "At that time I was not really mad at Susie. I was just angry and frustrated with myself because of all the stupid decisions I had made, including the cattle losses and my gambling debts. I knew we needed some money. It was all starting to press in on me. Then when I didn't wake up early enough to get to the rodeo on time, I popped. But I had developed a habit of using the least little thing that Susie did that I disliked as an excuse to take out my frustrations and anger on her. I convinced myself, *She is the problem, not me! If she didn't make me mad, everything would be okay.*"

And I agreed.

After that incident in 1984, Paul occasionally would blow up at me for no apparent reason. He didn't hit me, but he sometimes threw things at me, things such as wastebaskets, books, lamps, or chairs. He never hit me with any of the things he threw, but he would throw them close enough to scare me and to keep me dancing out of the way.

After every incident, Paul always repented before God and begged for my forgiveness. He was always deeply and sincerely sorry. "I will not do this again. I'm going to work on this," he'd say over and over. Then Paul prayed, "Oh, God, help me to deal with this, and to be able to control my anger."

He would cry and hold me and tell me that he was sorry. I cried too, and I always forgave him. That's the way we dealt with Paul's outbursts of anger. Once the anger subsided, we'd forget about it for a while. Then something would happen to set Paul off, and his anger would flare again. Over time, as Paul more readily vented his anger, the intensity increased.

During the time when I was working in Reba's office, Paul's jealousy and controlling nature extended all the way into the workplace. He continued to suspect that I was having sexual affairs with other men, once even accusing me of being interested in his best friend at the time, Mark Muggli. Mark and Paul had known each other since their college days, and Mark had been Paul's best man at our wedding. Mark met Reba's husband, Charlie, through Paul and went to work for Charlie as a ranch hand.

Mark was a good friend to both Paul and me, but Paul worried about those times when I was working in Reba's office by myself with Mark working outside on the ranch. Clearly, Paul's insecurities stemmed from his own immoral conduct during his college years—conduct that Mark had witnessed often—but Paul's suspicions of Mark and me caused even more tension in all three of our lives.

Even worse than Paul's false accusations were his possessiveness and intimidation. He wanted to know where I was, who I was with, and what I was doing every minute of the day. I knew Paul had the trip from the office to our house timed. He had me so intimidated that if I was supposed to leave work at five o'clock, I had to be home in so many minutes or he'd be looking for me. If I went to town, I faced an inquisition when I returned home. "Where did you go?" Paul asked. "Where have you been? Where did you stop? Who did you see? Who did you talk to?"

It was awful! I felt as though I had ceased to exist as my own person and that I was a puppet controlled by Paul. What really upset me was the fact that there was no reason for Paul's suspicions. I never cheated on Paul. I never even consciously flirted with another man after I was married. It was his own insecurity that made him want to control me. Nevertheless, when I went out, I got into the habit of keeping mental notes of where I was so I could later let Paul know what time I was there, with whom I talked, and what I did while I was out. I'd do whatever I had to do, then I'd hurry back to our house because Paul would be mad if I was not there when he got home. If I knew I was going to be late, I'd start collecting my thoughts on the way home so I could explain to Paul what had happened. "There's a new girl on the register at the grocery store, so it took me a little longer today." "They are working on the road down the way, and the highway crew stopped traffic for a while." It was ridiculous, but I did that sort of thing all the time during that period of our marriage.

Years later, when Paul and I finally went to some professional marriage counselors, one of the things we learned was that in homes where domestic violence exists, abusive relationships often start by the abusive partner interrogating his or her partner and by not allowing that person freedom to go anywhere or to have platonic relationships with other women or men. The abuser is perpetually suspicious. If his or her partner talks to someone of the opposite sex, the abuser immediately thinks that there is reason to be jealous. Often the marriage partner's protests of innocence only serve to further incense the abuser, causing him or her to respond violently.

Today, Paul and I know all that, but back in 1984, like many young couples, we were too naive, embarrassed, or proud to seek counseling. Marriage counselors estimate that many couples begin having troubles during their second year of marriage, yet most do not seek professional help until their seventh year of marriage. Had Paul and I sought help earlier in our relationship, it might have saved us both a lot of anguish.

Unfortunately, we did not seek help, and Paul's irrational behavior continued unabated. Although he was a good-looking, strong, well-built, intelligent man, Paul was extremely insecure. He had everything going for him, yet deep inside he had no confidence in himself. Consequently, it was difficult for him to have confidence in me.

His insecurities spilled over into his rodeoing, and his rodeoing frustrations spilled into our marriage. I had no doubt in my mind that Paul was one of the best rodeo cowboys in the world at that time, based solely on his talent and abilities. Yet when he got into pressure-packed situations, more often than not, he would totally blow it because of his insecurities and fear of failure.

Paul worried constantly about what his peers thought of him. Specifically, he worried about losing, fretting, "If I miss this steer, what are all the guys going to think of me?" Oddly, when Paul drew a difficult steer, he performed better. When he drew a steer that all the other rodeo cowboys considered to be weak and easy to take down, Paul frequently psyched himself out of the competition. He heard the inner voice of a demanding coach taunting him, *Everyone knows that's an easy steer. If you mess up, they will say, "There goes Luchsinger; he can't win anything."* It took the same skills to throw the tough steer as it did the easy one, but Paul didn't look at it that way. His self-imposed pressure caused him to fret so much that he was going to mess up, that he often did. When Paul failed to do well at the rodeo, his frustration came home with him and found its way into our relationship. It was a downhill slide. His insecurities led to failure, which led to frustration and lack of confidence, which led to anger and abuse in our relationship.

For instance, once Paul missed his steer in a rodeo in Denver. I was along with him on that trip, and when we got back to the hotel room after the rodeo, we had a big blowup. Because Paul had missed the steer, he hadn't made any money, and our traveling expenses for gas, meals, motels, and all the rest were eating away what little money we had. Paul was mad at himself for missing the steer, so it didn't take much to set him off. The argument started over some insignificant issue that neither of us can remember to this day. At the time, however, it seemed earthshaking in importance. Once again, Paul began to vent his anger on me. He wanted to argue, but I was tired and wanted to go to sleep, so I crawled into bed. I should have known better.

As he had done on other occasions, Paul pulled the sheets off the bed with me in them. I scrambled to my feet and tried to get out of the way. Before the night was over, I wound up hiding down in the corner of the hotel room closet, trying to protect myself from flying objects launched by Paul's anger.

In 1984 we were still trying to operate our marriage on the basis of "You do your thing, and I'll do my thing." It wasn't working, and both Paul and I knew it; but we insisted upon living separate lives even though we were married. Most marriage counselors encourage couples to have some personal interests, distinct from their marriage partner's interests, but few counselors ever recommend the type of lifestyle division Paul and I were trying to maintain.

Although Paul's priority was rodeoing, he did not balk when I wanted to borrow $10,000 to put up my half for a $20,000 sound system and an equipment trailer Pake wanted to purchase to further our singing career. We used part of that money to pay for our recording project, as well.

Paul was having a good year rodeoing, traveling again with our friend Roy Duvall. Pake and I were doing well too. We were working a couple of jobs each weekend and had even hired a band. We sang a lot of Dolly Parton's and Kenny Rogers' material as well as a few songs Pake and I had recorded.

We often played at the Dew Drop Inn at McAlester, thirty miles north of our home. Half the time our musicians were still trying to learn our songs in the middle of the dance. We'd get up on stage, start to play and sing, and suddenly in the middle of a song, everybody in the band was lost. It was terrible. I was embarrassed sometimes that we put on such a poor performance.

Paul tried to encourage me by saying, "Susie, don't worry about it. The people out there dancing don't know the difference anyway. They're drinking and dancing, and all they care is that you keep the music going; just keep playing." I appreciated Paul's attempt to console me, but it was not exactly what I wanted to hear.

In the spring of 1984, I became pregnant again. I continued singing with Pake on the weekends, but I didn't recognize that I was burning the candle at both ends. One night Pake and I were performing at The Rocky Ridge, a little nightclub in Stringtown. In the middle of the show, I felt my abdomen cramping badly. We were playing only seven miles from Chockie, so when the band took a break, I hobbled to the car and drove home.

Paul was at a rodeo, so our house was dark when I arrived. I stumbled in the darkness toward our front door. I had just gotten inside when I passed a huge amount of blood. I was terrified! What in the world was happening to me? I staggered around the bathroom in a daze. Although I did not know it at the time, I had just miscarried our baby.

I finally got the bleeding slowed down and myself cleaned up. I knew I wasn't okay, but I hurried back to The Rocky Ridge to finish the show. I had to go. I knew Pake would be waiting for me to go on. When we finished playing that night, we packed up our equipment and headed out to Sayre, Oklahoma, which is in the western part of the state. The pain had returned, and I was bleeding again, but I didn't say anything to anyone. I stretched out in the back seat of Pake's truck and bled during the whole drive to Sayre. I thought I was dying. Eventually the bleeding stopped, but I was extremely weak. We played shows that entire weekend, and I never missed a note. When we returned home on Sunday, I went to the doctor. The doctor examined me and told me that I would be okay with a little rest. Then he confirmed that I had lost our baby.

I was devastated. I really wanted another child. I had been hoping and praying for a little girl. Besides my love for children, I had also hoped that having another baby would bring Paul and me closer together. That sort of closeness would have to wait.

Chapter 16 ♪   # A FRESH
START

$\mathcal{B}$y mid-1984, our home had become a living hell. We both recognized that the verbal, physical, and emotional abuse in our relationship was destroying our marriage, but we didn't know how to stop it; nor did we know how to establish lasting changes. We loved and hated each other at the same time. As unusual as it might seem, when Paul and I weren't fighting, we got along great; we actually had lots of fun together. Our marriage even had frequent growth spurts. For a while, it would look as though things were really coming together. But then we'd have another bout with Paul's anger, and not only would our meager progress be wiped out; we'd be set back twice as far.

During the last week in July, Paul was rodeoing in Burwell, Nebraska, about seven hundred miles from home. On Saturday night after the rodeo, he drove home all by himself. Along the way, he picked up a speeding ticket for going seventy-six miles an hour in a fifty-five mile per hour zone. He was disgusted and exhausted by the time he arrived home around five o'clock in the morning.

Knowing I was taking a chance, I tapped Paul on the shoulder about 9:00 A.M. and asked if he wanted to go to church. Paul rolled over groggily. "Wha . . . go where? What time is it, anyhow?"

"Would you like to go to church?" I asked sweetly. "It's Sunday morning, and I thought you might like to go to church. It's okay if you don't want to go. I know you're tired, but I've been thinking about going to that new church down the way. I've heard some good things about it. I know the preacher there and he is a good speaker. But if you are too tired. . . . "

Paul looked at me as if I were out of my mind. I fully expected him to say, "Are you crazy, woman? Don't you know I have been driving all night long and I am dead tired?" Yet miracle of miracles, Paul did not respond that way. Instead, he replied sleepily, "Well, no, I mean, yeah, let's go." Paul slowly climbed out of bed, still rubbing the sleep from his eyes.

At that time in our lives, Paul and I had been attending First Baptist Church in Stringtown, the same church where we had gotten married. The pastor and his wife were deeply caring people and good friends to us. They were always there when we needed them. He was a wonderful pastor, but his approach to preaching was less "exciting" to Paul than the preachers on the rodeo circuit. We had met James Crowson, who was the pastor of Dayspring Church in Atoka, and we had liked him right off, but our loyalties to our own pastor and church kept us from attending Dayspring. Yet for some reason, that morning I felt like we ought to go to there. We didn't know anything about the folks who worshiped there, or much else about the church, but I just knew we were supposed to go.

The service had already started by the time we arrived, and the sanctuary was nearly full. The congregation was standing, singing contemporary praise and worship songs, something I had never before experienced. In our more sedate church in Stringtown, we sang a few hymns in every service, but the singing was much more somber and staid. This singing had *life!* It was as though I could sense God's presence all over the church.

We slipped into a row near the back and tried to look as though we knew what was going on. Paul was much more familiar with this sort of worship than I was because many of the rodeo cowboy fellowships were conducted in a similar fashion. Me? I was awestruck. Literally!

Suddenly, for no apparent reason, I started crying. Paul thought I was being emotionally touched by the music, but it was more than that. It was as though God was all over me. I could not hold back the tears, and I didn't even try to do so. Eventually, I sat down, but I continued to cry. I knew that the Lord was dealing with my life. I was a Christian, and I had already been born again and baptized. I had rededicated my life to the Lord back in 1982, yet my life was not where I felt it ought to have been. I wasn't sinning outwardly; I wasn't stealing, running around on my husband, or lying; but God was dealing with me about my heart attitudes. He was speaking to me about my life and my priorities; and of course, He was speaking to me about my relationship with Paul.

It was as though God were speaking directly to my heart, saying, "You're not happy. You are not content. You have never been content in what you are doing." I knew I needed to make a change in my life, but I wasn't even sure how to start, so I just sat in the church and cried throughout the service.

I don't remember a word Pastor Crowson said that morning. I just knew God was dealing with me. Although we did not make any outward commitments that morning—we didn't "go forward," or join the church, or anything like that—both Paul and I recognized that something significant was beginning to happen in our lives. We didn't want the service to end.

We decided to return for the evening service, and that night we took a seat right on the front row. Again God began speaking to my heart and mind. I sensed Him saying, "A house divided will not stand. You are going your way, and your husband is going his. I want you to go together as a family and sing about me. I want you to sing my praises."

At the close of the service, Paul and I walked to the front of the church and asked the pastor to pray for us. Pastor Crowson began talking to us about our lives and what God was saying to us.

Paul said, "God has been dealing with me about rededicating and recommitting my life. I don't know exactly what that means. Right now it just seems like a bunch of words to me, but I know God wants us to do something differently, something more than we are doing right now."

Pastor Crowson listened intently and prayerfully, then looked straight at Paul and me and said, "Here's what I think the Lord is saying to you. I think God wants you to go together as a family, and that He will make a way for your calling. I believe God wants Susie to sing for the Lord."

My mouth must have dropped wide open. Without my discussing it, the pastor was confirming the exact message that God had already spoken to my heart. The message hit home with Pau, as well. He had wanted me to travel with him and sing at the rodeo services ever since he had heard Dean Winborn and Wanda Jackson singing to accompaniment tapes.

Pastor Crowson talked with us further and prayed with us, sealing our fresh commitment to the Lord. Paul and I prayed too, repenting of our sins and asking God to give us a fresh start. We committed ourselves to doing whatever God wanted us to do, regardless of the cost. Later that night, Pastor Crowson gave us a book, *Called, Appointed, and Anointed*, by Janny Grine. The book was a great inspiration to us when we read it that week. The essence of the book's message is that if God has called you to do something for Him, He will provide for you. If He has truly called, appointed, and anointed you, He will use your efforts and people will be touched and spiritually healed as you obey Him.

That night Paul and I became convinced God wanted us to travel together as a family unit and that He wanted me to sing for Him. The message was confirmed to our hearts that as I sang for Him, lives would be changed, hearts would be repaired, and people would be healed. I just knew that this was what God wanted me to do.

When we got home that night, still basking in the afterglow of our renewed experience with God, Paul and I were talking casually when he said, "You need to call Pake if you are going to quit singing with him."

Quit singing with him! We had just invested $20,000 in our music career, had numerous singing dates booked, and had been trying to get a record contract in Nashville. Now I was supposed to tell my brother that I was going to suddenly quit and start singing about Jesus? I didn't even know if anyone would ever want to hear me sing Christian music. We had no idea how to start a singing ministry.

I knew Pake would not be happy to hear about my new commitment. Nevertheless, I also knew that Paul was right. If I was really serious about allowing God to have control of my life, the first step was to break off with my old lifestyle, and that included singing the "cheatin' heart" sort of country music in the bars and honky-tonks with Pake.

But that didn't mean it was an easy decision to make. I stepped outside into the night, pacing back and forth in front of our home, thinking about the ramifications of my choices. Paul came outside too, and was amazingly low-keyed and quiet. I think he knew that this decision was between God and me and if I was going to sing for the Lord, it had to be for Him, not simply because Paul wanted me to do so. Paul sat on the front porch for a while and watched me pace.

"What are you going to do?" he asked softly.

"I don't know," I replied. "I have to think about this."

Before I walked back in the door, God gave me a peace in my heart, and I knew what I had to do. I needed to walk away from that kind of life. Singing in the bars and clubs was no longer for me. I decided to sing Christian music.

It is important to understand that in the early to mid-1980s, there was no such music genre as "Positive Country," or "Christian Country," as we have nowadays. At that time, country music itself was a relatively small industry. In many parts of the nation, it was difficult to find a radio station playing country music, let alone "Christian Country." Even the Christian music field had experienced a swing away from traditional and southern gospel styles of music to a more contemporary sound. I was a country singer, not a pop or rock 'n' roll artist. Country was all I had ever sung; it was all I cared to sing. Consequently, when I decided that I would sing Christian music, for all I knew, it was a decision to bury myself in absolute obscurity.

Even though I had made up my mind, I still waffled when it came to breaking the news to Pake. "Maybe he and Katy are already in bed," I said to Paul, trying to put off calling them for a while. "I'd better wait until tomorrow to talk to them. No use getting them all riled up tonight."

Paul spoke kindly but firmly. "If you don't do it tonight, you won't do it. It is fresh on your mind, and your commitments to the Lord are renewed. If you put it off, you won't follow through on your decision." I could tell that Paul was trying to leave the choice in my hands, yet it was equally obvious that my husband felt adamantly about me making a categorical, irreversible decision tonight. And the best way to make sure I stuck to my promise was to call Pake tonight. Right now.

Slowly and reluctantly, I dialed Pake and Katy's telephone number. I talked to Pake first and said simply, "I am going to quit. I can't sing with you any more."

Pake had just gotten home from working outside. He said, "Whoa! Whoa! Wait a minute here. I don't understand what you are saying. It sounded to me like you said you were quitting."

"That's right, Pake," I replied. "I can't sing with you any more. I am going to church, and I am going to sing a different kind of music. I want to sing about Jesus."

"You what?"

"I'll talk to you about it more tomorrow. I just wanted to tell you tonight to let you know I am going to be making some changes." I knew if I stayed on the line any longer, Pake would try to talk me out of my decision. So I said a hasty good-bye and hung up. There! I had done it.

Paul was rejoicing. He had wanted me with him at the rodeos for a long time. Now, I was the one who had made the commitment to go with him and to sing wherever God opened the doors, or not at all.

Pake, on the other hand, was extremely hurt. It was hard for him to understand my decision. For the next few days, he hardly talked. When Pake spoke, it was as though someone had died. In a way, I guess I had. I had died to my own will, so I could do God's will.

When I talked to Pake's wife, Katy, a couple of days later, she dropped a bomb on me. "You know that RCA had been interested in signing you and Pake as a duet act."

"No, Katy. Pake never mentioned anything like that to me. No one ever told me that." Now I better understood why Pake was so upset. Not only was I walking out on our performance dates, I was walking out on a recording contract that Pake had worked so hard to achieve.

Looking back, I believe that God shielded me from learning about the potential contract until I made the decision to go with Paul and the family. Had I known about the recording contract, it would have been tougher to walk away from Pake and his dreams. I'm not saying that I wouldn't have done it anyhow, but it would have been more painful for me. Furthermore, I think God was much more interested in salvaging our marriage than my music career. He knew that Paul and I weren't going to be able to make it much longer, not with our relationship functioning the way it was. The idea of Paul going one way and me going another way wasn't working. That was our plan, not God's plan for marriage. We had entered into our marriage saying, "You do your thing, and I will do mine. We will have lots of money. We can do what we want to, and everything will be rosy." But from the beginning, that sort of relationship was not God's ideal for marriage. Otherwise, He'd have put Adam in the Garden of Eden with Eve commuting to and from Egypt on a camel!

I agreed to fulfill the remaining dates Pake and I had booked for the month of August. That would give Pake a chance to contact the places where we were scheduled for the remainder of the year and renegotiate a deal as a solo act.

I had long since quit my job in Reba's office. Now, after my last singing date with Pake in August, I hit the road with Paul and E. P. One of the first rodeos E. P. and I attended with Paul after our renewed commitment to the Lord and to each other was almost symbolic. It was held in Kansas City, the first official rodeo of the new season, and Paul won $1,800. It was almost as if God was saying, "See, I can take care of you. You concentrate on obeying me." We were ecstatic as we rolled down the highway in our little red and white Ford Falcon. A sense of peace pervaded the car. I hadn't sung in Kansas City, but that did not matter. For the first time, we were traveling the rodeo circuit as a family, not Paul with the guys and me staying at home with E. P. We were together, and we were happy. We sang praise choruses all the way home in the car.

Surely, our marriage troubles were over.

Chapter 17

DIFFICULT
LESSONS

*M*aybe it was because we were working together as a unit, or maybe it was simply less stressful for Paul, but in 1984 he had a tremendous year rodeoing. He made the finals again, the first time since 1981. To us, it was simply another sign of God's blessing upon our decision to follow Him more fully. I didn't do much singing during the fall of that year. I spent a lot of time with Paul and E. P. and began to enjoy being a mom and housewife once again.

Paul and I attended a few rodeo church services together, and occasionally the person in charge asked me to sing a song. I was always glad to accommodate, even though I only knew two Christian songs and had to sing both of them *a cappella*. I began to buy the most "country-sounding" accompaniment tracks available and started learning the songs. I went along with Paul to the 1984 National Finals Rodeo competition, with no thoughts about singing. I was just excited that Paul was back where he wanted to be, on top of the rodeo world. But once we arrived, I was asked to sing several songs for the main meeting of the Cowboy Christian Fellowship, the organization that sponsors the Cowboy Churches at rodeos around the world. That was a great honor because there were more than one thousand people attending the service. The crowd included cowboys, their families, and rodeo fans from all over the United States, Canada, and various parts of the world.

I sang three songs during the service. When I was done, Jeff Copenhaver, the president of Cowboy Chapter of Fellowship of Christian Athletes, stood up and said, "We are going to receive an offering, and I just feel impressed to give this offering to Paul and Susie." He went on to tell how we had recently given our lives totally to the Lord. Paul and I were shocked! More than that, Paul was downright embarrassed. After all, he had been winning at rodeos all year long and was a competitor in the finals. He was almost insulted that anyone wanted to give him a handout. Paul recalls his feelings that day:

> I wanted to crawl under the seat. When I realized they were actually going to receive an offering on our behalf, I wanted to jump up and say, "Hey! Don't take an offering for us; I am a competitor here!" But the folks at that church meeting gave us $1,154 that day. Sure, we needed the money because we were so far in debt, but taking an offering for us pinched at my pride. I was so embarrassed, I wanted to make them take the money back, but Jeff Copenhaver wouldn't hear of it.
>
> When Susie and I returned home, I went to our pastor and told him what had happened. I said, "We can't take that money."
>
> He pulled out his Bible and said, "Listen, this is what the Scriptures say." He read Luke 6:38, "Give, and it shall be given unto you; good measure, pressed down, and shaken together, and running over, shall men give unto your bosom." Then the pastor said, "Paul, God is going to use other people to bless you and Susie. If He wants to use men, then receive it."
>
> So we received it. I still felt uncomfortable about taking the money, but we were grateful for the kindness of Jeff and the Fellowship of Christian Cowboys.

Looking back on the incident, it is now easy for us to see that God was proving again that He is faithful and He will take care of us. It was a confirmation of what Pastor James Crowson had told us the night we had renewed our commitment to the Lord—"that He would make a way" for us. Even when it seems there is no way, He will make a way.

In March of 1985, Paul, E. P., and I stopped by Roswell, New Mexico, to visit with Willard and Donna Moody, a couple that has greatly influenced our lives spiritually. Willard was once a champion rodeo cowboy, having been to the NFR six times as a calf-roper, and Donna was a barrel racer. They spend most of their time these days training horses and telling people about the Lord.

I was three months pregnant at the time. One morning, Paul and Willard were up early—about 3:00 A.M.—getting ready to go to the rodeo in Lubbock, Texas. They were almost ready to go out the door when I felt some cramps in my abdomen, so I hurried into the bathroom and discovered that I was spotting severely. Paul was concerned, but I made light of the situation. "Now get on out of here or you're going to be late," I told him. "I'm okay; I'll be fine. If I need anything, Donna is here." Deep down, I sort of resented that Paul would even consider going to the rodeo with me bleeding. But at that point in our marriage, I did not show my true feelings.

Paul and Willard headed off to the rodeo. Not long after the men left, I started cramping more severely. I kept bleeding, and it seemed the flow of blood was increasing. Finally, Donna said, "Come on, Susie. I'm taking you to the hospital."

When we arrived at the Roswell hospital, the doctors in the emergency room quickly determined that I was about to miscarry our baby. They tried their best to stop the miscarriage, but to no avail.

This was the second baby we had lost, and I was emotionally devastated by it. Losing an unborn child, to me, is as awful as losing any other child. Even though I was not able to see or touch our baby, I knew the baby was there, and I would soon be feeling it move within me. Although I didn't know the child, I was bound to that baby, mind, body, emotions, and spirit. I grieved the loss of our child as much as I would have had we lost any other member of our family. My response must have surprised the attending physicians. The doctors stared at me silently, coolly detached from the situation. It was tough enough to lose the baby, but it was even worse to be in a harsh, sterile room, a strange place where I didn't know any of the doctors or nurses, with no family around to help ease the pain in my heart. I sat on the cold, uncomfortable, examining table covered by white paper and cried and cried and cried.

I went back to Willard and Donna's home and waited for Paul. When Paul returned from the rodeo in Lubbock, I was lying down in the guest bedroom. He came into the room quietly and sat down on the bed. I said, "Paul, I lost the baby. I don't know what was wrong, but the doctors said they just couldn't help." Paul was terribly disappointed, but understanding. He took me in his arms and held me, and said, "It will be all right. We'll try to have another baby as soon as you are able." Paul tried his best to console me, but there was a distinct emptiness, not just in my womb, but in my heart. I had really wanted that baby.

I can't exactly say that I am thankful for my miscarriage experiences, but over the years God has used them many times to help me be more compassionate and empathetic with those who lose a baby. I know a little of the hurt they are feeling. I don't have any pat answers for them—except to trust that God is still in control—but I do understand the questions that tear at their souls.

On a positive note, I did my first solo album in 1985. I selected ten songs that sounded as "country" as I could find, yet still had strong Christian messages. They included "I Won't Walk without Jesus," "Reign on Me," and "This World Is Not My Home." It was a simple album in many ways, but there seemed to be a strong spiritual anointing on it. To this day, it remains one of my most requested albums.

Because we now had a tape of songs to sell, and more sound tracks to sing to, it wasn't long before Paul felt that I should be singing at every rodeo in the world! He started entering as many rodeos as he could, not simply so he could compete, but so I could sing and he could give his testimony at the Christian cowboy services. Paul assumed that the same logic he used for rodeoing would work for ministry opportunities, too. His philosophy in rodeoing was to enter as many rodeos as possible, because that increased his chances of winning. He'd say, "You're out there anyway; why not be busy?" Applying the same formula to the ministry, he felt that the more rodeos in which I sang and he gave his testimony, the more effective we were going to be, and the more tapes we were going to sell, and the more people we were going to touch. It was a "bigger is better" mentality that was so easy to slip into, thinking we must do more and more, faster and faster. In the meantime, we wanted to have more children, and we were trying to work on our relationship because it was still such a mess.

In 1985, we went to more than one hundred rodeos. Paul's dream of us being on the road as a family was certainly coming true. He loved it! Besides needing much less rest than I do, Paul is a "people" person. They energize him. I am just the opposite. I love people, but they tend to drain me. After being with a crowd, I need time to get away by myself to recharge my emotional batteries. But neither Paul nor I understood that at the time, so we kept on traveling more and getting busier. All the while, my physical and spiritual reservoirs were nearing dangerously low levels.

Another dream of Paul's was being fulfilled too. In early 1985, Paul was ranked the number one steer-wrestler in the world. For a fellow who had never even ridden a horse competitively until he was in college, it was no small achievement for Paul to ascend to the top spot in the sport within a few years. Paul couldn't have been happier. We were serving the Lord together; we were traveling as a family in a pickup truck and camper combination; and he was sitting on top of the rodeo world. What could be better?

Me? I was just happy that Paul was happy.

By June, Paul had slipped to number three in the rodeo rankings, and he was determined to get back to the top. He won $5,700 in the rodeo at Reno, and that shot him back up to number two in the world. From Reno, we headed to Calgary, Canada, for the big Fourth of July rodeo. Most rodeos paid anywhere from $1,000 to $15,000 to the winners, with the average being about $7,000, but Calgary had a whopping $50,000 bonus in addition to their regular rodeo purse. Whether it was for money or pride, I wasn't sure, but when Paul ran his first steer at Calgary, he did exceptionally well. I could tell he wanted to win this one. He was probably thinking that if he could just win this rodeo we would be on our way to getting out of debt.

But God had a more important lesson He wanted Paul to learn.

The Calgary rodeo lasts all week long. Since Paul drew a steer on the first day and the last day of the rodeo, rather than sitting around doing nothing all week, he entered the rodeo in Ce'real, Alberta. On Sunday morning, as was our custom, we attended the Cowboy Church service. The Christian Cowboy Fellowship had arranged for a television crew to attend the church service that morning, and they wanted to feature a rodeo cowboy. Since Paul was sitting atop the world rodeo standings, he was a natural choice for the TV crew. After the service, the TV crew followed Paul everywhere he went, filming a feature story on a day in the life of a champion rodeo cowboy. The crew filmed Paul getting ready for the rodeo, sitting in the "box" just before the gate opened, and ripping out to run his steer. They also filmed me singing at the Cowboy Fellowship. The show aired on Canadian television coast to coast.

There are good and bad steers in steer wrestling—good if they run straight after they leave the chute and if they fall easily after you've caught them. A bad steer does just the opposite. That day in Ce'real, Paul drew the best steer in the herd, but when he looked at the contestants' draw-sheets and saw which steer he had drawn, he knew immediately that something was wrong. The officials had made a mistake. This was the second rodeo performance that day. They had ended the previous run of the cattle and had started another run on the same cattle on the same day. Rodeo rules say that a cowboy cannot run a steer that has already been run in a previous performance that day.

Not only had Paul drawn a steer that had already been run that day, but the first and second place bulldoggers had run him too. Paul remembers that steer well. He says:

If it had been a bad steer, and I had known they had misdrawn, I would have asked the rodeo officials to redraw the cattle. I would have said, "No, that steer has already been run." But I had drawn the best steer. Instead of reporting the mistake, which the Lord was telling me to do, I was seeing dollar signs. I rationalized my actions in my heart by saying, "Hey, if the guys in charge aren't smart enough to figure it out, I'm not going to tell them."

In a way, I naively figured that my getting the best steer was a blessing from the Lord. The Lord had been dealing with me lately about dishonesty and showing me that any shading of the truth compromised my integrity. But I just shucked off the conviction as though I was brushing off the dust from my clothes after wrestling a steer. I should have paid attention.

I didn't say anything to anybody about which steer I had drawn. I didn't even mention it to Susie. I just prepared to run my steer, figuring I'd soon be lining up at the pay window.

There was one slight disadvantage to running that particular steer, however. The steer had a habit of "setting up," which means he stopped quick, short, and hard. That makes a steer hard to catch. When the steer sees the cowboy and his hazer—the guy who is trying to keep the steer running straight—tearing after him on horseback, the steer will sometimes stop so suddenly the cowboy will go right over the top of him.

To prevent that from happening, I told my hazer, "Let's bump this steer a little bit and see if we can make him take one more jump." Usually when a hazer bumps the steer, the animal will respond by jumping as it is running, which gives the cowboy a little longer to catch him.

When I went out to run my steer, everything worked just as my hazer and I had planned. He bumped the steer and sure enough the animal jumped. But then the steer stopped short and turned its burly head in my direction, just as I was sliding down to catch hold of his horns. The steer's horn plunged into my chest all the way up to my collar bone. Had I come in a little lower, the horn would have pierced me right in the lung.

I heard a dull thud and felt a sudden pain in my chest when the steer hit me, but I didn't know that he had gored me. I just thought he had hit me really hard. But the pain in my rib cage roared in my brain. Fortunately, the steer simply jerked his head around and pulled the horn straight out.

I rolled onto the ground, blood gushing from my upper chest. The first thing I thought about (as soon as I realized what had happened) was that I had removed myself from the Lord's protection by willingly going along with running the wrong steer. Right there on the ground, before any cowboys even got to me, I said aloud, "Lord, I am sorry. I know you were telling me that I should have reported the mistake on my steer. I understand what you are saying to me."

Gary Green, a fellow steer wrestler, came running up to me, saying, "Paul, Paul, are you all right?"

I was sitting on the ground, and all I could think about was, *Oh Lord, I am sorry.*

"Paul, can you hear me? Are you okay?" Gary said frantically in front of my face.

"Yeah, I am all right," I managed to grunt. "It hit my collarbone," I said. By this time, Susie had rushed into the arena with a terrified look on her face.

"Paul, Paul! How bad is it? Are you okay?"

"I think he just hit me hard," I told her.

"No, the horn went in," Gary argued. "Just look." He lifted my arm and blood gushed from the gaping wound.

I heard the announcer's voice over the arena's public address system, calling, "Is there a doctor in the house?"

A young surgeon from Calgary was in the audience that day, in town along with his wife to visit her family. He came out of the crowd and examined me and suggested I be taken to the clinic in town, where he could sew me back together.

At the clinic, before the surgeon began working on me, I said, "I don't know if you believe in Jesus or not, but I am going to pray before you go cutting on me."

"You do what you have to do," the doctor said. "It doesn't matter to me." So I prayed. Afterward, the doctor took x-rays to see if any bones were broken. None were. The steer had gored all the way through my pectoral muscles, however, so the hole in my chest required twenty-seven stitches.

Once the bleeding was contained, the doctor's main concern was infection. A steer's horns have all kinds of bacteria on them, and a horn puncture is considered highly infectious. Usually, when a rodeo cowboy is gored, he must spend days in the hospital with drainage tubes in his body and antibiotics pumping intravenously through his system to prevent infection.

But I knew I didn't want to stay in the hospital. I had to get back to Calgary because I had another steer to run! I repented and prayed, asking the Lord to help me, then Susie and I headed back to Calgary, a distance of about four hundred miles.

On the way back, I drove the camper, and Paul lay in the back, groaning, each bump in the road agitating his injury. I could tell he was hurting badly, but he was obsessed with running his second steer at Calgary, so I kept going. He needed only to score a slightly above average run, throwing the steer in less than ten seconds, and he would qualify to compete for the $50,000 bonus money.

Paul realized that the puncture to his pectoral muscles severely limited his strength and pulling ability, but he had the Justin Healer Medicine Team at Calgary bandage him up tightly so the muscles wouldn't tear any more where the steer had gored him. When he tried to bulldog that day, however, he couldn't hang onto the steer's horns, and the steer jerked away, taking with it Paul's hope of a quick fix to our financial problems.

Paul had to sit out for several weeks as his body recuperated. The doctor in Calgary had told Paul, "It will probably be about six weeks before you will be able to do anything physical. You will know you're healed when you can do a push-up."

Miraculously, within two weeks, Paul was doing one hundred push-ups. Furthermore, he did not have a trace of infection. Paul and I are convinced that the Lord simply touched him and caused the normal healing processes to be speeded up!

The only lasting negative result of the accident was that Paul dropped in the national standings because of being sidelined. He made the 1985 finals, nonetheless, placing number fourteen in the top fifteen.

Throughout the latter part of 1985, I sang at several meetings for Donna and Coy Huffman, cofounders of Pro Rodeo Ministries. One day, we went to Federal Way, Washington, where Donna had been teaching a women's church group how to pray more effectively.

Although I had masked my emotions fairly well most of the time, I was still deeply grief-stricken over the second miscarriage we had suffered. Paul and I were thrilled and thankful to have our son E. P., but we wanted more children. I had told Donna the whole story, how I was tired and frustrated with our failed pregnancies and how I really wanted to have another baby.

That day, in her Bible study, Donna taught the women that if you ask the Lord for anything in Jesus' name, and if you believe in your heart, you will receive that which you ask.

I stared back at Donna in disbelief. I had faith, and I prayed regularly, but I was much more comfortable praying for nebulous things such as more love for my husband, blessings for the missionaries, and world peace. I wasn't used to asking God for anything so specific, so . . . so *tangible* as a human baby.

You can't be serious, I thought as I listened to Donna.

"Yes, I'm serious," Donna said to the class. "Be specific in your prayers, and tell the Lord exactly what you want. He loves you and knows what's best for you, but there's nothing wrong with you letting Him know what's on your heart."

So I took her literally. I knelt down beside my chair to pray. Donna had said to be specific, so I said to myself, *All right, I am going to be specific.* I prayed, "Lord, I'd like a perfectly healthy, curly blonde-haired, blue-eyed, baby girl— with a good disposition! Amen."

"Done!" Donna said, as if we were ordering a Christmas present over the telephone. I got up from my knees and felt a peace in my heart and mind that I had not felt prior to praying.

Within a few weeks, I found out that I was pregnant. There was no doubt in my mind that I was carrying a little girl.

Chapter 18

BEGINNINGS OF
MINISTRY

*D*uring the 1985 National Rodeo Finals, Paul and I knew that God was dealing with us about starting some sort of ministry in which he would speak and I would sing. We were already doing that whenever we went to Christian Cowboy Fellowship meetings, so we didn't see that having an official status would change our heart concerns. We talked to our rodeo ministry friends, Glenn and Ann Smith, and they convinced us that we should think more seriously about starting a bona fide ministry. On their advice we established Psalms Ministries, Inc.

The biggest change for us as a result of saying we were a ministry—beyond the tax and paperwork hassles that go along with it—was that it turned our focus upside down. Previously, we went to the rodeos primarily so Paul could compete, and maybe—just maybe—we'd have a chance to share our testimony at the fellowship meetings or somewhere else. Now, we began to think in terms of looking for ministry opportunities, and if there was a rodeo opportunity for Paul that was okay. If not, that was all right too.

Paul had begun to sour a bit on rodeoing toward the end of 1985 anyhow. The goring incident in Calgary may have been more significant than Paul had originally thought. Although it did not set him back physically for long, it dampened his enthusiasm enough that he did not do well in the finals. I could tell that Paul had lost a bit of his spunk for rodeoing, but I was not about to say anything. Paul would have to realize that for himself.

Paul continued rodeoing in 1986, while we increased the number of services in which we ministered. The majority of our ministry still took place at rodeos, holding Cowboy Church on Sunday mornings. Paul was well known in rodeo circles as a top steer-wrestler, and most folks around the rodeo knew the McEntire family. Those who didn't know about Grandpap's or Daddy's legacy at least knew about Reba as a rising country star.

In 1984, Reba had won the Country Music Association's award for Female Vocalist of the Year, the first of four straight times she would receive that award, a record in itself for country music artists. In 1986, she won the highest honor an active CMA performer could achieve, the Entertainer of the Year. Because of all the name recognition in our family, Paul and I were like a celebrity couple to the rodeo crowd. Hundreds of people came to hear us tell them about Jesus. Of course, some came to see Paul, and some came to see Reba's sister, but we were always careful to give God the glory and let Him shine.

About that time, people started inviting us to minister in their churches too. Before this, our ministry had been almost exclusively to rodeo folks. We weren't sure how churches would take to a former country music singer and a rodeo cowboy. We were shocked when churches not only embraced us but asked us to come back again and again. In the church services, like the Fellowship meetings, I would sing some songs from my album, and Paul would give a testimony or speak briefly from the Bible. We didn't do things fancy, and we probably made a lot of mistakes, but God blessed our honesty and our sincere efforts to tell people about Jesus.

Russ and Anna Weaver were key people in helping Paul and me get established in the church ministry. Russ and Anna were home missionaries associated with the Assemblies of God denomination. Their mission field was not in the jungles of Africa or the mountains of Mongolia; their mission was to the rodeo circuit. They traveled the country with their three boys in a truck and camper rig and spent their lives talking, befriending, counseling, and sharing the gospel message with rodeo cowboys and their families. When Russ and Anna were in town, Russ competed in calf-roping, and they usually conducted a Cowboy Fellowship meeting at the rodeo site, as well as the Sunday evening service at the closest Assemblies church. They often asked Paul and me to accompany them. Paul shared his rodeo cowboy testimony, and I sang. It was a wonderful way to be introduced to mainstream Christian ministry circles.

Looking back, we now realize how kind it was for Russ and Anna to present us to their friends. Those churches were their support base. For the Weavers to bring in someone like us, opening the door for us and helping us to get started in the ministry, was extremely humble and unselfish. Beyond that, it was risky faith for Russ and Anna to endorse us the way they did. Paul and I were both relatively new Christians, and although to most onlookers it appeared that we had the perfect marriage, that was far from the case. Of course, Russ and Anna were unaware of the abuse that was taking place in our home. Although they had occasionally seen Paul's temper flare in my direction, no doubt they thought that any friction between Paul and me was long since in our past.

Regardless, Russ and Anna believed in us. Russ always managed to tell the congregation to whom we were ministering, "God is doing something big, right here with these two young people. You are on the grass roots of something big."

Working with the Weavers also gave us an opportunity to sell a few tapes after each service. The first album was so popular that soon we were thinking in terms of recording another album, which we did later in 1986. For the next ten years, I recorded a new album every year.

At nearly every rodeo that Paul and I went to in 1986, we ministered in at least three services. The change in our focus was increasingly obvious. In 1985, Paul entered nearly one hundred rodeos, and we ministered at about thirty services. In 1986, we ministered at about one hundred services, and Paul entered only thirty rodeos. Because of his continued problems with a chronic sickness, Paul began to think seriously about giving up the rodeo all together.

He started booking more and more singing dates for me, at most of which he spoke or shared a testimony. As the news spread that we were available for such services, the phone started ringing off the hook at our house. Our mailbox was jammed daily with new opportunities for us to go somewhere and share our story. Little did people know that the toughest part of the story was still a work in progress.

Several rodeo preachers took us under their wings and helped us during those days. Besides Russ and Anna Weaver were Coy and Donna Huffman, Glen and Ann Smith, Larry and Debbie Smith, Randy Weaver (Russ's brother), Wilbur Plaugher, and Willard Moody, a few of the rodeo preachers with whom we worked. Singing about God was different than singing "tears in your beer" songs in honky-tonks, to people who weren't paying attention or were too drunk to know what I was singing about. Now, I felt that the audience was getting something life changing. It wasn't simply entertainment; it was the Word of God, and the Word brings life! Paul and I were especially thrilled when we were able to help someone else discover the Lord. That was more precious than gold to us. Good thing, too, since there wasn't much gold in the kind of work we were doing. Money was scarce during those early years of our ministry. It was a tremendous blessing for us to get as much as fifty dollars in an offering. If we got enough money to buy something to eat and to buy gas to get us to the next town, we were content. The money didn't matter.

The Lord had already taught us that He could take care of us, and He had given us a clear word that He would make a way for us, so we didn't worry much. God always provided for us, and we never lacked for food or money to buy enough gas to get to the next concert location. It was a wonderfully liberated way to live!

Near the end of January 1986, we went to the famous Billy Bob's nightclub in Fort Worth, the biggest honky-tonk in Texas, to help conduct the first ever Cowboy Church in the middle of Billy Bob's rodeo arena. The service was held Sunday morning at 11:00, just as in many other churches.

Only during this service, the preacher wore a black cowboy hat, blue jeans, and cowboy boots; nearby some curious onlookers were playing pool and video games. About 250 people were seated on folding chairs in the dirt and sawdust of the rodeo arena. Others sat in bleachers behind the arena rails.

Jeff Copenhaver opened the service by saying, "Welcome to Cowboy Church. It's nice just to be here acknowledging God with or without the stained-glass windows." Paul gave his testimony, as did bull rider Bobby Del Vechio; I sang some songs, and Jeff Copenhaver preached. A collection was received, with contributors tossing their offerings into cowboy hats as they were passed. The management of Billy Bob's was so impressed with the Cowboy Church that they wanted to make it a regular Sunday morning feature at the club.

On the way to Fort Worth, I had noticed that E. P. did not seem to be feeling well. Then he started to complain about his stomach aching. When I mentioned it to Paul, he just laid his hand on E. P. and prayed. I believe in prayer, but when E. P. kept complaining about his tummy, and slept only fitfully on the way to Fort Worth, I was concerned that this was something more than a tummy ache. When I brought it up again, Paul became irritated with me that I didn't have the faith to believe E. P. was okay.

Paul and I assumed E. P. was merely hungry. Once we arrived at Billy Bob's, we got him something to eat, and that seemed to help. During the service, E. P. enjoyed playing with the other children who were there, climbing on the railings that surrounded Billy Bob's arena.

Afterward, we went to visit Russ and Anna Weaver at their home. By that time, strangely, E. P. did not want to play with the Weaver's three boys who were around his age—nearly three years old—and some of his best buddies. Nor did he want to eat anything that night. Instead, E. P. only wanted to crawl up and sit in Paul's or my lap. I knew something was wrong with our boy when he didn't want to play, but I didn't say too much in front of Paul. In his effort to raise E. P. as a tough little guy, Paul was always pretty hard on our son. Whenever E. P. was hurting for some reason, Paul usually encouraged him to simply brush it off and keep going. "Oh, just get tough and go along with it," he'd say. Paul admits today, "That was one of my big problems, not only with Susie but with our E. P. as well. I had very little sympathy or compassion."

Actually, Paul's attitude was influenced by three factors. First, Paul had received little compassion during his own childhood, so he had no models to emulate when it came time for him to express compassion toward E. P. or toward me. Paul thought he *was* being compassionate, but his idea of showing compassion was a far cry from what most folks would consider as caring or showing empathy.

Second, Paul tended to spiritualize everything by saying, "We have faith; God is the Great Physician here, so let's just pray and trust God to heal him." Paul did the same with me. If I told Paul, "I have a headache," he'd respond, "Oh, that's a negative confession. Just confess you're healed and trust God to heal it, and He will take care of you. Don't take any medicine; you don't need aspirin. Just trust God."

I'd say, "Paul, that's easy for you to say. I am the one with the headache." And I'd take an aspirin.

I was glad Paul had great faith, but his comments not only made me feel that my faith in God was insufficient but that I was unimportant to Paul, that he didn't love me, that my pains—large or small—didn't really matter to him, that I, in fact, did not matter to him.

Paul has always had an aversion to taking medicine of any kind, so when he became a Christian, he was easily swayed by the theology that emphasized using more faith and less medicine. Paul now says, "My misunderstanding of biblical faith gave me a basis to say to Susie, 'Well, you just don't believe God.' Then we would get into an argument over who had more faith. It was ridiculous."

The third reason why Paul was always quick to make light of an injury or an illness was economic. We did not have health insurance. Similar to football players, hockey players, and athletes in other rough contact sports, insurance rates are horrendous for rodeo cowboys. Unlike athletes in other sports, most rodeo cowboys are self-employed, although the PRCA does have a group health plan. Regardless, to pay for health insurance on Paul and our family would have been out of the question. Besides, because of Paul's ulcerative colitis, we had little hope of getting a company to insure Paul.

Not only did we have no insurance; we had very little money. Any time E. P. got sick and I suggested, "Let's take him to a doctor," I could almost predict what Paul's response was going to be.

"No, we don't need to take him to a doctor. He will be all right. Just trust God."

Paul was not being selfish. He treated himself the same way. That night in Texas, however, E. P.'s condition continued to worsen. Shortly before daybreak, he woke us up, moaning in his sleep, calling, "Daddy! Daddy!" The child was delirious. He was so sick, shivering, and shaky, it was almost difficult to hold his fevered little body. He kept saying to Paul, "Oh, Dad, I'm so thirsty. Can I have a drink? I'm so thirsty."

We rushed to a doctor. The doctor checked E. P. but could not ascertain what was wrong with him. "He could have an intestinal flu," he said, "but most intestinal flues do not produce such pronounced effects, even in a child." Finally, the doctor took E. P. and thumped him on the bottom of his feet. "Let's get some blood samples," he said. Then he took x-rays of E. P.'s chest and abdomen.

"All I can come up with is appendicitis," the doctor said eventually. "But two-year-olds don't usually get appendicitis." The doctor was clearly baffled. "Wait here a minute. I'm going to make some phone calls and see if I can get some help." The doctor left the room, and Paul and I prayed for E. P. for the umpteenth time.

When the doctor returned, he told us, "His white blood count is around 60,000, which is extremely high. This all points to appendicitis. I think we need to get your boy to the hospital right away."

When we arrived at the hospital, the doctors there immediately began preparing E. P. for surgery. He was screaming for all his little lungs were worth as the doctors put the intravenous needles in his arm. As he went to the operating room, the attending physicians refused to allow E. P. to keep his "security blanket," and that hurt him even more than the needles. Little E. P. was screaming, "Mama! Daddy!" It was as though he was crying out, "How can you let these mean people do these things to me?"

The doctors discovered that E. P.'s appendix had burst. The doctors told us that his appendix had been in an unusual place, more toward his back, which made the problem worse. Thankfully, we had gotten E. P. to the hospital in time, and the doctors were able to treat him. He remained hospitalized, however, for seven days.

After the initial operation, there was nothing else we could do but sit there with him each day and try to make him comfortable. Keeping a two-year-old in one place for seven days—even a sick two-year-old—was an ordeal.

At some point after the danger to E. P.'s life had passed, the admissions officer at the hospital asked Paul what insurance plan we were covered under.

"We don't have any insurance," Paul told the man.

"Well, just exactly how do you plan on paying your bill?" the man snarled.

Paul replied, "I am sorry. We don't have any insurance, and we don't have any money." He said, "I know we owe this debt, and we will pay every penny, but we will just have to pay you what we can. I think we can pay about ten dollars a month right now."

The admissions officer nearly choked on that one. The bill for E. P.'s surgery and hospital stay was more than $7,000. Ten dollars a month was not the accountant's idea of an adequate payment.

"Excuse me, sir, but approximately how much was your income last year?"

"Around $40,000," Paul told him.

"Well, it seems to me that with an income of $40,000 you should be able to pay substantially more than $10 a month," the man sniffed.

"You don't understand," Paul told him. "Sure I made $40,000 last year, but it cost me $38,000 to get it. We don't have enough money to pay a large amount right now, but don't worry, you'll get your money."

The man behind the desk was probably already looking for the phone number of a collection agency.

That week, at their usual service in a nearby Assembly of God church, Russ and Anna Weaver told the congregation of our plight. They then received an offering for us which topped $500.

We kept enough money to get home and gave the hospital the remaining money. Paul said, "We will pay you when we can, but we will pay."

When we got back home to Oklahoma, we told my sister Alice, who worked for the Department of Human Services, about what had happened in Texas.

"Let me see what I can find out," Alice said. She discovered that our state had an emergency aid program for children under twenty-one years of age. We qualified for the program, and the emergency fund paid every penny of E. P.'s hospital bill. Again, the Lord had made a way for us where there seemed to be no way.

Chapter 19

UNCHALLENGED
ANGER

$\mathcal{W}$e had a strong competitive streak in our family. When E. P. was just a baby, my mama reminded us that Reba had walked at only six months of age. That was all Paul needed to hear. He was convinced that he could teach E. P. to walk in less than seven months. He almost did too. E. P. was slightly over seven months old when he took his first steps. It didn't matter to anyone else but Paul (and maybe Mama) that he didn't beat Reba's record.

Although Paul loved E. P. dearly, he frequently became frustrated if E. P. did not catch on right away to what Paul was trying to teach him. Sometimes, Paul would get impatient with E. P. and spank him for no reason at all when E. P. couldn't do what Paul had told him to do. "Dadgummit," Paul bellowed, "I said do it!" Poor little E. P. was scared stiff of Paul. The more Paul would yell, the more nervous E. P. became, and the less he was able to do what his daddy was demanding, which caused Paul to become even more angry. It was a vicious, no-win cycle.

While E. P. was still of preschool age, some friends gave us a dog as a gift. It was a cute little pitch-black puppy we named Ebony. That dog loved E. P., and E. P. loved Ebony. Sometimes, though, as a means of playing with Ebony, E. P. would kick at the dog.

One day, Paul saw E. P. harassing Ebony. Paul asked E. P., "Did you kick that dog?"

With stark terror in his eyes, E. P. answered, "No, Daddy." That infuriated Paul. He never stopped to consider that lying comes all too naturally to children, that nobody has to teach a child to lie, but we have to teach our children to tell the truth. Instead, Paul's main intent was to teach E. P. not to lie. But E. P. was just a little boy, scared that he was going to get a spanking. What was he going to say?

Paul turned E. P. over his knee and spanked him with his hand until E. P.'s bottom was beet red.

I was accustomed to Paul's unreasonable anger being expressed toward me. I shook in my shoes and sometimes feared for my life when Paul got mad, but I had been around him enough during his fits of anger that I was no longer shocked at his outbursts. When I saw Paul's anger directed toward E. P., however, I was terrified. I wanted to call out for help from somebody, but I didn't even know how to bring up the subject. Besides, whom could I tell? Who would believe me? Most of our friends and family members saw only the happy-go-lucky side of Paul. They had no idea what anger lurked within him. Beyond that, since I assumed that Paul's anger was directly related to me, I thought that if I could just figure out what I was doing to set him off, I might be able to handle things on my own, without anyone else getting involved. My tendency was to wait and hope that given enough time, the bad things would go away without any sort of confrontation. I no longer do that. Nowadays, although I am still reluctant to confront anyone, I am learning that sometimes I must deal with my problems head-on, even if that requires a face-to-face confrontation. Back then, I closed my mouth and suffered silently.

As a result, I allowed the situation to go on unchallenged.

Sometimes Paul's anger seemed totally unrelated to anything that was going on in our lives. To this day it is difficult for Paul and me to pinpoint one particular issue that sparked his violence. No specific words set him off. No lifting of the eyebrows made him angry. No one act of repeated negligence could we point to and say, "Every time that happened, Paul lost his temper." On the contrary, Paul's explosions inevitably came after a cumulative buildup of steam over several days, weeks, or months of seemingly insignificant issues, which then resulted in a sudden violent blowout.

One day, for example, I was doing the accounting bookwork associated with our ministry. I had my ledger books, checks, receipts, and bills spread out all over a long table in our house. I also had some cassette tapes to send out to people who had ordered them. I was sitting at the table working when Paul came in. It was obvious that he was angry about something, because he totally ignored me. When I caught a glimpse of his clenched teeth, however, I knew trouble was coming, but it was too late to get out of the way. After trading a few comments with me, Paul began violently kicking anything that happened to be in his way.

One of Paul's frequent targets when he became angry was the kitchen trash can. Now, he went for it with a vengeance. He kicked the plastic can over so hard, egg shells and other garbage splattered all over the kitchen. Perhaps by kicking the trash, Paul was indirectly taking out his anger on me, since he knew that later I'd clean up the mess. On this day, the kitchen trash flew all over the floor as Paul began to vent his rage. Then Paul turned toward me and my work at the table. With one mighty sideways motion of his arms, Paul swept all of my accounting materials off the table onto the floor, where they landed among the egg shells and trash already there. With another strong swipe of his arms, Paul knocked me out of the chair onto the floor among the mess. I skidded on my elbows for a couple feet after I hit the floor.

"Paul! What's wrong with you?" I screamed. His eyes darted back and forth in his head, as he looked down on me and hollered, "I'll show you what's wrong with me!" And with that, Paul began kicking me in my backside with his hard leather cowboy boots.

"Paul!" I screamed again. "You're hurting me!"

Paul did not answer, nor did he relent. He kicked me again, and I curled up on the floor like a whipped puppy. Paul kicked me again, violently. When I was a young girl, my daddy kicked Reba, Alice, and me in the rear every once in a while when we did something wrong, or sometimes just to get our attention. I knew what it was to be kicked by a man. Being kicked in the behind by a parent or a spouse, or anyone else for that matter, is an extremely demeaning gesture. It hurt when Daddy used to kick us. But I had never been kicked as hard as Paul kicked me that day.

Tears flooded from my eyes, as I cried out to Paul, "Paul, please! Please quit!"

"Get up!" Paul roared.

I tried to get up, but I hurt so badly that I could barely make it to my knees. I knew instinctively that if I did not make an effort to stand, Paul would make me get up one way or another. *Better that I get up under my own power,* I was thinking, when suddenly I felt his muscular grip on my shoulder.

"Get up, I said!" Paul yelled as he grabbed me by the shoulder and jerked me off the floor.

I staggered to my feet and brushed my forearm across my face, trying to wipe the tears away.

Paul wanted to talk it out, so he continued yelling at me, but I was sobbing so much that I could not even speak. I just stood there in pain and cried.

"Oh, here you go crying again," Paul continued to yell at me. I still was not sure what it was that had ignited his fury, but I started apologizing for whatever it was that I had done.

Paul refused to accept my apology. "Yeah, that's just what my mom always said. She always told my dad that she was so sorry, but nothing ever changed. You sound just like my mom."

For a fleeting moment I thought about the way Paul's mom and dad related to each other, but I knew better than to argue with Paul about the vast differences between his mom and me. I simply began cleaning up the mess Paul had created. At first Paul threw the stuff back down onto the floor, so I stopped. After a while, Paul got down on his hands and knees and began to help me clean up the mess.

"I'm sorry, Susie," he said sincerely. "I don't know what got into me. I am so sorry." Tears poured down Paul's face now too. Paul seemed so truly sorry for what he had done that it touched my heart. I couldn't help feeling compassion for him. "Please forgive me, Susie," he said through both our tears. "I'm sorry. It won't happen again."

"I forgive you, Paul," I said as I held his head in my lap and stroked his hair. "I know you didn't mean to hurt me." Even as I spoke the words, I knew it would not be the last time I would suffer pain at the hands of this man.

Despite Paul's occasional blowouts, we continued ministering and rodeoing through the spring and summer of 1986. I was pregnant, and "great with child"—which I was convinced was a girl—but we continued our normal heavy schedule. One day as Paul, E. P., and I were driving through Dallas, on the way to another rodeo and ministry event, I looked up and saw a billboard advertising Lucchese (pronounced: "Lew-Kay-See") boots, a premier cowboy boot. "Hey, Paul! Wouldn't that be a great name for our little girl!" I said excitedly. We had considered several names but hadn't settled on anything. When I saw *Lucchese*, I knew that was it! Paul agreed that if our baby was a girl—which I knew it was—we would name her Lucchese Luchsinger.

Lucchese was due on the first of July. The week before that, Paul and I ministered in an Assemblies of God church in Dale, Texas, and experienced one of the most powerful moves of God we had ever encountered in one of our services. I sang only one song, "Touch Through Me," written by Dottie Rambo, before the Holy Spirit began to draw people to the front of the church, where they fell to their knees, crying and repenting. We had not tried to manipulate people into responding; we hadn't done a thing to promote any kind of response at all. God simply moved into that service and took over. It was marvelous!

After the service, we loaded up the camper and headed back home to wait for the arrival of our baby. I still recall changing my clothes in the back of that moving camper. Now that I think of it, with my history of miscarriages, that could easily have been a disaster had Paul swerved quickly or hit an unexpected bump. But we were still sky high from the service. We were assured of God's presence, and nothing could darken our spirits. We had a baby on the way any day now.

The day after we got home, I had my regularly scheduled appointment with Dr. Maggi, my obstetrician. He examined me to see how the baby was doing. "Doctor Maggi, I've had a funny feeling," I told him. "I feel like something is wrong." It was then that I told the doctor that I had a history of herpes, which dated back to my college days. Dr. Maggi's face turned ashen. "You have what?" he asked, clearly concerned. "If you have herpes, you will have to have a cesarean section with this baby. Because if the child passes through the birth canal, it could contract herpes or possibly develop other birth defects, and you wouldn't know it until it was too late."

It was less than a week before our baby's due date, and Paul and I had been planning on having a natural birth. I knew he would not be thrilled to hear Dr. Maggi's report. Paul had gone over to the pediatrician's office to line up care for our new baby while Dr. Maggi had been examining me.

Paul was in a good mood when he returned to pick me up. As I got into our truck, he asked excitedly, "Well, what did he say?" I was reluctant to tell him about the doctor's serious assessment of my condition, so I hesitated a moment before answering. "Well?" Paul urged, the anticipation of being a father again written all over his face.

I said, "Well, I told Dr. Maggi that I had a funny feeling . . . and it felt a lot like the time I had herpes. He said that if it really is herpes, then when the baby is born, we're gonna have to have it c-section."

Paul responded, "Oh, we can't do that! We ain't gonna do that."

"Paul, the doctor said if I have herpes, and we have the baby naturally, the baby will most likely contract herpes or some other defect that could damage our baby's brain. That's why we need to do the cesarean."

"We just aren't going to do that," Paul said adamantly.

I was upset and heavy-hearted with guilt and shame for my past misbehavior, but Paul was making matters worse. I knew he was concerned that we had no insurance coverage, and with the average cesarean operation and hospital stay, we could easily run up a hospital bill of eight to ten thousand dollars. We hadn't expected that, and it was a bit of a shock to Paul. But it was no less a shock to me!

"Let's go back in to see the doctor," said Paul. "I need to ask him some questions about this."

When we sat down with Dr. Maggi, Paul asked him, "What do we have to do to clear your mind and to clear Susie's mind that we can have this baby naturally?"

The doctor replied, "We will have to do some tests, but since I have already examined Susie today, she must remain undisturbed for twenty-four hours before we can do a culture to see if there is any herpes resident."

Paul said, "I want her to have this baby naturally. I don't want her to have a cesarean section."

The doctor knew our financial situation, but he said, "Doing a cesarean section is never our first choice either, Paul. But sometimes it is necessary for the life of the baby or for the life of the mother."

"I understand," Paul answered. "But if at all possible, we'd like to have this child naturally. When will we know for sure?"

"It will take approximately a week to get the tests back," Dr. Maggi replied, "since they will have to be sent to Dallas. As I said, we cannot take the culture today, so you will have to come back tomorrow. We'll do the culture, and I will send it off immediately for analysis. Then in a few days we will need to do another culture. All together, we will need about a week."

We argued all the way back home about how we should have our baby. I was convinced we should simply go ahead with the cesarean section and not take any chances. Paul was equally convinced that God would help us have the baby naturally, even if it took a miracle to do so. No matter how long we talked, we could not come to an agreement on it.

Agreeing did not mean that one of us should simply acquiesce to the opinion of the other. To us, it was a spiritual matter. We believed what Jesus had said in the Bible, "If two of you agree on earth about anything that they may ask, it shall be done for them by My Father who is in heaven" (Matt. 18:19, NASB).

When we arrived at home, we called a good friend of ours, Duane Sheriff, whose spiritual sense we trusted. All three of us got on the phone together to discuss the situation. God really gave Duane wisdom in talking to Paul and me. Duane asked me, "Susie, what can you believe God for?"

I said, "I can believe God for the time it takes to get those test results back. I can believe for that."

"All right," Duane said. "Can you go along with that, Paul?"

Paul replied, "Yeah, I can go along with that, but I believe this baby is coming naturally."

"That's fine," Duane answered, "but you two have to be in agreement." This was the first time Paul and I ever really understood the importance of being in spiritual agreement as husband and wife as we approached the Lord with our prayers. We knew that Jesus had said, "If you ask Me anything in My name, I will do it" (John 14:14, NASB). And we believed that, but we had neglected the matter of agreeing in prayer together. Maybe it never had occurred to us because we were so used to disagreeing with each other in so many other areas of our lives. Yet Jesus had told His disciples, "If two of you agree on earth about anything that they may ask, it shall be done for them by My Father who is in heaven" (Matt. 18:19, NASB). Duane emphasized that this needed to be our mind-set and heart attitude if we were going to expect God to intervene in our situation. So Paul and I agreed together in prayer and asked God for an extra seven days.

The first test was done the next day, and it came back negative. A few days later we did the second one, and then we waited. Every minute seemed to take an eternity to pass. Finally, the second test came back negative as well. It was safe for us to have a natural delivery, which was a good thing because our baby was due any hour now.

On July 8, exactly seven days from the time we took the tests, Lucchese Joy Luchsinger was born—naturally.

God had taken care of us once again, making a way where it seemed there was no way. God was teaching Paul and me that we needed to be united in our hearts, not simply in words. He wanted us to believe Him together, to trust Him, as well as work together for Him.

Lucchese was such a blessing to our lives. She was a healthy, happy, blue-eyed baby, a true answer to prayer. She had very little hair for more than a year; then, suddenly, little, curly ringlets began popping out all over her head. Blond ringlets.

Everyone who saw her asked, "Where does she get that beautiful, curly, blond hair?"

At first I was reluctant to say what I truly believed. I'd answer, "Oh, you know, everybody in my family has curly hair."

Then the Holy Spirit reminded me, asking me, "What did you pray for?" I recalled my prayer, when I asked God specifically for a healthy, blue-eyed, blond, curly-haired baby girl with a good disposition. I realized I had not been telling the whole truth when folks asked me about Lucchese. Furthermore, I had not been giving God the glory He deserved. The next time someone asked, "Where does she get all that curly, blond hair?" I told them, "Lucchese is a special answer to a special prayer—and she has a sweet disposition, too!"

I thank God for Paul's perseverance. Had it been left to me, I might have simply gone along with the doctor's opinion. I would have given birth to our baby, but I would have missed a miracle. Paul's perseverance, however, had a negative side as well. Eight days after Lucchese's birth, we were back on the road again, on our way to another rodeo, the Cheyenne Frontier Days, another ministry opportunity, and more domestic violence.

Chapter 20 ♪   # HELP AT LAST!

*I*n recent years, many people have asked Paul and me, "How long after you became Christians did the domestic violence in your relationship stop?"

It didn't.

Some people are uncomfortable with the fact that the abuse continued in our relationship even after Paul and I became Christians. They would much prefer a nice, simple solution, a spiritual utopia in which a person trusts Jesus and lives happily ever after. I know that there are times when God miraculously and instantaneously changes someone. Other times, He changes the circumstances that someone is facing, and the problem is solved.

But things didn't work out quite so neatly for Paul and me. We loved the Lord, and we loved each other, but the abuse continued to occur, popping up unexpectedly like a jack-in-the-box. The music played pleasantly and then, suddenly, surprise! After we recovered, we tamped everything back down into the box, and the music played sweetly again for a time. But before long the inevitable explosion occurred. We lived each day thinking the violence was in the past, yet fully conscious that at any moment, it might happen again.

Maybe that's why I wasn't surprised when Paul blew up again in Albuquerque in late 1986. Two things about the abuse in Albuquerque, however, distinguished it from all the previous situations. One, for the first time Paul's beating me caused marks on my body in visible places. And two other people saw the results of his rage.

As usual, we were in our hotel room after the rodeo when the argument broke out. The chronic diarrhea that had plagued Paul since his senior year in high school was giving him trouble again. He was getting sicker and sicker all the time. He could hardly keep food in him for more than thirty minutes. He would eat his meal and then, a short time later, have to race to the bathroom. When we were traveling, Paul would have to stop for a restroom break every thirty to forty-five minutes.

Besides the physical problems, Paul was having trouble dealing with our financial pressures and the stress of mixing rodeo and ministry. We were both constantly tired, and it was getting harder and harder to keep up with everything. Paul had been struggling to make the National Rodeo finals again, and time was not on his side. He could not afford to have a bad day at the rodeo. Unfortunately, he did not do as well as he had hoped in Albuquerque, so it didn't take much to light the fuse of his anger. In addition, Paul and I had continued to have disputes over the kids, and my loyalty to them, which often seemed to Paul like I was making excuses for them.

This time, with E. P. and baby Lucchese in the room, Paul slapped me full in the face with the open palm of his hand. He hit me so hard, I literally flew across the room and landed on the floor. Usually, when Paul got angry I tried to protect myself, but I knew better than to lash back at him. I rarely even tried to confront him during his fits of anger. But this time, for some reason, I came back at him, calling him a few names I thought I had forgotten how to say.

I lunged at Paul and scratched him across the face. That infuriated him all the more. He literally picked me up and threw me out of the way. Then he continued by kicking me again and again as I tried to squirm away from his blows. He beat me until I stopped moving on the floor.

The next day I awoke with a huge "goose egg" where my eye should have been. My face was black and blue around my eye where Paul had slapped me. Fortunately, he had hit me with his palm open. Had he closed his fist, he might have knocked my eye out.

As usual, Paul was apologetic about his words and actions, but oddly, we did nothing to resolve the problem. Like many couples involved in domestic violence, we had grown accustomed to Paul's outbursts of anger. It seemed almost "normal" for us to have to deal with the aftermath of another one of his tantrums.

This time, Paul was going on to the Pendelton rodeo, and from there to Omaha and Abilene. In the meantime, I would travel to Deming, New Mexico, to visit with Paul's parents. The grandparents had not yet seen their new granddaughter Lucchese, so Paul had arranged for the kids and me to stay with them after Albuquerque while he went on to the other rodeos. He planned to join us at the end of his trip, But when I saw myself in the mirror, I wasn't sure if I wanted to leave the hotel room, let alone see Paul's parents. But Paul left early the next day, so I had to drive on to Deming.

Paul's parents welcomed the children and me warmly. They were delighted to meet their new grandbaby as well as to see E. P., whom they had not seen in quite a while. Both Paul's mom and his dad noticed my black eye, but neither of them said a word. They didn't even ask me what had happened. Maybe, because they had experienced domestic violence in their own relationship, they did not think it unusual that I'd show up with my face black and blue. Or maybe they simply thought that I had fallen at the rodeo or at home. Whatever they thought, they kept it to themselves, and I was too afraid and embarrassed to tell them anything.

My eye was still blackened when a few days later Paul and I returned home to Chockie. My sister Alice saw my eye, and exclaimed, "What in the world happened to you?" I told her that Paul and I had gotten in a fight. Alice immediately flew into her "big sister" role and started making plans for me to leave Paul. "Okay, Susie, let's go get the kids and get you out of there. There are lots of places you and the kids can go where he'll never find you."

"No, Alice. I'll handle it," I said softly.

"You really look like you are handling it!" Alice retorted hotly, as she reached toward my face as though she were going to touch the swollen skin where Paul had hit me. Instinctively, I jerked my head away. I knew Alice was furious at Paul just then, and not at me, so I let her remark pass by.

"Alice, I said I will handle it," I spoke more firmly and deliberately.

Reba and Charlie never caught on that the abuse was happening. Nor did Pake or my parents. My family members may have assumed that Paul and I were fighting occasionally, but they would never have imagined the reality of what was going on behind closed doors. None of our parents were "snoopy"—they lived by the policy, "Don't get into their business. Let them work it out on their own."

Why didn't I say anything about the abuse to my family members or to anyone else? I'm not completely sure. Part of the reason may have to do with my personality and me being the youngest in my family. I still carried insecurities with me from my childhood, when my lisp and my stuttering kept me from being able to express myself very well. I could still hear the teasing of my family members when I tried to speak up for myself as a little girl. They'd say, "Ch-ch-ch-ch," not realizing that their seemingly harmless teasing was searing straight into my heart. To me, it was as though they were saying, "You don't have anything to say, and you can't say it anyway."

A more subtle but just as real reason why I didn't say anything had to do with a misguided sense of pride. I was afraid of our marriage not appearing "successful," as I was sure it wouldn't if anyone found out about the abuse. Beyond that, I didn't think my family would forgive Paul for what he had done to me, as I had forgiven him.

So, even as an adult, though I longed to cry out for help, I was afraid to say anything about it. I closed my mouth and didn't even try to tell anyone what was going on in our home. I simply tried to appease Paul in any way possible.

Paul admits today that in 1986, he increasingly felt that his violence in our marriage was a permissible vent for his anger. He says:

> Violent outbursts were becoming a pattern in my life because I got away with it. I had discovered that I could control Susie by my anger. Being a high-control person, I wanted that control. I would have

done anything to get it, or keep it once I had it. Now I can see that my desire to control Susie was sinful, that I was not allowing her to be the unique person that God made her to be. But back then, any-time Susie did something I didn't like, I would get angry. If she didn't keep the books the way I liked, or if she didn't discipline the kids the way I liked, if she didn't talk the way I liked, or if she did anything at all, and it wasn't the way I liked it, I was liable to fly off the handle. At best, I would simply get belligerent about it, but many times I became more violent.

If other people knew about my abusive tendencies, nobody was saying anything. Our family members didn't say anything. Other guys on the rodeo circuit didn't say anything. Nor did anyone in our church say a word. Nobody ever confronted me about the abuse—until my friend Jim Bode Scott stood up to me.

Jim Bode Scott had led Paul to the Lord back in 1978. He and Paul remained friends, and Jim Bode's wife, Marcie, and I became friends as well. When our travels took us anywhere close to Billings, Montana, we made a special effort to spend a night or two (and often a week or two!) with Jim Bode and Marcie. They are some of our dearest friends in the world; yet they did not have a clue about what was going on in our home.

By 1987, Paul's debilitating condition had been definitely diagnosed as ulcerative colitis. This, the doctors discovered, was the culprit behind all those years of diarrhea and headaches Paul had suffered. He underwent an operation on his intestines and had to spend four weeks flat on his back while he recuperated. His condition improved, but the colitis was not alle-viated. In November, we decided to visit Jim Bode and Marcie at their place in Montana.

Paul's moodiness and frustration over his operation improved dramati-cally when we got around our friends. Jim Bode and Marcie had a guest bed-room in their basement, so we had private living space when we wanted it.

Things were going along well—Paul was laughing and enjoying shar-ing stories with Jim Bode and Marcie—and I started to loosen up and let down my defenses a bit. I laughed more readily and talked more freely, feeling comfortable and safe with our good friends.

Then one night, we were upstairs after supper when tension flared between Paul and me over the discipline of our children. I took more liberty in voicing my opinion (as I usually did when in mixed company), and Paul motioned me to go down to the basement for a "talk." When I got to the bedroom, I realized Paul was angrier than I expected.

"Why do you always make excuses for the kids?" he asked.

I came back quickly with what was on my heart. "Well, why do you always have to be the strong arm, demanding they be so perfect at other people's houses?" The look on Paul's face instantly told me that I had gone too far—I shouldn't have an opinion at all.

Paul grabbed the neck of my shirt and shoved me up against the wall.

"You listen to me," he said through clenched teeth. His breath was hot and heavy, and his eyes darted frantically back and forth. "I'm the authority here. Don't you ever go against that authority in front of the kids. Do you hear me?"

By that point, I was willing to do anything Paul asked. I pleaded with him, "Okay, okay; just please let me go." Probably because Paul knew our friends were upstairs, he released me with no further outbursts.

But I was scared. I knew I needed to do something, but what? Jim Bode and Marcie were some of our dearest friends, but would they understand if I told them what was going on between Paul and me? Would they still want to be our friends? Or would they reject us and want to keep their distance from us? Maybe I should just keep quiet as I always did. No, I would talk to Marcie.

It must have been the Holy Spirit who gave me the strength to go up to Marcie's bedroom and confess the turmoil that was going on in our marriage. Marcie listened compassionately as I described some of our problems, but when I told her about Paul's violent temper outbursts, including the incident that had just happened downstairs, she became animated. "I'm going to talk to Jim Bode about this," Marcie said. "Something's got to be done!"

Marcie told Jim Bode the whole story, and Jim Bode immediately went down to the basement, shut the door, and had a heart-to-heart talk with my husband. Paul later told me the contents of that conversation. "Paul," Jim Bode said, as he stuck his index finger in Paul's chest, "that's not the way to treat a woman, and it's sure not how God intended marriage to be. There's more to life than living in turmoil with the woman you love."

Conviction came upon Paul, and his shoulders slumped as he realized he had been found out. He knew that he had handled the present situation with me completely wrong; but more importantly, he realized that Jim Bode was right, that he was not treating me the way God intended a husband to care for his wife.

Jim Bode wrapped Paul in his big arms and said, " Now, brother, we're going to walk through this together, every step of the way."

This was the first time I had ever said anything specifically about the domestic violence in our relationship. It was also the first time anyone other than my sister Alice knew for sure that something serious was going on, and it was definitely the first time Paul was confronted by anyone concerning his behavior.

That was a turning point in our marriage. Hope was renewed.

No, the abuse did not stop overnight. Nor did we instantly turn into the ideal Christian couple. But for the first time, somebody whom Paul respected knew about what was happening in our home. Paul opened up to Jim Bode and told him the whole sordid story. I did the same with Marcie. For the first time, our lives were laid bare.

Rather than reject us, Jim Bode and Marcie did the opposite. They opened their hearts to us and said, "We are here for you." Jim Bode kept his promise to walk with Paul every step of the way. He and Marcie have been faithful to Paul and me through the years by calling to check on us and keeping us both (not just Paul) accountable for our actions.

At the time they found out about our troubles, Jim Bode and Marcie were working on their own relationship, not because it was bad but because they knew they had something good and wanted to make it better. In the process, they had heard about a week-long marriage counseling program, and they had scheduled themselves to attend. They recommended the counseling program to us. Beyond that, they arranged for Paul and me to take their place to attend the program during the time they had scheduled for themselves.

Most important of all for me, until Jim Bode and Marcie started talking to us and getting into Paul's face and saying, "Hey, Bud, this is not the way it is supposed to be," I felt that I was somehow causing Paul to be angry. I always felt sorry for him and believed that I was the problem, not Paul. Now, for the first time, I understood that although I may have contributed to the problem by some things I said or did, it was Paul's responsibility to control his anger, and it was not my fault when he did not. That may seem obvious to many people, but to me, it was a revelation.

A few weeks after our visit with Jim Bode and Marcie, Paul and I attended the week-long Christian counseling program at Elijah House, a ministry directed by Paula and John Sanford in Coeur d' Alene, Idaho. During our time there, we learned some basic communication skills and some important ways to diffuse Paul's anger. The sessions taught us to use terms such as "I feel" and "that makes me think" and others, focusing the statement on our own personal feelings rather than verbally lashing out at each other. For example, we practiced statements such as, "I feel that you are treating everyone else kinder than you are treating me" rather than "You treat me like a pile of cow manure."

The week we spent there was not a cure-all, but it was the beginning of a process through which God would bring health and healing to our marriage. The program taught us how to forgive each other in our hearts, not simply with our words. It taught us how to better express our emotions in more open communication. It also taught us the importance of bestowing spiritual blessings upon our children. This was especially important to Paul and me because we were aware that E. P. and Lucchese, even at their young ages, had definitely been negatively affected by the abuse in our home.

The counselors at Elijah House presented a balanced approach to dealing with our problems, intermingling doses of spiritual truths and psychological principles. They did not try to "wow" us with a battery of psychological tests and then spend the entire time telling us what the little black marks on paper meant. Instead, they talked a lot about what the black and blue marks on my face meant.

They gave us a long list of words to use when trying to express certain emotions. And they emphasized our need to learn the difference between emotion and basic facts. Consequently, Paul was able to express to me how he was feeling about a certain set of facts. He could say, "That made me mad when you said that."

About that same time, Paul discovered a tape series, *Communication, Sex, and Money,* by acclaimed speaker and author Edwin Louis Cole. The series provided some simple keys for improving communication between a husband and wife, and between a parent and child. In addition, Cole dealt with biblical concepts of sexuality, including subjects such as "What is the purpose for sex?" and "Why did God give us the sexual relationship?" Paul says, "For most of my life, I thought that sex was something dirty, a way to use a woman for my own gratification. But Ed Cole's message helped me to understand the beauty of sex and the blessing God intended it to be within marriage." Cole also explored a man's attitude toward money, another sensitive area to Paul, since we seemed to be constantly struggling to make ends meet, which caused tension in our relationship.

That same year, Paul and I learned a lot from *Nova Shalom,* which eventually became known as "Marriage Ministries International." Through this group, Paul and I took a thirteen-week marriage class, discussing a man's and woman's distinct roles in marriage from a biblical perspective. We enjoyed the class so much that we became instructors and taught the class in our home church for the next two years!

We learned that most women communicate differently than most men. Prior to this, when Paul said something to me, I heard what he was saying, but I didn't always catch the full meaning of what he was trying to get across. Similarly, sometimes he heard me saying one thing when I meant something totally opposite. We learned to clarify our statements to each other, especially those that were potential powder kegs. We discovered the helpful communication practice of repeating what the other person had said, and then asking, "Well, you are saying such and such? Is that what you mean?" And the other person was free to say, "No, that is not what I am saying at all. This is what I mean." We forced ourselves to express ourselves in words, rather than rely on body language as we had done often in the past, which led us to misunderstand each other. We found that many potential arguments could be prevented if we took a little more time and effort to make sure the other person truly heard and understood what was being said.

The communication principles were so simple even a child could understand, yet in our hectic, pressure-packed lifestyle, neither Paul nor I had been doing a very good job of expressing what we really meant to say to each other. Even more fundamentally, we learned some principles that would help us begin to build our relationship on a much firmer foundation. We studied the biblical basis of love and learned how to say "I love you" in ways that are most meaningful to the other person.

Our relationship improved immensely, but we still had occasional flare-ups. One day, Paul was in a bad mood, and it looked as though his temper might get the best of him. I waited until he was in the shower, then I took the phone outside and called Jim Bode. I said, "Jim Bode, you need to call Paul in about ten minutes; it's bad."

"Okay, Susie, I will," he promised. "I'll call right away."

Within a few minutes after Paul was out of the shower, Jim Bode was on the line with him and was helping him diffuse his anger. Jim Bode acted as though he didn't have any idea what was going on. He simply called Paul and said something such as, "Hey, how are things at home?" With a little nudge from Jim Bode, Paul opened up and began to talk about what was bugging him.

We repeated that scenario frequently that year. Just as it seemed Paul might explode, I'd have Jim Bode call and try to diffuse his anger. I felt a little safer knowing that in Jim Bode I finally had someone who would stand up to Paul and confront him. Sometimes Paul's anger had something to do with me; many times it did not. Regardless of the cause of Paul's anger, Jim Bode could almost always calm him down—almost always.

Later, Paul chided me for acting as the Holy Spirit by prompting Jim Bode to call, but honestly, there were times when God beat me to the phone and had Jim Bode call without me even asking!

Although the incidents and the intensity of the abuse slowed down after Jim Bode started confronting Paul, occasionally things happened so quickly there was no time to call Jim Bode or anyone else for help. Often such incidents happened right before major concerts. We fought about all sorts of things—what Paul thought I should share from the platform; nursing the baby close to the time I was to go on; getting ready on time; the sound system not being set right; or our records, tapes, and other ministry materials not being set up correctly. Most of the time we had travelled all day and we were just worn out. Sometimes even the smallest detail having to do with some aspect of our ministry would set us off. Then we'd have to patch things up and go speak and sing about Jesus as though everything in our lives was wonderful. In spite of ourselves, God still used us to touch the lives of many people.

We knew that if our marriage was to survive, much less our ministry, we needed to make some changes. Our faith was real, but both Paul and I were off track in some ways. Paul complained that I was practicing my Christianity much like "the world," by going to church on Sunday, while running my own life the rest of the week. I had a Bible, but I didn't read it a lot. Paul was much more radical in his faith than I was, but he was also very critical of me, constantly emphasizing, "You have to know the Word" and "You have to read your Bible and memorize verses." Paul felt he was a lot better and a more mature Christian than I was.

On the other hand, I felt that Paul didn't have a close, loving relationship with God. All he had was a bunch of rules and regulations. If he or I violated one, we were going to be in trouble with God and each other. I felt that all Paul had was a pile of life-stifling doctrine. Besides, if he was such a great Christian, what was he doing banging me around so much?

What bothered me even more than the physical abuse was Paul's lack of compassion toward me. For instance, in June 1988, on our way to Calgary, Canada, we scheduled a concert on Sunday evening in Birney, Montana.

The day after our concert, we were scheduled to go inner tubing down the Tongue River, just to have fun and relax.

I suspected that I was in the early weeks of being pregnant, but I kept cramping as if I was about to start my menstrual period. Before we got going that morning, I told Paul, "I don't know if I should go today. I'm feeling pretty poorly."

He encouraged me, "Oh, come on, the trip will relax you and do you good."

I admitted I didn't want to miss the trip, and out the door I went with sunscreen in hand.

The river was really lazy that day, so we had a nice, slow float downstream. Everyone was on their own inner tube except Lucchese and E. P., who were sharing a small craft. As planned, it was a very relaxing day. So relaxing, in fact, that I felt completely better—as if I'd been healed! We said good-bye to our hosts, Peavey and Jennifer Bonham, and headed west toward Billings to visit Jim Bode and Marcie.

On the way there, however, the cramps came back full force. I thought, *Here we go,* and lay down on the back bed of our motor home all the way to Jim Bode and Marcie's home.

We were so glad to see the Scott family. Jim Bode and Marcie have shared so much of our lives. Little did I know they were about to share one of the worst times of our marriage.

The pain in my abdomen continued getting worse. After a day's visit with Jim Bode and Marcie and their children, Paul suggested that we all travel to Red Lodge, Montana, a distance of about fifty miles from the Scott's home. It was going to be great fun, all together in our motor home. We planned to stay the night, take in the town the next day, and then return to the Scott's home.

Off we went to Red Lodge, and we had a great time together. The Scott kids are close to the same age as ours, and they especially enjoyed "camping out" in the motor home. Everyone was enjoying our little escape, and I didn't want to dampen the enthusiasm by dwelling on the pain in my abdomen, but it continued to irritate me. I tried to shake it off and pretend that I was fine. To help get my mind off the pain, Marcie and I went shopping in downtown Red Lodge. When we returned, however, the pain and bloating were worse. I couldn't wear my own clothes and only felt comfortable in very loose clothes that I borrowed from Marcie.

When I talked to Paul about my condition, he tended to ignore it, as if it would just go away. He said, "We believe in God's healing. You'll be all right."

Finally, I took action on my own by taking a pregnancy test. It was positive. By Sunday, I told Paul, "I'm bleeding, and I think I need to go to the doctor. Something's not right."

I received no acknowledgement from Paul. He acted as though he had not even heard what I had said.

I had been keeping in contact with my doctor at home, and he had cautioned me, "If your shoulder starts hurting, you better get checked." It sounded strange, but he said if my shoulder started hurting, it was an indication that there was trouble in my abdomen. That night, as we were playing Pictionary, the pain in my left shoulder was more than I could bear. The next day, the pain had subsided, but the bloating was getting worse. I asked Paul again, "Don't you think we should go check this out?" Again, no answer.

Marcie knew most of the gynecologists available at the hospital, so she phoned to see who was on call. She wanted to make sure I would have a good doctor if Paul chose to take me to the emergency room. Of course, our backup plan was to go ourselves, but we wanted Paul to make the decision. That secured, I made the next move.

Jim Bode was practicing his calf-roping in the arena, and Paul was with him untying the calves. I marched up to Paul as he leaned against the fence and told him, "Marcie phoned the emergency room, and there's a good doctor on call. They suggested I come in right away."

Paul gave me the answer I had expected all along. "The emergency room! Why, that will cost a fortune!" I had figured that the root reason for Paul's reluctance to go to the doctor was money and now, there it was. He had said it.

And I had had enough. "You'd take your horse to the vet before you'd take me to the doctor!" I yelled. With that, I turned on my heel, marched to the motor home, and vowed to teach Paul a lesson by bleeding to death!

Meanwhile, Jim Bode rode over to Paul and, without missing a swing on his rope, asked, "What do you think Jesus is more concerned with right now, how much faith your wife has to be healed, or your compassion for your wife?"

Enough said. It only took a few seconds before Paul followed my footsteps into the motor home and said, "Get dressed, we're going to the doctor."

At the hospital, the doctor performed numerous examinations and tests. He determined I was indeed pregnant, but the baby was not in the womb. He told me he would do a laparoscopy (a scope with a tiny light on the end) through my navel to see if he could fix whatever was wrong without making a larger incision. Once the anesthetic took effect, I was completely unaware of the next four hours.

I later learned that inside my abdomen, the doctor found where my right fallopian tube had been "blown out" by the pressure of the embryo being lodged there shortly after fertilization. The pain I had been feeling was this tiny life growing within the confines of a space no larger than a pencil lead! The doctor, bless his heart, was able to repair the tube, drain over a pint of blood off my abdomen, and sew me up. I lost the baby, but had the pregnancy continued, it might have resulted in my death as well as the child's. I awakened to a husband by my side who had once again learned a lesson about human compassion and God's amazing grace.

I asked the Lord, "How many more lessons will it take?"

That's why to have the support of Jim Bode and Marcie was a lifesaver. I have often wondered since, had they not intervened in our lives would both Paul and I still be alive? Today, we laugh when we tell the old story of the married couple who on their fiftieth anniversary were asked if they ever considered divorce.

"Divorce, never!" one of them answered. "Murder? Many times."

Back then, for us the punchline was not a joke.

Chapter 21

WHY WE DIDN'T
GET DIVORCED

*I*n 1996, an interviewer asked Paul and me, "When you two were going through the worst periods of your marriage problems, why didn't you say, 'Look, let's put an end to this facade of a marriage. Let's just get away from each other, walk away, go get a divorce, and forget it.' " The interviewer pressed, "It would have been easy for you to say to one another, 'We don't belong together; you are not meeting my needs, I am not meeting yours; you are interfering with my career, and I am interfering with yours; we are thwarting each other's self-expression, so let's call it quits and go pursue our own goals.' Yet you chose not to do that. Why did you not get divorced?"

The answer has to do with both practical and relationship issues. Practically speaking, our family was already experiencing extreme stress in 1987. Daddy hadn't been feeling well, so his doctor sent him to St. John's Hospital in Tulsa for tests. The tests revealed that Daddy had blockages in three arteries near his heart and needed triple bypass surgery immediately. Daddy came through his surgery with flying colors, but the seriousness of his operation caused everything else to pale in significance—including Paul's and my troubles.

About that same time, Reba and Charlie were having

troubles of their own. Their marriage had been floundering for several years. I knew how strong-willed Charlie could be because I had worked with him in Reba's office after I came off the road. Charlie wanted to control everything about Reba's career, but especially he wanted to control Reba. My sister just wasn't wired that way. I knew she had loved Charlie when she married him, but by her own admission, by the middle of 1987 she and Charlie were having trouble carrying on a civil conversation.

Nevertheless, I was shocked when one day I received a telephone call from Reba while Paul and I were at a Cowboy Campmeeting out in the middle of west Texas with Willard and Donna Moody. I knew Reba would not have gone to the trouble to track me down unless something pretty serious was happening. As soon as I was done singing, I hurried to a telephone and called Reba back. I could tell the moment I heard her speak that something was dreadfully wrong. "Susie," she said quietly, the pain evident in her voice, "I've left Charlie."

I was flabbergasted. I said, "Reba!" I was still in my "ministry mode," and without even thinking about it, I immediately took it upon myself to save Reba and Charlie's marriage. I spoke adamantly with my older sister. "Reba, you don't want to divorce Charlie; you shouldn't divorce Charlie; you don't have any right to divorce Charlie."

I should have known better than to try to talk Reba out of her decision. When Reba makes up her mind on something, it's a done deal. She may deliberate about a matter for a long time, but once she has arrived at what she intends to do, it would take somebody a lot more persuasive than I am to be able to change her plans. Still, I felt obligated to try.

"Reba, you need to stay with Charlie."

"Susie, you don't understand."

"Now, Reba, really. You and Charlie need to go into counseling—"

"No, Susie. There's not going to be any counseling. It's over. And I'm going on with my life."

"Reba, please! Let Paul and me come and talk to you about it, and let's pray together about this decision."

Reba was adamant. "Susie, I have already prayed, and I have made up my mind. This is not a healthy relationship for me to stay in."

I continued trying to talk sense to Reba, hitting her with every spiritual principle and marriage principle I could think of.

Reba listened to my tirade for a few minutes and then said a hasty good-bye. Much later, I realized how badly Reba must have been hurting when she called me. She wasn't looking for answers; she wasn't trying to save her marriage; she had already made up her mind. She just needed me to love her, to tell her that life was not over, that God still loved her and He could heal her broken heart. But I didn't do that. I took my Bible and used it as a sledgehammer to drive my sister lower into the pits. I didn't believe in divorce (and I still don't), but when Reba reached out to me at that moment, I foolishly judged her without even trying to understand. I've always felt sorry about that. By "Bible-thumping" my sister when she needed me the most, I caused a rift between us that has taken a lot of years to repair. Despite my well intended but self-righteous efforts to keep Reba and Charlie together, they divorced in November 1987.

Although Daddy's heart problems and Reba's divorce were factors that tended to take the spotlight off Paul's and my problems for a while, they were not the main reasons why Paul and I did not walk away from our marriage. When thoughts of divorce went through my mind, three factors forced the thoughts away. First, I really, *really* loved Paul. I didn't want to go away from Paul. Plenty of times I thought about killing him; I even planned how I could do it. But I loved the guy, and I believed he loved me, even though at times he had a strange way of showing it. Besides, I knew that if I divorced Paul, it would not be an amicable divorce. We would not part friends and share visiting rights to our children. None of this "Oh, we're divorced, but we're still good friends" stuff for us. Once we entered into divorce proceedings, I knew there would be no holds barred. There would be no surrender; it would be war, with the survival of the fittest. And most likely, there would be no reconciliation.

Besides, the worst part of our relationship was not the physical abuse. The emotional abuse was much worse, in my estimation. That mental torment would not have ended merely because a judge declared our marriage to be dissolved. To me, the emotional baggage that would inevitably come with the divorce would have been much worse than enduring the occasional beating when Paul lost his temper.

Today, I can honestly say that I love Paul more than I did on the day we married. Sure, I still get aggravated and mad at him. But through that hard time, we grew closer together. Our relationship with God and with each other has become much stronger.

The second and more important reason why Paul and I stayed together was that neither of us regarded divorce as an option. We are Christians who believe the Bible to be the final word in our lives. Several places in Scripture, the teaching is clear: Marriage is for life, and it is not God's will that anyone be divorced. In the Old Testament, for example, it says:

" 'I hate divorce,' says the LORD God of Israel, 'and I hate a man's covering himself with violence as well as with his garment,' says the LORD Almighty. So guard yourself in your spirit, and do not break faith" (Mal. 2:16, NIV).

Clearly from this passage, God intends His married children to stay together. Yes, the violence referred to here is abhorrent to God, but so is taking the easy way out by getting a divorce.

Some people may say, "Well, that's the Old Testament. Jesus was not so rigid. Oh? Really? Look at this part of what Jesus taught about divorce and marriage:

"And it was said, 'Whoever divorces his wife, let him give her a certificate of dismissal'; but I say to you that everyone who divorces his wife, except for the cause of unchastity, makes her commit adultery; and whoever marries a divorced woman commits adultery" (Matt. 5:31–32, NASB).

Mark's gospel contains a similar passage quoting Jesus:

And He said to them, "Whoever divorces his wife and marries another woman commits adultery against her; and if she herself divorces her husband and marries another man, she is committing adultery" (Mark 10:11–12, NASB).

Some people have said, "Jesus' law is a law of love rather than rules and regulations." Maybe so, but Jesus didn't loosen the marriage bonds. Notice what He said to some Pharisees who asked Him why Moses allowed divorce in Old Testament times.

He said to them, "Because of your hardness of heart, Moses permitted you to divorce your wives; but from the beginning it has not been this way. And I say to you, whoever divorces his wife, except for immorality, and marries another woman commits adultery" (Matt. 19:8–9, NASB).

Here Jesus was spelling it out so anyone could understand. The only permissible reason for divorce is "immorality," sometimes translated marital infidelity, sex outside the marriage. All other divorce is sin on the same level of seriousness as adultery—which in Old Testament times was punishable by death. Jesus even includes the person who marries a divorced person in this condemnation. I had never heard these verses discussed much in sermons, but when I read the Bible for myself, they jumped off the page at me. Making the message even stronger was the fact that this message was coming straight from the mouth of Jesus.

Granted, not too many people are quoting Jesus on these points nowadays, but as a relatively new believer, I took those words of Jesus seriously. The words of the apostle Paul were equally as straightforward. He wrote:

"To the married I give this command (not I, but the Lord): A wife must not separate from her husband. But if she does, she must remain unmarried or else be reconciled to her husband. And a husband must not divorce his wife" (1 Cor. 7:10–11, NIV).

Did that Scripture tie me there so Paul could beat on me? Absolutely not, but to me the biblical message was clear. I believed that I was meant to stay married to Paul; I did not rule out a temporary separation, which I believed the apostle's instructions allowed, but I never took that step. The reason I did not seek temporary shelter someplace apart from Paul was that he was always so sincerely repentant after an incident of abuse occurred. I could tell that he honestly did not want to act this way, yet when feelings of anger overwhelmed him, he often gave in to them and lost control. I knew, though, that he truly wanted to change.

Why didn't Paul just leave if he was so angry and unhappy? I joke with him now that he wanted to stay and be miserable. Paul puts it this way:

Our agreement was for marriage; divorce was not an option. I recognized, too, that Susie was really trying to be a Christian wife and mother. And, although for the first seven or eight years of our marriage I constantly accused her of being unfaithful to me, that was my problem, not hers. It stemmed from my own insecurities. I knew in my heart that Susie was loyal to me and that she loved me as no other woman ever had or ever would.

Did thoughts of running off or going out and having sex with some other woman ever go through my mind? Yes, they did. But why would I want to trade a lifetime with a woman I loved, and who loved me unconditionally, for five minutes of pleasure with someone I didn't care about and who didn't care about me?

I really didn't know what true unconditional love was when Susie and I married. I thought I knew what love was, but I didn't. As we grew in our relationship, I went from 'Man, I really like this woman!' to 'I love this woman with all my heart' to 'I don't ever want to live without her' to 'After God, she is the most precious thing on earth to me.' That is what happened in our relationship. I truly admire Susie for staying with me. She is the picture of a woman operating in God's amazing grace. And that is why divorce was not even an option to me. I felt that we were going to work it out, one way or another. I didn't know how at first, but thankfully, God met us in our ignorance. He began to use Jim Bode and Marcie Scott and others in our lives to bring me to my senses.

A third important issue held our marriage together when it would have been easier to walk away. Paul and I knew what divorce would do to our kids. They love their dad, and they love me. Neither Paul nor I wanted to subject our children to being forced to give their loyalty to one parent or the other. They would not know where to begin to pick sides, and we would never want them to have to do so. What misery that would be for them! Some marriage counselors say that disgruntled married partners should not stay together simply for the sake of their children. I strongly disagree. If for no other reason, marriage partners should strive to stay together because their children deserve to have their own mom and dad as they are growing up. I pray that those parents who are having difficulty in their marriages would look past their selfish desires and realize they have made choices that will impact their lives and their children's lives forever. We try to stay together for the benefit of others around us, why not for our own children? It's not fair to make the children pay for two adults' mistakes. Certainly, stepparents can do an admirable job of parenting, but a child will always be connected to his or her own biological (and spiritual) parents.

Because of all these factors, we never seriously considered divorcing. Please understand, although Paul and I do not regard divorce as an option, we do not condemn or look down self-righteously on anyone who has gone through a divorce. We understand the hurt, pain, and shame that accompanies the breakup of a marriage relationship. We have seen in the lives of our own family members how devastating divorce can be. Somebody always gets hurt in divorce. We do not ever intend to add one ounce of guilt or pain to those who are already bearing much more than they deserve. We understand when someone says, "I just cannot take anymore!"

At the same time, we would be remiss if we did not say that God's standards have not changed, that His standards concerning marriage are high and they are stringent. That is not to fence us into an intolerable relationship; it is to protect us from the influences that would tear us apart—which sometimes include ourselves. God is in the business of restoring lives. If we walk away from a marriage without putting forth the maximum effort to save it, we might well be giving up too soon. We might miss the miracle that God wants to perform right before our very eyes.

That's what God did in Paul's and my relationship. In doing so, God brought a man into our lives who not only helped prevent a divorce but was instrumental in stopping the violence in our home as well.

Chapter 22

THE MUSIC AND
THE MAN

*T*hroughout the late 1980s and early 1990s, Paul and I were on the road nearly every weekend, speaking and singing about the Lord. When our children turned school age, we enrolled them in Faith Christian School in Atoka, Oklahoma. At first we tried leaving the kids with baby-sitters when we had to be gone, but because of our exten-sive travels, we eventually decided to use the services of a nanny, Kimmie Zucal. Later on, in 1995, I began to home school our children so we could be together as a family. We traveled in a variety of vehicles to get us where we were ministering. We started in a pickup truck and a camper and grew into a forty-foot Holiday Rambler motor home. Then in 1994, we purchased a Silver Eagle tour bus.

We ministered wherever there was an opportunity—at rodeos, state and county fairs, churches, schools, and civic group functions. We especially enjoyed going to some of the more rural locations, places where many "big-name" shows have to pass by because they can no longer afford to play to small crowds. Although each service was different, our normal procedure was for me to sing a variety of songs, then Paul would give his testimony, followed by some more music. At the close of most programs, we invited people to meet Jesus Christ and encouraged believers in the audience to renew their commitments both to the Lord and to their marriage partners. So much of the emphasis in our service was on husband-wife relationships, I sometimes got embarrassed for any single people who showed up to hear us.

Paul continued to rodeo after his operation in 1987, however not nearly as frequently. As Paul was prone to do, he still condemned himself for having the operation in the first place. He felt that if he had done the "right" things such as eating a special diet and reducing stress, his body would have healed itself—with God's help, of course. Paul has always been hard on himself, criticizing and judging himself and others by a standard that is impossible to live up to. Often, as I watched him beating up on his own self-image, I wondered, *Whose expectation is he trying to meet?*

During that time, we ministered at numerous rodeo cowboy fellowships and cowboy camp meetings. The camp meetings were always a tremendous time of fun and faith mixed together. Often, the cowboys gathered and camped out among the mesquite bushes of West Texas. The hosts supplied a cook and their chuck wagons. Most people slept in their motor homes, but a number of folks pitched their tents under the wide open sky. We ate together with the cowboys and their families, had Bible studies, and then held services at night. It was wonderful to be out there in the open range, just worshiping God—although we sometimes had to pray with one eye open for rattlesnakes.

Our ministry with the rodeo cowboys and their wives was timely. The pressures of the rodeo lifestyle put a strain on even the healthiest of marriages, and not surprisingly, many rodeo marriages fall apart. During the services, Paul and I talked openly about our marriage troubles, especially the matter of the verbal, emotional, and physical abuse. We also talked a great deal about some of the things we were learning as a couple, and how to make our marriage better. The cowboy families were glad to hear Paul and me talk about some of the tough times we had come through in our marriage. They seemed encouraged to hear that it was possible for a rodeo marriage to survive, and they were eager to learn any ways they could improve their family relationships.

In the mid-1980s, RCA Records signed my brother Pake to a recording contract. I was thrilled when "Every Night," a song off Pake's album, broke into the Top Ten in country music. Pake had worked long and hard to land a recording deal, and he deserved all the success he could get. Ironically, after scoring a top ten hit, Pake quit the mainstream music industry and returned to ranching and selling insurance. He was content to continue singing locally with his three daughters, Calamity, Chism, and Autumn. Like all of "The Singing McEntires," Pake learned that success in the music industry isn't always what it's cracked up to be.

During this time, God continued to use my music, often in ways I could never have imagined. In the late 1980s, Paul and I met Ken Stemler, who was then serving as the commissioner of the Professional Rodeo Cowboy Association. Ken is the person most responsible for bringing in some of the big-money sponsorships that the sport of rodeo enjoys today.

But God was doing something even more significant in Ken's life. Ken lived in Colorado Springs and was regularly commuting sixty miles to Denver to see a psychoanalyst to help him sort out some personal problems. Ken often listened to my tape, "Susie McEntire Luchsinger" during his commutes, and the Lord began turning his life around. Ken recalls: "I would play Susie's tape to help pass the time, and soon noticed the songs were helping me more than the psychoanalyst!" Ken Stemler gave his life to the Lord and today is working in Christian ministry.

Shortly after Ken became a Christian, he was so excited he wanted to help Paul and me in our ministry. Ken was convinced that the best way he could do that was to help us record another album of music, similar to the one God had used to touch his life so deeply. Ken went with Paul and me to Nashville, where we met with Vic Clay, the producer who helped us find the right songs, hire the studio musicians, and book the best studio possible for our project. The album that resulted was titled "First Things First."

In many ways, the album was a first for me. Most significantly, it was my first album on which I used "real" live musicians backing me up and playing the songs just the way the producer and I wanted them. Prior to this project, I had always recorded my voice to pre-recorded soundtracks.

Yet the album also caused more trouble between Paul and me. Paul thought that I was enamored with (and attracted to) the studio musicians and my producer in particular. Often during the recording process, Paul would become bored and frustrated at the many takes required to get a part just right. After several hours in the recording studio, he'd say, "I'm going to take E. P. back to the motel."

When I didn't return until late at night or the wee hours of the morning, Paul became suspicious. "Why does it take so long to record a song?" he wanted to know. "Weren't you about finished with it when I left?" he interrogated.

"Well, we ordered a pizza and took a break," I'd explain.

"Oh," Paul replied sarcastically. "You had to eat with all your friends."

I knew it was futile to argue any more, or it could easily turn into an all-out fight. At one point in the recording process, Paul was so suspicious that he accused me of having an affair, which was absolutely ludicrous, and Paul knew it.

When it came time for me to record a new album in 1989, we used Vic again. Paul and I were short on money, so Vic said, "Let's just get the album done and see what God's gonna do." He let us ride with the money we owed him, so we could pay for the studio time and the musicians. The recording went well, and we named the album, "God's Still in Control."

And He was!

In 1988, we moved from the "Weaning House" to eight miles west of Atoka. In October I became pregnant again, and on July 17, 1989, our second son, Samuel, was born. He was due on July 9, but I guess he liked his home in my womb a little too much. We finally induced labor on the 17th. The birth was difficult because Samuel's head had turned sideways, but he was born strong and healthy—eight pounds, fifteen and a half ounces—with blue eyes and blond hair. Samuel was the largest of our babies. He was so cuddly, warm, and energetic (and still is!). Samuel's personality was friendly and open right from his birth. To this day, he has a friendliness and openness that I have seen in very few children. But he can be stubborn, too. My mama says he's a typical "Smith"—a little bullheaded at times!

We were back on the road within eleven days of Samuel's birth. It seemed that our schedule had taken on a hectic life of its own. I was enjoying the music and the ministry, but I longed for the day when I could just be a "normal" mom to my kids and wife to my husband.

Not long after that, still wondering how we were going to pay Vic for our new album, I sang at a women's retreat in McAlester, Oklahoma. Jane Hanson, the president of Women's Aglow, an international women's ministry, was the speaker for the retreat. After she heard me sing, she approached me and said, "Our national conference theme is "country," and you'd fit in great. Could you come and sing at San Antonio in November?"

I said, "Sure," and put the date on our schedule.

Three days before we were to leave for San Antonio, Paul and I got into a terrible argument. We knew we needed a mediator, so we went and got our friend Philip Miller. Paul, Philip, and I were in our minivan when Paul's temper began to heat up. We parked a few miles outside Atoka so we could talk without interruption. Philip was sitting in the front passenger seat and I was sitting on the middle seat, behind them. I said a few more things that Paul didn't agree with, and he started seething. Poor Philip was trying to be the mediator between Paul and me, but he was totally unprepared for what happened next.

Suddenly, Paul flung one arm toward Philip and one arm toward me, grabbing us both by the nape of the neck. Philip tried desperately to reason with Paul, but I knew his efforts were futile. There was no reasoning with Paul when he got angry; he was right and everyone else was wrong. Although he did not hit either of us, he had clearly lost control. This was the first time Paul had ever been so unreasonable and violent with me in front of another adult. Philip and Paul had been friends for years, but Philip had never before encountered this side of Paul.

When Paul's rage subsided and we were able to carry on a relatively calm conversation, Paul said abruptly, "We're not going this weekend."

Knowing that I might be risking another outburst from Paul, I objected nonetheless. "We can't just cancel. They're depending on us," I said.

"We can't even get along with each other," Paul replied. "I don't want to stand up in front of a bunch of people and pretend to be these nice Christian people."

For some reason, I felt a strong sense of spiritual boldness. "Paul, we're human—just like everybody else in this world—and we make mistakes just like everyone else. That's why Christ died, isn't it?"

I grinned at Paul, and as he enfolded me in his arms, he said, "Yeah, I keep forgetting that Christ forgives me. The hardest thing for me to do is to forgive myself."

"Well, you just need to go through those steps of seeking His forgiveness and then reminding yourself by faith and believe what God has done for you." With that, Philip breathed a huge sigh of relief, and Paul and I went home and packed up the motor home to head toward San Antonio and the Women's Aglow conference.

At San Antonio, we discovered that eleven thousand women were expected for the conference. I pondered and prayed about which songs I should sing. Many music artists make it a practice to give the audience their latest "single" off their latest album. It just makes good sense to promote the material that is being advertised in stores and magazines and being played on the radio. But I try to choose my songs according to the occasion and in obedience to the promptings of the Holy Spirit. I never want promotion to get in the way of ministry.

That night, rather than doing material from my latest album, I felt I should sing "Jesus Fan" and "Blood Bought Church," both from my third album. I started singing, and the people immediately leaped to their feet and began clapping their hands and praising God. By the time I was through my second song, every one of the eleven thousand people in the hall was standing, shouting, applauding, or praising God in some way. Paul later said that the women in the room were so loud, the sound engineers had the knobs on the sound system turned up to the point where they peaked out, and still the engineers could not hear me singing over the crowd.

To say the least, I was "pumped" when I left the stage that night. When the evening speaker finished, Paul and I went to our product table where we had tapes and T-shirts available. When the women were dismissed, it was like a herd of cattle coming toward a feed truck! They completely engulfed our table, calling out, "I want a tape! I want a tape!"

Paul was so overwhelmed that he finally had to say, "Whoa, whoa, ladies! Now you'll have to slow down for this ole' Oklahoma cowboy!" We had brought a small number of tapes because we had assumed that this was simply a small meeting of women where we might not need as many. Were we ever wrong! The first night of the conference, those ladies scooped up every piece of product we had! And they were calling out for more.

Paul and I called our friend Philip back home. We arranged for Philip to get all the tapes we had in storage and put them on a plane in Dallas to get to us in time for the sessions the next morning. Sure enough, the tapes arrived in San Antonio right before the morning sessions ended. Again, the women thronged our table and grabbed every tape we had. They were still clamoring for more when the last one was gone.

When we left San Antonio the next morning, we had enough to pay for the album with money to spare. Not only that, but as a result of this conference, Women's Aglow extended an invitation for us to go to their conference in Australia in 1990. God truly did have it all under control!

Soon we began having more ministry opportunities outside of rodeo circles. That was especially true after my singing career took off again in 1991. Paul didn't mind the switch. After all, he had risen from a novice rodeo cowboy and had gone all the way to the National Finals Rodeo five times. He had accomplished most of his goals as a rodeo cowboy. If there was any awkwardness for Paul, it came as we made the transition from him being the main breadwinner in our family to me bringing in the majority of our income. That was tough on a self-sufficient cowboy's ego.

I did my first music video, "God's Kept Me," in 1991. Then in 1992, things really took off. With my music now receiving airplay across the nation on both country and gospel radio stations, I was named "Country Gospel Artist of the Year" by Nashville's *Gospel Voice* magazine. The other performers nominated for the award that year were Ricky Skaggs, Glen Campbell, and Paul Overstreet, three men I admired immensely, not simply for their outstanding musical ability but because they maintain a strong testimony for Jesus Christ in their lives and in their music. More and more, I began to consider that maybe God could use that country music after all.

That same year I received the "Female Vocalist of the Year" award from the International Country Gospel Music Association, as well as the "Video of the Year" award for my "So It Goes" video. No doubt all the publicity from these awards brought me to the attention of Integrity Music in Mobile, Alabama. Integrity had begun as an upstart company designed to produce "Praise and Worship" music. In a matter of a few years, the company had soared to the top of the genre, surpassing such well established Christian music companies as Word and Maranatha! Music in their sales of praise and worship music.

In 1992, Integrity was looking to expand their horizons by entering what they felt was a burgeoning new field of Christian music known as "Positive Country" in some circles and straight out "Christian Country" in others. The company had noticed the success of mainstream country artists who, although they rarely sang about Jesus in their music, were espousing Christian ethics and morality and the importance of family relationships. Ed Lindquist, cofounder of Integrity, felt that I would fit in well with their plans, so by 1993, I had recorded my first album with them.

The album was titled "Real Love" and was produced by multiple-Grammy-award-winner Paul Overstreet. Paul was one of the most successful songwriters and artists in his field, having written dozens of hit songs for himself as well as artists such as Randy Travis, who had a mega-hit with Paul's song, "Forever and Ever, Amen." Paul's list of songwriting credits reads like a Who's Who of the country music industry. Even more than his musical ability, Paul combines a down-home, gentle spirit with an irrepressible sense of humor and a passion to produce the best music possible.

"Real Love" was Integrity's first release in the fledgling Christian Country field. Four songs from "Real Love" went all the way to the number one spot on the Positive Country music charts: "I Saw Him in Your Eyes," a song that was my testimony about Grandma Smith; "I Don't Love You Like I Used To," written by Paul Overstreet and my current producer, Billy

Aerts; "For Pete's Sake," written by Mike Curtis and Lenny Le Blanc; and "There Is a Candle," written by Chris Rice. Two of those songs were extremely special to me. "For Pete's Sake" was a touching song about a couple whose marriage was breaking up, but they decided to stay together for their child's sake. "I Don't Love You Like I Used To" was almost an autobiographical lyric about Paul's and my marriage. The "hook" line of the song, however, is followed by the most important message: "I love you more." As I said previously, that's the way I feel about Paul today. I love him more today than I did the day we married.

Ironically, I almost didn't record "I Don't Love You Like I Used To." Paul Overstreet had played it for me early on as we were looking for potential material to record. I loved the song because it was so parallel to Paul and me, but it was more mainstream country and I wasn't sure how my listeners would react. We were nearly done recording when Don Moen, vicepresident of Integrity, asked Paul Overstreet, "What about that song, 'I Don't Love You Like I Used To'? Wouldn't that be great as a duet?"

"A duet? With who?" Paul Overstreet asked.

"Well, you and Susie could sing it," Don replied.

"That might work," Paul said, as he mulled over the idea in his mind.

Paul set about playing the song for the studio musicians, and we cut it that same day. "I Don't Love You Like I Used To" became a signature song for me and gave the country music world the chance to see my husband Paul on the video. I will always be grateful to Paul Overstreet for his willingness to take a chance at the last minute.

In 1993, *Cashbox* magazine, one of the most prestigious magazines in the music industry, named me "Top Female Vocalist" in the Christian Country field. That same year, *Gospel Voice* presented me with their "Performance Excellence" award for my album "No Limit." I was overwhelmed, to say the least. I had never fancied myself as a lead singer; I was a backup singer, remember? Now here I was getting all these awards that I felt I really did not deserve.

Paul and I continued ministering around the country. We didn't change anything about what we were doing, but the publicity from my musical success brought more people to the churches and auditoriums to hear us. Our schedule grew busier and busier, because now, in addition to ministry opportunities, we had an obligation to our record company to help promote my music. We spent hours on the road going from one radio station to another, visiting with DJs and personally introducing ourselves and our music to them. I also did hours and hours of interviews for magazines, newspapers, and books. That's a nice element about country music that is not always found in other musical genres nowadays—the dee-jays and radio personnel still invite and appreciate that personal connection with the artists. I was pleasantly surprised to find that some of the dee-jays remembered me visiting them nearly a decade earlier when I accompanied Reba to radio stations to promote her music.

Along with the success of my music came several endorsement offers. I was cautious about becoming involved in that part of the business. If I put my name on something, I want people to be assured that I believe in that product. I consented to represent three clothing lines: Roper Western Apparel; Spencer's, a children's clothing company; and Crumrine Jewelry. I still enthusiastically represent all these companies.

In 1994, I received the "Entertainer of the Year" award from the International Country Gospel Music Association. I also received the "Female Vocalist" award from the Christian Country Music Association as well as the "Vanguard Award" for being one of the leaders in our industry. *Gospel Voice* magazine, a publication directed toward the Southern Gospel field of music, selected me as their "Christian Country Artist of the Year."

That same year, I was nominated for three Dove Awards by the Gospel Music Association. I was nominated as "New Artist of the Year," an interesting designation since I had been singing Christian music since 1985; I was also nominated in the categories "Country Song of the Year" and "Country Album of the Year." I didn't win any of those awards, but as Paul and I attended the gala awards show, I couldn't help thinking, *This is a long way from Chockie!*

I was awed and humbled by the awards and the kind words of recognition by so many people whom I admired. I tried my best to return all the honor and glory to Jesus because when you get right down to it, He's the only one really worthy of our praise. Besides, I was just doing what I loved to do, singing songs about love and life, and relationships, what I like to call "songs for the soul."

Doors were beginning to open for Paul and me to minister in places and to groups that I had never dreamed would be interested in hearing me. One such group was Professional Athletes Outreach (PAO), a nondenominational, biblically based ministry geared to professional athletes in all the major sports. Each year, the organization sponsors several week-long conferences in which the pros come with their spouses and learn how to better handle the primary relationships in their lives. In February 1993, at the urging of J. Pat Branch, another cowboy minister, Paul and I attended a PAO conference in Costa Mesa, California. We were excited about going, since we were always looking for ways to make our marriage better.

The following February, Paul and I went to PAO again. One of the speakers at the event that week was Ken Hutcherson, a former defensive linebacker for the Dallas Cowboys and the Seattle Seahawks, who now pastors a thriving church in Kirkland, Washington, near Seattle. Ken Hutcherson—"Hutch" to anyone who has known him for more than two minutes—is a huge bear of a man, six-foot, two inches tall, weighing 270 pounds, with a quick smile and a contagious laugh. It is impossible not to listen when Hutch speaks.

Hutch gave his testimony the first night of the conference, and I could see Paul's eyes lighting up as he listened. Paul could relate to many of the things Hutch was saying, but more importantly, it was obvious that Paul had an instant respect for Hutch. Frankly, I had not met many men that Paul really respected. Hutch had a seminar during the conference on the topic "How to Study Your Bible." Paul attended the session and was amazed at Hutch's simple yet profound approach to the Scripture.

At one point during the conference, Paul and I talked to Hutch about our hectic schedule and how we might get a better handle on it. Hutch gave us some helpful, practical suggestions. I could tell Paul admired a man who could cut to the heart of a matter and offer sound, biblical principles for daily life. Hutch, Paul, and I spent a lot of time together that week, and we developed a fast friendship that would change our lives.

When we first met Hutch, he did not know about the abuse that had taken place in our home and was still occurring occasionally. As we got to know each other better, however, he picked up on the fact that Paul was having trouble dealing with his anger. In April 1994, Hutch offered to make himself available to us for counseling, but on one condition.

"If you want to counsel with me," said Hutch in his linebacker's tone, looking Paul straight in the eyes, "you will have to be accountable to me."

"What do you mean?" Paul asked.

"I mean I want to know exactly how you are doing in your relationship with the Lord and with Susie, and I won't take any sugar-coated answers."

Paul nodded in understanding as Hutch continued.

"I mean that if you ever hit that woman again, I will come wherever you are and find you, and let you know how it feels."

Paul's eyes widened. He was surprised to hear this pastor say he was willing to become physically involved in responding to any future abuse.

Over the next few months, Paul and I counseled with Hutch by means of long-distance telephone calls, or meeting at various places around the country as our traveling schedules intersected. Hutch recognized that Paul felt badly after he abused me each time, so he was convinced that Paul needed to be trained to "feel bad" *before* the abuse took place, not just afterward. To do so, Hutch felt two processes were important for Paul. One, he had to know that he was accountable to someone else, that he be given a motivation that would mean more to him than allowing his anger to go uncontrolled. In other words, he had to understand that the consequences of abusing me were not worth the momentary release of stress and anger that he experienced when he let his anger get the best of him. Like all abusers, Paul needed to know that it was going to hurt him if he hurt me.

Second, he needed to learn how to become accountable to himself. Since Paul was the only person who knew when the first angry thought sparked, he was the only one who could put out the fire before it turned into a raging blaze. Right there, Paul needed the inner strength that would help him be willing to change. Certainly, some of that inner strength would be the result of basic spiritual disciplines, such as Bible study, prayer, Scripture memorization, and attendance at church services, but the real strength came from a recognition that Paul at his best could not handle this himself. He was going to need God's assistance to help him choose to change on a daily basis. He was going to need to be controlled by the Holy Spirit moment by moment.

Paul willingly committed himself to the two areas of accountability Hutch required of him. For Paul, it wasn't simply that he was worried that Hutch might whip him in physical terms; but the fact that Hutch was willing to deal with Paul on a physical level helped Paul understand just how serious this situation was. Unquestionably, Paul's not wanting to tangle with Hutch was probably a deterrent at times when, otherwise, Paul might have flown off the handle. But Paul wrestled steers for a living! He was not going to be intimidated by any man, not even one Hutch's size. It was not Hutch's threat that caused Paul to control his anger; it was his caring. It was the fact that Hutch cared enough to get involved to the point of saying, "Here's the line, Paul. Don't you dare cross it, or you will be dealing with me." That is what impressed Paul about Hutch.

Some might criticize Hutch's method of using fear as a motivating factor, saying he was trying to scare Paul into being good. Hutch, however, is quick to say, "Sure, I'm using fear, but it is fear based upon love, understanding, and concern. Just as a child learns that there are consequences for crossing certain lines in life, an abusive spouse needs that same reminder."

Paul agrees. "It wasn't the fear of Hutch that helped me," he says. "It was the fact that Hutch kept bringing things back to my own responsibility. He would not let me get away with saying, 'Well, Susie made me do it' or 'I was stressed out, so I took out my frustration on Susie or the kids.' He kept saying, 'You are the man. You are responsible for your actions. Nothing or nobody apart from you *makes* you do anything. You may have had some bad experiences in your upbringing. Your parents may have made many mistakes in the way they raised you, but the bottom line is that YOU are responsible.'

"Another important principle that Hutch drove home to me was that abuse is nothing but a bad habit. It is *learned* behavior. I hated to admit it, but I knew Hutch was right. I had learned that I could control Susie by using anger. Once I knew that I could get my way by my angry outbursts, it was easier to slip into those destructive patterns. Hutch helped me to see those patterns for what they were—not something I had inherited geneti- cally, not something that because of my environment I was compelled to give in to, not something that could not be conquered, but simply habitu- al behavior patterns that must be broken and replaced with new, positive patterns."

Hutch invited Paul to the Seattle area to attend a men's retreat. Paul went and had a tremendous time of fellowship with the men of the church Hutch pastored. Paul began to toy with the idea, *What would it be like to actually live in a place where I could stay under the care of Hutch and the guys?*

Hutch and his wife, Pat, invited our family to come to Washington to stay with them for a while. We went to visit them for a few days and ended up staying more than a month! During that time we lived in the same house with Hutch and his family. We ate our meals together, played together, worked together, and we studied the Bible together. What the Hutchersons were teaching us, however, was not something that could be gotten out of a book. It was a lifestyle. We could see how their family func- tioned. We could observe them in fun times as well as stressful times.

As the pastor of a growing church as well as a popular speaker on the conference circuit, we knew that Hutch and his family had to deal with many of the same sort of demands as those in our lives. The way they approached everything in life was a lesson for us. In the Bible, Jesus did something similar with His disciples. He not only taught them the Word of God, He modeled it in front of them. That's what the Hutcherson fam- ily did for us. Paul and I and our children, E. P., Lucchese, and Samuel, will be forever grateful to a man and his family who cared enough to put their words into action. I know Hutch helped save our marriage; he may well have saved our lives.

Chapter 23

A SISTER'S
                                     # LOVE

*I*n the aftermath of the O. J. Simpson trial, President Bill Clinton called for a greater focus on the issue of domestic violence. October 1995 was declared National Domestic Violence Awareness Month, and the weekend of October 27–29, USA *Weekend* ran a feature article on the physical and verbal abuse in Paul's and my marriage. When we saw the article, we were sick. Paul and I had given them an in-depth, honest, open interview, relating how abuse had been a part of our marriage, but that God had changed our lives and we were now two new people. Unfortunately, the paper chose to play down that part of our story; they barely mentioned the positive aspects of our relationship and focused almost entirely on negative elements from our past. We felt that USA *Weekend* had exploited us.

The paper estimates that 39.1 million people saw the article that weekend. One of those people was my sister Reba McEntire.

Reba had known that there was friction between Paul and me since the early days of our marriage. She wasn't surprised to learn that we had been having sustained troubles throughout the years. But she was shocked and furious when she learned just how bad the trouble was and how intense the abuse had been.

As soon as the article hit the press, I called Reba. I knew she had seen the newspapers. The papers that carried our story all made sure that Reba's name was used in the headlines. I wanted to speak to her and find out how she was dealing with the fallout from the article. Paul wanted to speak to her, too, and when he did, Reba tore into him. Reba said, "Paul, I don't believe a man should be hitting a woman for any reason whatsoever. I'm mad at you! I can't believe you'd do these things. I don't even believe in hitting an animal, let alone you thumping on my sister!"

Paul told Reba that things had changed, that the abuse was not happening any more, and that he had placed himself in an accountable counseling relationship with Hutch.

Reba was not convinced. "Paul, if you ever touch her again, I'll be there."

"Why didn't you say something like that ten years ago?" Paul asked. Reba later said that she suddenly realized that her words were an idle threat to Paul. Reba and Paul were a thousand miles apart, and besides, he was not going to be afraid of her. Paul told Reba about how he had responded positively when Jim Bode Scott had confronted him in 1985, and then how Hutch had told him that if he ever hit me again, that Hutch would intervene. Reba was still skeptical.

I got on the line with Reba, and she asked first of all, "Susie, are you okay?"

"Yes, I'm fine," I told her. "The phone has been ringing like mad since the article came out, but physically I am okay."

"Susie, if Paul has a problem, let him go fix it, but don't you and the kids stay there."

"We're fine, Reba. Really, we are."

"Susie, if you want to leave, I will help you."

"No, Reba. It's okay. We're handling it." I spoke to my sister sincerely from my heart. "Reba, things have changed. They only printed the bad. Paul and I are madly in love. He's a wonderful husband and daddy. I know what the article said, but it's not like that now. We want people to see how God can change people if they are willing to be changed."

For the next few weeks, everywhere Reba went, in every interview she did, the question of Paul's and my relationship came up. People constantly bombarded Reba with questions such as, "Why didn't you do anything?" Reba's answer was always, "What could I do? How could I have intervened? Why don't you try to intervene?"

In fairness to Reba, she really had no idea what Paul and I were going through. In 1987, after her divorce, Reba had moved to Nashville and was now happily married to Narvel Blackstock, her former tour manager. The two of them built a significant musical empire in Music City. She and I did not see each other frequently, but when we did, I wasn't going to unload a bunch of my problems on her. I never told her about the abuse in my home. She may have guessed, but she could not have been certain. Once Reba had heard Paul yelling at me at the front of the bus when I had been working with her as a background singer, but she thought it was just a normal marital spat. She closed the door to the back of the bus and returned to bed. Another time she and Pake had seen Paul being rough with E. P. at Mama's house. But neither Reba, nor Pake, nor Mama and Daddy ever had a clue that Paul had been beating and kicking me. Alice knew about the black eye I had received in Albuquerque in 1986, but as the older sister, she had absorbed some of my pain and kept it to herself. No one but our children had ever seen Paul strike me.

I told Reba, "The best thing you can do for Paul is to love him. That's all. Please try to love him—for me."

I appreciated Reba's concern for me. I knew she was just trying to protect me. After all, I'm still the little sister in the family, and Alice, Pake, and Reba have always watched out for me. I'm glad they do. More than that, Reba and I were always best friends.

People often ask me, "What was it like being Reba McEntire's sister as the two of you were growing up?" I sometimes return the question, asking jokingly, "Well, what was it like to be your sister or brother as you grew up?"

We never thought anything of it. We didn't grow up thinking that someday Reba was going to be a superstar. Our childhood, as I have described it earlier, was similar to that of most kids in our part of the country.

Growing up, we were the best of friends, yet we were also the best of fighters. "I hate you!" we'd scream at each other. Of course, I'd get after my kids for saying anything like that, and so would Reba. But when we were kids, we were pulling hair, scratching, biting, and kicking. A few minutes later, we had made up and everything was fine again.

Reba and I shared a bedroom with Alice. We had a little nine-by-twelve-foot bedroom, just large enough to hold a dresser with a mirror, a set of bunk beds, and a small closet. As Reba says, "And it wasn't a walk-in closet, I promise you!"

Alice and I slept in the top bunk, and Reba slept in the bottom bunk. Underneath the top bunk, exposed coil springs hung down. The reason I remember those springs is because Reba blew her nose a lot, then she would stick her Kleenex in the holes in those bed springs.

Mama always washed clothes on Saturday, as that was her only day off from her job as secretary and bookkeeper to the superintendent of Kiowa School. Another reason why we didn't wash clothes every day was because Mama had a wringer washer. That old-fashioned machine made washing clothes easier than doing them on a washboard, but not much. We had about three or four rows of clotheslines that Mama always filled to capacity on wash days. Meanwhile, Reba and I were in our bedroom trying to decide what really needed washing. We would be sorting through the clothes, and I remember Reba having all of her clothes piled up on the dresser. She never hung them up; they were always piled on the dresser. (Of course, I've forgotten where mine were!) I walked in the room one time and she was sorting them into smaller piles: "Can wear again," or "Better wash it." I attempted to sit down on the bed, but as I did, I stepped through a pile of Reba's clothes she had taken off the dresser and separated onto the floor. Reba flared at me, "What are you doing, stepping on my clean clothes?"

I said, "Clean clothes? I thought they were dirty! They're on the floor." Reba took offense at that, and I mean we got into it, scratching, slapping, and squalling. Thirty minutes later, we were the best friends, making mud pies outside and playing down at the roping pens.

Reba and I don't get together much these days, but we try to make the annual trek to Mama and Daddy's for Thanksgiving. We are still emotionally close, but now it is a different sort of closeness; it is a closeness of the heart, rather than of physical proximity. I am very proud of what Reba has done with her life and career, but nobody can achieve as much fame, fortune, and popularity as she has and not be changed to some degree.

For the most part, being known as Reba McEntire's sister has been a positive experience for me, both in and out of the music business. Often, in her concerts, Reba tells the audience about me and that I sing Christian music. Reba used to do a medley of hymns in her show, and she always included "The Man in the Middle," a song from my first album.

Many people have shown up at one of my concerts because they first heard about me at Reba's concert. Others see an advertisement in the paper and think, *Well, Reba is sensational. Her sister can't be all bad! Let's go check it out.* Amazingly, some people may not even know that they are searching for God, but they will come to our concerts, or buy my album, and God will do something special in their hearts. Numerous people have given their lives to the Lord because Reba has referred them to my music.

Reba's reputation goes before her, and before me, too. It has opened thousands of doors for me to go into places to sing, where most Christian singers might not be able to go.

Being compared to Reba is sometimes a hassle, I must admit. There's only one Reba, and although we may look and sound somewhat alike, we are taking different approaches to our music. It bothers me sometimes when people refuse to recognize that. One prominent Nashville-based album critic once wrote concerning my music and me, "Reba McEntire, she certainly is not." I suppose such comparisons are inevitable, but they do sting. Once people get to know me, and hear me sing, and hear what I have to sing about, and what I have to say, they don't compare Reba and me anymore.

Reba McEntire is one of the best entertainers in the world, regardless of the style of music. I respect her singing skills, her elaborate staging and costume changes, and her showmanship. Reba's and my goal in singing music is for people to have fun, to laugh and cry and have their emotions touched, but I want to minister to their spirit as well. Both of our prayers are that when our listeners walk out of a church or concert hall, they will be changed, that they will have gotten something, a tool that can change their lives, that they will have new hope.

A woman from Albuquerque once asked me a question that has given me an entirely new perspective on Reba's success and comparisons between what she does and what I do. The woman asked me point blank, "Do you think that God made Reba famous just for Reba?"

I did not know how to respond to that question. I said, "I don't know, I never thought about that."

Apparently, this woman had. She said, "I believe God made Reba famous not only for her, but for you too—to pave the way for you to go and tell people about Jesus." A few weeks later, I was in an entirely different part of the country, when someone else told me the almost identical thing.

One day I was thinking about that idea, and God revealed something similar to me, personally. He said, "You didn't have anything to do with the family that you were born into. Why would you be upset as to where I put you? For I know the plans I have for you."

I was blown away! God had my music, my ministry, my life all planned out, and He knew what was going to happen before I was even born. He also knew the talents and abilities that He had given to Reba. Whether she used them for country music or some other purpose, God put those talents and abilities in her. And then He placed me, not as the first child, or the second, but after the third child, right after Reba. So it all fit when God spoke to my heart and said, "You didn't have any choice of what family you were born into, who your sister was going to be, or what order you were going to be born into the family. I am the one who placed you there. This is my doing."

That message gave me an incredible sense of peace and confidence that God has placed me right where I am supposed to be. It doesn't matter what people say to me, or about me, as long as I know I am doing what the Lord wants me to do.

Chapter 24

DEEP WOUNDS
HEAL SLOWLY

Some time in 1994, I began to do a deep self-evaluation, asking myself some tough questions about what I really wanted out of life. Did I want to be a music superstar? I could honestly answer, "No, I don't." Did I want to have a world-renowned ministry like that of other music artists? No, I didn't. Although I have a passion to share the good news about Jesus with everyone I meet, I have come to understand that I do not have to be on stage to do that. Did I want my name on magazines, books, and albums everywhere? Not really. I had tasted enough of that honeycomb to know that a few of those sweet morsels go a long way. Those things feed the flesh but do nothing positive for a person's spirit. That was not what I truly wanted to be. When I got completely honest with myself, I realized all I ever wanted to be was a good wife to my husband and a good mom to my kids.

Samuel, our then five-year-old, brought that issue into better focus for me when he was thrown from a horse while he, Paul, and E. P. were helping Daddy round up cattle on his ranch. Thin and slight of frame, Samuel landed hard in a creek bed, broke his left thigh bone, and cut his head. My baby had known plenty of bumps and bruises in his life—they go with the territory when you live on a ranch—but I had never heard his little voice wail in such painful cries.

At the hospital the doctors put a pin in Samuel's leg and put him in traction. It was pitiful to sit there for hours on end with our little boy who could barely sit still under ordinary circumstances. Samuel was always doing something, running, jumping, playing, and having a good time. Now, he could not move because of the pain in his little body. Worse yet, the doctors said his recovery might take months.

It other ways, 1994 had been a good year. Paul was being faithful in his accountability to Hutch. In music, I had been voted the top honors in my field by my peers. My songs were at the top of the Christian Country music charts. We were out of debt and living a debt-free lifestyle. So many things were going well for us. But when I looked at Samuel in that hospital bed, nothing else mattered.

I went for a walk, and I talked to God along the way. I had all the usual questions that folks have when an accident occurs or things don't turn out quite the way you had planned. "Why, God? Why Samuel? Why now?"

As I talked to God, I said, "Lord, a lot of people would say that You have left us, or You don't love us, but I am not going to turn my back on You. We're going to walk through this, loving You more and more." I didn't know if I was expressing things in the right way or not, but it didn't seem to matter. It was such a relief to talk to the Lord and tell Him my feelings and know that He still loves me and accepts me.

An amazing transformation took place in my heart during that walk. When I got back to the hospital, Samuel was still just as miserable. Nothing had changed concerning his condition. But suddenly, I not only saw little Samuel in that hospital, but I felt tremendous sensitivity toward the nurses and doctors and other patients in the hospital as well. We are all hurting in some way, I realized, and we all need to know that God is there, that He loves us, and that He cares. I saw that God could use my moments of pain to help someone else survive what they have to deal with.

Samuel's accident also let me know how much people cared for us. We cancelled all of our concert dates and stayed at the hospital with him. During that time, we received all sorts of cards and letters of encouragement. Many people sent toys and other gifts for Samuel. Some people sent money to help us meet the financial need. (We still had no insurance!) It was a special outpouring of love during a time when we really needed it. God again proved His faithfulness to us.

Samuel was back on his feet after a few months, and our family was back on the road. My new album, "Come As You Are," was doing well. The calls were coming in again, along with requests for personal appearances and ministry opportunities. Paul and I had not yet learned how to say no to a chance to speak and sing in a church or concert hall, so we started crisscrossing the country once again.

Besides traveling with me, Paul was still working hard running cattle. He put up a roping arena out of six-foot iron panels so the kids could rope and ride. We had just sold our house and forty acres of land in Atoka and were planning to move back to Chockie soon.

Paul and I wanted to get out of debt once and for all, so we decided to move into Mama and Daddy's original home, which had been vacant for a while. Paul and I were happy to reduce our monthly housing costs, and Mama and Daddy were happy that we would be living in the old homestead to "watch things" for them.

Before we moved, one evening in early April 1995, Paul and the kids were out in the arena roping, when Paul decided that since we were moving and would have to move the steers as well, we needed to deworm and put fly tags in our cattle's ears. In addition, we had one calf that weighed about 450 pounds that needed to be castrated. "Come on," Paul called. "Let's get these calves done before dark."

I felt that Paul was asking for trouble. We were not prepared for this job. Paul's knife was not sharp, and he did not have enough antiseptic medicine for the calf. Nor did he have the right syringes to give the animal the shots, but none of that bothered Paul. He had made up his mind, and now we were going to castrate the calf, no matter what. It was typical of Paul that having put off getting the animals ready earlier, we now had to rush to get everything done on time.

"Hurry up, let's go," he called.

I just rolled my eyes and thought, *Oh, Paul. Why now?*

The only chute that Paul had to work in was not a "squeeze chute," a chute that held the cattle still while being worked on. Ours was just a wide open, roping chute that allowed the cattle to move while he was trying to work on them. He was trying to replace the cattle's ear tags, which were made of heavy plastic. To do so, he had to cut the old tag out of each animal's ear with his dull knife and insert the new tag, then clamp it together on the other side, all while the animal was basically free to move.

Paul was having an awful time. The knife may not have been sharp enough to cut a steer's ear, but it could sure slice up a man's hands. Paul's fingers were becoming more bloody by the moment, and the blood was not from the animals.

Finally, I couldn't take it anymore. I said, "Paul, come on. Give it up. Tomorrow is another day. We'll get this then. Let's worm them up at Daddy's, where we can use the squeeze chute."

As he did so many times, Paul completely ignored me.

"We're running out of daylight," I said.

Paul did not respond.

"Paul, please!" I begged.

"No, no; I want to do it *now*. I can do it." A red flag went up in my mind. I recognized one of Paul's weaknesses shining in his eyes, even in the dim light. Paul was convinced that he could overcome any obstacle by his sheer strength. God had been dealing with Paul about that very attitude, and had been showing him that his own physical strength was insufficient. Regardless of how strong Paul was, he was never going to be strong enough to deal with all the things that God wanted him to do.

Perhaps I should have called that to Paul's attention at that point, but the timing didn't seem right to me. I could tell he was on the verge of exploding, so I kept my mouth shut.

About that time, along came the 450-pound bull calf that needed to be castrated.

"Wait, Paul, please!" I begged him again, but I could see that he was already grabbing the bull calf by the head. "What are you going to do?" I asked, knowing full well what he intended to do.

"We're going to cut this bull," Paul answered matter-of-factly. "Okay, I'll put the rope around his horns, then I'll trip him, and E. P. can hold the feet."

I looked at Paul in disbelief. I knew what he was asking E. P. to do was extremely dangerous. If the bull calf squirmed or got loose while Paul was trying to castrate him, the animal could kick E. P. right in the face. At twelve years of age, E. P. was a good-sized, strong boy, but he was no match for a 450-pound calf.

Paul was still giving instructions. "And Susie, I want you to sit on the calf's neck and hold him down."

Can you imagine what it might be like trying to sit on 450-pound bull calf's neck while he was being castrated? It did not sound like a place I wanted to be sitting.

I rebelled. I looked over at Paul, his hands a bloody mess, and I said, "No."

"What did you say?" Paul bellowed.

"I'm sorry, Paul, but no. I cannot do that." I've always been afraid of horses and cattle anyhow, probably stemming back to my many bad childhood experiences with the animals.

"I just can't do it, Paul."

"Yes, you can!" he roared. "Come on. Get down here!"

"No! And E. P. doesn't need to do that, either. He could get kicked in the face."

Paul dropped his hands to his sides, looked at me with unmasked disdain, and said to E. P., "Turn him loose, E. P."

I could tell that Paul was furious, so I did not stick around there. I started to climb the fence in the direction of our house. "Get your horse to the barn, Samuel," I heard Paul yelling. Meanwhile Paul began letting all the cattle loose, as if to say, "Okay, if you're not going to help, we won't get the job done at all!"

I had just climbed over the fence on my way toward our front porch when suddenly I heard a "whooshhh" sound zinging past my ear. Then I heard a dull thud as a landscaping post slammed into the ground like a spear, landing just to the side of me. I knew Paul could have easily aimed the post at my back as I was going over the fence, but I also knew that he had thrown the post hard enough and close enough to my body to make a strong statement.

I did not look back. Nor did I acknowledge in any way the post thrown in my direction. I continued on toward the house.

The kids later told me that Paul then proceeded to yell at them. "Just go on! Get out of here!" he screamed at E. P. and Lucchese. He pulled them off their horses and kicked them in their rear ends. "Get out of here, I said! Get up to the house," Paul roared. The kids came running into the house, crying, "Mama, Daddy kicked me! Daddy kicked me!"

I went outside to where I was grilling some steaks, and thought, *Oh, no; what's going to happen now?*

I was about to find out.

Paul stomped onto the porch, stepped through the front door, and slammed it hard behind him. He picked up one of our benches and threw it out the back door. He then raised an end table high in the air and smashed it on the floor. Then Paul crushed the remote control for our stereo unit.

Then he came out back to where I was tending the steaks on the charcoal grill. I had raised the lid on the grill, and Paul grabbed the top of it and slammed it down as hard as he could. Glass from the front of the grill top shattered everywhere, on the patio, in the food, and down inside the grill.

Paul was raging out of control, but he never touched me. He never struck me with his hand or with any of the things he smashed, nor did he kick me. Looking back, I can see that it was not so much that Paul was out of control—it was more that he willfully allowed himself to lose control.

When Paul went inside to where the kids were in their rooms, I went around the house and got inside our Ford Explorer. I locked the doors and contemplated what I should do. I had a car phone, and it was the first time in our marriage that I ever considered calling the police. After calming down a bit, I decided against summoning the local authorities. I felt that

God had put godly people in our lives to help us, and for the most part, we had been on the right track. This was no time to call in people who might not understand what we were working through.

After a while I risked walking back into the house. I began trying to salvage what I could of our dinner, putting what was left of the food on the table. Already Paul had begun to clean up the mess he had made. The kids were all in their rooms, trying to avoid their father, but Paul had apparently calmed down and was no threat to them or me.

Soon Paul approached me and said, "Susie, I'm sorry. I did wrong. I apologize." Paul looked over the damage that he had done to our home and began to cry.

"It's all right, Paul. It's just stuff." I wrapped my arms around him. "We're gonna make it."

A little later, our family sat down at the supper table, and as we bowed our heads to pray, Paul said jokingly, "Lord, forgive these kids for acting like heathens." We all laughed, and the kids and I knew we were back on track again, when Paul asked the kids to forgive him.

In August, while we were doing a series of concerts in the northwestern corner of the country, we took a brief break and stayed with Hutch and his family for a few weeks. It was great to see them, and we hated to leave. But all too soon, we were loading up again. We needed to head back to Oklahoma, but we decided that since we were only a few states away, we would sweep through Montana and spend the night with Jim Bode and Marcie Scott on the way home. What could be better? Spending time with Hutch and Pat and then spending time with Jim Bode and Marcie—why, it would be like going on a spiritual retreat. Or so we thought. . . .

We left the Seattle area at about nine o'clock in the morning, drove all day and night, a distance of 860 miles, and arrived at Jim Bode and Marcie's home around 1:30 A.M. We were all extremely tired, but Paul said we needed to leave by 7:00 A.M. in order to get back to Oklahoma in time for our next scheduled date. Paul has always been a stickler for being on time. If he is supposed to be somewhere, he doesn't mind arriving a half hour early, but it irritates him to be even one minute late. Because we needed to leave so early, we all agreed to get up at 5:00 A.M. to be able to spend a little time with Jim Bode and Marcie.

When the clock went off, we reluctantly dragged ourselves from beneath the covers, still weary from yesterday's journey and not too excited about another long day on the road. Jim Bode and Marcie got up about the same time so we could visit a while before we had to leave. Jim Bode wanted to talk to Paul alone—no doubt to see how he was handling his anger—so he and Paul decided to go someplace. "Now be ready to leave when I get back," Paul said as he and Jim Bode were going out the door.

"Okay, we'll be ready," I said as Marcie and I smiled knowingly.

When Paul and Jim Bode returned, the kids and I were ready to leave. Just before the guys came inside the house, however, Marcie suggested that I take some of her special diet soup with me for lunch on the road. I had just started a soup diet, so I was glad to accept Marcie's offer. We were transferring the soup from her large container to a smaller one as the guys came into the kitchen.

"Hey, I said I wanted to leave as soon as I got back," Paul groused when he saw us pouring out the soup.

"Oh, calm down," Marcie chided him. "This will only take a minute. You'll be glad you took the time a few hours from now."

Paul did not respond well to Marcie's rebuke. "No, that's not the point. I said I wanted to leave at 7:00 A.M. And when I say 7:00, I mean 7:00."

I could tell Paul was getting hot. I knew that he was still fatigued from driving all day yesterday, and this was not a good time to mess with him. In our counseling, we had learned to watch for triggers that might set off outbursts of anger; and for us weariness and fatigue were high on the list. I tried to diffuse the rising temperature by saying, "Paul, we just need two minutes to get this soup in the thermos."

Paul turned and railed at me, "I don't care about any soup! I said be ready to leave when I got back, and you're fooling around in the kitchen."

"Oh, Paul, quiet down," Marcie said firmly. "You're the only one around here acting like a fool." Marcie was one of the few women in our circle of friends who was willing to confront Paul.

Paul looked at Marcie as though he were going to say something nasty, and then he caught himself. He turned toward me and said, "Let's go, let's go. Go get everybody together."

But Marcie wasn't finished yet. "Hey, buddy," Marcie challenged him, "you don't need to act like that. Besides, it's not even 7:00 yet."

They argued over the time. Marcie said, "Well, I've got five till, and you said you were leaving at seven."

"Oh, yeah? Well, I've got five minutes after," Paul countered. This was getting dangerous. Marcie wasn't backing down from Paul, and Paul wasn't backing off any, either. Instinctively, I stepped back from the two of them.

Just then, Jim Bode came in and shouted, "Hey, what's going on in here?"

"Oh, he's acting like a fool," Marcie retorted while looking at Paul.

"Well, maybe I am!" Paul shouted. "What's it to you?"

Jim Bode's face turned beet red. He did not like his friend speaking to his wife that way. He turned toward Paul and roared, "You just think you are so tough. You can talk like that to a woman. What about a man?" He threw his glasses off and started across the kitchen toward Paul.

My steer-wrestler husband's reflexes may have slowed a bit over the years, but he still recognized a potential attack when he saw one. In a flash, Paul reared back and punched Jim Bode right in the face. Jim Bode looked like a slapstick cartoon character as he flipped onto his back and landed on the kitchen floor with a loud thud. He could not have been more surprised if he had seen a ghost.

But it didn't take Jim Bode long to recover. He shook off Paul's blow and started to get to his feet. Paul stood over him, ready to pounce like a tiger. Paul later said, "In the old days, before I became a Christian, I would have jumped on Jim Bode while he was down and just started pounding him. But now, I could only stand there in amazement myself. I thought, *Whoa! This isn't right. I have just decked my best friend in the world!*"

Jim Bode did not wait for an apology from Paul. Both he and Paul were former state wrestling champions, so he got up and grabbed Paul in a wrestling hold right there in the kitchen.

There were Paul and Jim Bode, wrestling around on the kitchen floor, slamming into things, knocking over chairs, crashing into the walls. The sounds alone, which were coming from the two men, were chilling. Grunts and groans and gasps combined with Batman-style "Whooms," "Booms," "Splats," and "Ker-pows!" The scene looked and sounded like two gorillas fighting in a cage.

Obviously Paul and Jim Bode were too old and too tired for this sort of altercation, but they continued until neither of them could budge from the floor—yet neither would surrender, either. They stubbornly clung to each other, arms and legs intertwined in wrestling holds, like two spent bears after a fight.

"All right, you guys. That's enough!" Marcie yelled.

Paul and Jim Bode ignored her and squirmed all the more on the floor. Finally, Jim Bode did a cross-face wrestling move on Paul, smacking him right in the eyes. Paul let go of his grip on Jim Bode, and the two warriors staggered to their feet. Already, the flesh around Paul's eyes was puffing up like a goose egg and turning a familiar color of purple and black. Jim Bode's face was streaked with scratches, as though a cat had clawed him.

The two men stood there for a moment, so out of breath they couldn't move, not knowing whether to laugh or cry. Finally, they started laughing and hugged each other. After a good laugh, we all sat down and talked for the next thirty minutes about what had happened. We discussed how this incident could have been avoided. We all agreed that Paul could have assessed the situation and instead of flying off the handle, he could have helped get us down the road. All of us agreed, too, that five minutes really didn't matter. Most of all, we realized that wanting our own way—basic selfishness—was a major cause of the strife between us. Only a friendship such as we have with Jim Bode and Marcie could grow stronger through such an incident.

After a while, Jim Bode said with a laugh, "Go on, get out of here." Jim Bode waved his hand toward the door as he spoke. "You're going to be late."

"And don't forget the soup," Marcie called after us as we headed toward our car.

Ninety-nine percent of the stress in our lives, I am convinced, was caused by our incessant travel schedule. People who do not travel for a living sometimes have difficulty understanding how exacerbating and draining it can be. Multiply that level of stress by five, and you have an idea what our travel schedule was doing to our family. Our regular travel schedule went something like this: Leave home early Friday morning to get to the airport; fly to our first concert location for Friday night. Do the concert, then drive to the next day's concert location. Do that program, then drive to our Sunday morning concert location. After the morning service, we were back on the road again, heading for our evening concert location. Late Sunday night, or early Monday morning, we'd fly back to Dallas and drive the two and a half hours to our home, where we tried our best to be good parents to our kids. Week in and week out, that was our schedule. After a while, I almost dreaded to see another weekend approaching.

In late August, Paul and I were again staying with Hutch and Pat. One day we were on an airplane, returning to Washington from a concert trip to Texas. We were cruising along above the clouds when Paul looked over at me and asked, "Susie, what do you dream about?"

I recognized by the tone of Paul's voice that he was not asking me for a list of nightmares or nocturnal fantasies. I could tell that Paul was serious. He was asking about my hopes and dreams for our future.

For some reason, the very question coming from Paul caused my eyes to well with tears. I thought for a moment and then replied, "I dream about being a housewife, being with my kids, being home—we're here and there and everywhere."

At one time, Paul probably would have reflexively responded, "We can't do that! How will we live? Who's gonna pay the bills?" Not anymore. He was still a tough, pragmatic, rodeo cowboy, but as I looked in his face I saw something that even a few years ago I would not have thought possible. There was compassion and concern in his expression and, yes, tenderness. He truly is a changed man.

Paul looked out the window for a moment, then back at me and spoke softly, "We can change that. We don't have to go as hard as we've gone.

Let me work for a while. Let me do that for you. You can be a mom, because that is what is most important to you." We had tried the broad way and found it to be exciting and busy, but unfulfilling and leading to destruction. We had tried the narrow way, which leads to life; but we had crammed it so full of people, events, concerts, and ministry, it almost seemed too crowded to enjoy. Now, at last, we were taking the tender road home.

Back in the 1970s, the sequel to the heartpounding movie *Jaws* was being heavily advertised. The familiar music theme played as an announcer said something like, "Just when you thought it was safe to go back in the water again. . . ." And then from out of the depths came a great white shark to terrorize the beach community all over again.

I've known that feeling. Just when Paul and I seem to be doing so well, and things in our home are calm and easy, suddenly something happens that poses a potential disaster—and it hasn't always been Paul's fault. As the man of God in our home, Paul has bravely been willing to take responsibility for his failures, and I appreciate that. He has consented to share our story in this book in hopes that other men and women can find hope and the courage to change. But we would be less than honest if we didn't say that, at times, I could be just as cantankerous as Paul.

One night in November 1995, Paul and the kids and I were in our living room at the Chockie house watching a sitcom on television (we only get two channels, so our viewing selection is rather limited). Suddenly, Paul said, "Ain't nothing good on TV anyway."

I disagreed. I started listing shows that I thought were worth watching. "Well, there is a good show on—"

Paul quickly cut me off. He glared at me and said, "Is supper done yet?"

"Yeah, it is," I replied curtly. "That's why I came in here in the first place, to tell you it's ready, and then we got interested in this program."

We all went out to the kitchen, and as I was getting the chicken-rice-and-broccoli casserole out of the oven, Paul said something that really ticked me off, and I lost my cool.

Without thinking, I whirled around from the oven, casserole in hand, and threw the whole pan right at Paul!

He let out a surprised yell as he jumped backward to avoid the hot, flying casserole. As he did, he kicked the pan sending chicken, rice, and broccoli all over our kitchen.

I took one look at the mess and thought, *Uh-oh! I've done it now. He'll be after me next.* As Paul continued angrily kicking the aluminum casserole pan around the kitchen, I quickly went to the front room and said, "Come on, kids. Let's get out of here. Get your coats."

I thought briefly about packing a suitcase, but there was no time. E. P., Lucchese, and Samuel and I bolted out the door and hopped in the car. I went to turn the ignition key—we always left the keys in the car at our Chockie house—but the keys were not there. Nervously, I thought, *How did Paul get out here and take the keys?*

We ran to Paul's pickup truck, looked in, and . . . no keys there, either!

"Get in kids," I commanded, "and lock the doors." We were all breathing so heavily, the windows fogged up in the chilly evening air almost immediately. Then I did something I had rarely ever done during Paul's past explosions.

I said, "Kids, let's pray for Dad. Only God can deal with him now." We prayed, and then we sat in the truck for another five minutes. Paul did not emerge from the house.

Finally, I felt sure that he was not going to come after us. "Okay," I said to the children, "let's go in and see what the damage is." We started to get out of the truck, and as Lucchese moved out of the middle seat, I noticed the truck keys where she had been sitting. I'm convinced that those concealed keys were no accident; the Lord wanted us to unite and to lean on Him, rather than running away from the situation.

The kids and I walked quietly back into the house and down the hall toward the kitchen. I could hear sounds coming from the kitchen, but they were not the sort of sounds I had come to expect during one of Paul's blowups. I heard the sound of sweeping.

Sure enough, as we drew closer the kids and I saw a sight we will never forget: Paul sweeping up the mess and dumping the ruined casserole in the trash.

As I entered the room, Paul looked up at me, smiled, and said, "Hungry?"

Paul and I both got a lot of ribbing from the kids for that incident. "Mom, you threw that food at Dad!" and "Yeah, Dad; we were really thinking that you'd come out that door and get us" and "Can you believe it? Dad in here sweeping the floor?"

I could believe it. And I rejoiced, because I realized that Paul was not going to hit me. God really had changed his heart. It was more evidence that Paul was a new man.

One of the traits I love and admire most about my husband is his openness to change. When the Holy Spirit convicts him about some sin in his life, that sin becomes revolting to Paul. He hates it and tries his best to deal with it. Similarly, when the Holy Spirit shows Paul a biblical principle that he needs to incorporate into his life, Paul is quick to obey. He has a very teachable spirit. In fact, our friend Hutch says that Paul may have the most teachable spirit he has seen in a long time. As I mentioned earlier, people often ask me why I didn't divorce Paul and make life easier on myself. I suppose I saw what others could not see—that open, teachable spirit, the desire deep inside Paul to love and obey God, and his desire to be rid of the old Paul Luchsinger.

God has taught Paul many important biblical truths—too many to fit into one book. Before I share with you some of the things God has taught me through our marriage troubles, it is only fair that Paul should have a chapter to tell you about one of the most life-changing experiences in our marriage.

Chapter 25

LEARNING THE
HARD WAY

*W*hat does it feel like to slap, kick, or toss around a woman in anger? How does it make a man feel? Believe me, it does not make a guy feel like more of a man. It made me feel like I was the scum of the earth.

Looking back, it is hard for me to believe that I did the awful things that I did to my wife. After the Lord, Susie is the most precious person in the world to me. What caused me to treat her so badly? What was I thinking, feeling, and doing before, during, and after my outbursts of anger directed toward Susie? These are just a few of the questions people want to know when they hear our story, and, frankly, these are some of the tough questions I still ask myself.

Usually, leading up to my temper tantrums, I became extremely quiet and introspective. As Susie said earlier, I was angry at myself for some of the mistakes in judgment I had made. I was angry for allowing us to get into financial bondage. Often I felt guilty for some of my past sins, even though I knew they were forgiven. Sometimes I was mad because I had performed poorly at a rodeo. All of these things weighed heavily on my heart and mind. Since Susie and I weren't good at communicating with each other, instead of talking about what I was feeling, I'd sink into silence. My anger and guilt turned inward and led to further depression. Increasingly, I retreated into my own mind in my attempts to find the answers to my problems. When I started turning inward, I'd lapse back into my upbringing, drawing from the only well I had when it came to dealing with my feelings—the way my mom and dad had treated each other. Unfortunately, that well was filled with contaminated water and cluttered with filthy words such as "leave," "you're so dumb," and all sorts of other hateful words and feelings.

Although I knew in my heart that Susie loved me more than anyone else in the world, more and more, she became the target of my animosity. I'd tear her down in my mind, silently calling her horrible names, and mentally casting aspersions at her. As my anger began to build, I'd start vocalizing some of the demeaning things I was thinking about Susie, calling her names and insulting her out loud.

Our usual pattern went like this: I was already stewing, then Susie would say something that irritated me, or maybe she bucked my opinion or authority. At first, I'd let it slide and act as though it hadn't bothered me, but then something else would happen, or she'd say something else that bugged me. One thing built on another until, finally, some little thing—often totally unrelated to the first thing that had angered me—set me off and I grabbed Susie, threw her down, and started kicking her.

People have asked me, "Paul, how could you do such a thing? What were you thinking about as you were abusing your wife?"

That's just it; I didn't think about it. I merely reacted. Had I taken time to think through my feelings, I would not have responded violently, but, instead, I allowed myself to lose control.

Why didn't I stop after the initial outburst? Domestic violence, like any sin, has a progressive aspect to it. It keeps getting worse. Once I started to express my anger toward my wife in violent ways, each time it went a little further, moving from angry feelings, to thinking hateful thoughts about her, to verbally abusing her, to physically beating on Susie. Had it not been for God using Jim Bode Scott and Ken Hutcherson to intervene, I'm afraid to think how Susie and I might have ended up. Domestic violence does not get better with time; it will increase in frequency and intensity.

Did I know I was doing wrong? Of course. After the first blow, I knew I was wrong. As a man—especially as a Christian man—I knew I was expressing my anger in inappropriate, sinful ways; but while I was doing it, I didn't care. I'm ashamed to admit it, but the truth is, it felt so good to vent my anger that I was oblivious to the pain I was inflicting on Susie. Not until it was all over did I realize how badly I had hurt my wife.

As I was abusing her, my attitude often was, *Our relationship is over, anyhow, so what does it matter? I'm out of here. I'm leaving!* Although I never left, I was tempted to on many occasions. As Susie said earlier, divorce was never a serious option. But in my anger, I thought about it frequently; and at my lowest points of depression, I thought about it constantly.

When I slapped or kicked Susie, my attitude toward her was never, "I'll show you!" or "You're gonna pay for that," or "I'm going to punish you!" No doubt, some perpetrators of domestic violence have those intentions, but I didn't. My thoughts were simply, *I'm angry, and I'm going to take it out on you. You're the cause of my anger.*

I often yelled at Susie, "I hate you! If you just wouldn't do those things, I wouldn't be angry." That was a lie, actually a double lie. First, I didn't hate Susie; I loved her. And second, I was angry within, and nothing Susie said or did caused that. I didn't like myself, so I was taking it out on her.

Interestingly, I rarely got into fights with any of my friends, other than the incident in which I punched Jim Bode and a fist fight I once got into with my brother-in-law, Pake. There was rarely anyone with whom I became so angry that I started swinging or kicking. Usually, if I got mad at someone, that was simply the end of our friendship, and I'd blow them off and forget about them. Yet I allowed myself to get so angry at Susie that I physically abused her. It didn't make any sense.

One minute I'd be furious with her, slapping her, kicking her, and taking out my anger on her, not wanting anything to do with her. The next moment I'd see her as a helpless, hurting woman—my wife, the mother of my children, the woman I love—yet I had done those awful things to her. Immediately, when I came to my senses, I'd feel a deep remorse for my actions and a sincere concern and compassion toward Susie.

I'd apologize to Susie and recommit myself to working harder to control my anger. And I'd do it . . . for awhile. Together, Susie and I tried to find answers through counseling, books, and other sources, but, inevitably, the anger returned.

We knew we needed to do something radical.

In January 1996, Susie and I decided to take a one-year sabbatical and move to the Seattle area to sit under the teaching of Pastor Ken Hutcherson, my mentor, and to fulfill Susie's dream of being home with her family. We felt—and Hutch agreed—that it would be helpful to spend more than a few vacation days together every so often. What I really needed was to watch, listen, and learn from Hutch on a prolonged basis, to be with him in ordinary, day-to-day situations, as well as to see how he operates under pressure. Susie and I didn't regard him as some sort of guru who had all the answers we would ever need, but God had used Hutch in my life to help stop the madness. Maybe Hutch could help me to start doing the things that are right. Susie and I both agreed that it was worth a try.

Through a series of what some people might call coincidences, but what Susie and I consider to be God's amazing goodness to us, we moved to Redmond, Washington, not far from Seattle, and rented a house just down the road from Hutch and Pat. Hutch and I talked by phone or in person almost every day. We spent long hours together, just being open with each other. Hutch enjoys animals almost as much as he enjoys people, so he invited me to keep our horses at his place. At least twice a day, morning and evening, I was over at Hutch's place to feed the horses. He and Pat made themselves available to Susie and me day and night. Of course, our family attended services at the church Hutch pastors, and we became involved in many of the ministry programs of the church. We attended weekly Bible studies, spiritual retreats, and all sorts of other activities with the church. I became involved in Hutch's discipleship group, a small group of men who meet weekly for a concentrated Bible study led by Hutch. In that group, we study nothing but Scripture, not books about the Bible, not Bible lessons or commentaries, just the Bible. Hutch always says that the best commentary on the Bible is the Bible. One of his favorite phrases when talking about Bible study is, "Concentrate and connect." In other words, if you really want to understand the Scriptures, you have to concentrate and study, not merely read the words on the page. But beyond that, it is important to connect one passage of Scripture with the rest of the Bible. The common thread that connects the Scriptures, from Genesis to Revelation, is Jesus Christ. Rather than simply taking a verse here or there and trying to make it fit your lifestyle, Hutch teaches that we are to align our lifestyle with what the Bible says.

Susie became involved in a women's Bible study group, as well as other activities through the church. After a while, since we weren't on the road ourselves as much, Susie even started singing in the church choir.

Throughout 1996, Susie and I grew spiritually by leaps and bounds. Although we had heard many fine pastors and Bible teachers, neither of us had ever experienced having the Scriptures come alive as we did when we listened to Hutch. Part of it can be explained by Hutch's spiritual gifts and anointing; and no doubt, part of it can be attributed to the simple fact that our hearts were open and we were ready to receive what God wanted to teach us.

The climax came in October, when Susie and I attended a marriage seminar taught by Sam and Mary Glynn Peeples. It seemed that all the things that Susie and I had been learning since we had first gotten serious about living the Christian life eighteen years earlier, and everything Hutch had been teaching us for the first nine months of 1996 suddenly came into focus through the Peeples' messages. That seminar changed my life.

For the first time, I saw the reason why I had such difficulty containing my anger. As they taught on Isaiah 53:6, "All we like sheep have gone astray; we have turned every one to his own way; and the LORD hath laid on him the iniquity of us all" (KJV), that Scripture became a mirror to me. Suddenly, I saw myself for how I really was—selfish! And that selfishness was sinful. The Bible teachers pointed out that the root of the problem was not simply my sinful actions but a basic selfish nature within me that cried out, "I want what I want when I want it!" They showed me the difference between my transgressions and my iniquity—the difference between my sinful actions, words, and thoughts—and the nature within me that caused me to be that way. I had always lumped all those negative things together— transgressions, iniquities, they all sounded bad to me. But as a result, no matter how hard I tried to change my exterior actions, I couldn't do it, because my heart had not been changed.

In the past, when I didn't get what I wanted, I'd get mad and blow my stack. Now I understood why that happened. It was my selfish nature rearing its ugly head.

Other people had given me their opinions as to why I lost my temper so easily, and many of their suggestions were helpful, but they never really got to the heart of the matter: Why was that anger there within me, ready to explode at the slightest provocation? Even fine Christian counselors to whom Susie and I had spoken frequently did not deal with the root problem but rather dealt with the symptoms. The symptoms were merely the outward expressions of my anger. Dealing with them alone could not change me. As Hutch often told me, "We're not interested in simply putting a new coat on the person; we want a new person inside the coat." Sitting in the Peeples' seminar, I began to understand what Hutch meant by that.

I realized that in the past, I had wanted Susie to be what I thought she should be; and, of course, she wanted me to be and do what she wanted. No wonder we had problems. We were two selfish people trying to see whose will was going to win. Since I was bigger, stronger, and louder, my selfish way usually won. Marriage isn't designed to work that way. God made us both special in unique ways. As we come together in mutual cooperation, and put our own selfish natures to death, we submit to each other. As I submit to God, Susie submits to me—and that's a wonderful thing when a godly woman is submitted to a godly man. But I couldn't change Susie. In fact, contrary to pop psychology that told me I couldn't change anyone else but myself, I now saw from the Scripture that I was unable even to change myself! Fortunately, the seminar did not stop there.

As I listened to Dr. and Mrs. Peeples, I was reminded of the answer to my problem, an answer so simple that I had been missing it. I don't mean

to be trite, but the answer is *Jesus*. One of the most loved and quoted verses in the Bible says, "For God so loved the world, that he gave His only
begotten Son, that whosoever believeth in Him should not perish, but
have everlasting life" (John 3:16, KJV).

As I listened to the Peeples teach, I realized that for years I had been
trying to be good on my own, instead of trusting Christ to be good through
me. I had tried to *act* like Jesus, instead of *being* like Jesus—or better yet,
allowing Him to be Himself in and through me. I had been trying my best
to control my own anger, instead of submitting my will to Christ and allowing Him to deal with my anger. While it may seem simple to some people,
the truth hit me like a lightning bolt that my only job—really the only
thing that I *can* do—is to submit my will to the lordship of Jesus Christ on
a moment-by-moment basis. That means He's the boss. He's in charge.
When things go well and even when they don't, Jesus is still Lord of my
life.

In a practical sense, whatever Jesus would do is what I want to do. And
whatever Jesus would not do, I shouldn't do either. Jesus certainly would
not go around kicking or slapping a woman. Why? Because His will was
submitted to the heavenly Father's will. That is the way my will is to be on
a daily basis, as well.

One of the most helpful aspects of the Peeples' message was their
emphasis on "maintenance," keeping our wills submitted to Christ and our
spiritual lives together on a consistent basis. They referred to Proverbs 4:23,
"Keep your heart with all diligence, For out of it spring the issues of life"
(NKJV). I began to understand that I had to keep my heart in a right relationship with God. I couldn't depend on Susie, Hutch, Jim Bode, or anyone else to do that for me. I was responsible to submit my will to the Lord.
King David once prayed, "Search me, O God, and know my heart; Try me
and know my anxious thoughts; And see if there be any hurtful way in me"
(Psalm 139:23–24, NASB). I have to do the same thing. I have to ask God
to search my heart. I have to be willing to say, "Okay, God, what do you
want me to do? Even if I am *right* in this situation, how do I need to handle it?"

In the past, if I thought I was right about something, there was no discussing it. My attitude was, "I'm right, by golly, and everyone is going to line up and we're going to do this thing the right way." I may have been right, but my attitude stank. And everyone in our family suffered because of my rotten attitude. If I didn't get my way with Susie, I'd simply fly off the handle, and before long she would fall in line. My actions were selfish, sinful, and totally wrong.

Susie didn't make me angry. I had an angry, bitter heart. As Dr. Peeples put it, "The circumstances or the events of life, or the people around me, do not make me the way I am. They *reveal* the way I am." If I have anger or bitterness in my heart, it is going to come out when the pressure is on. But if my heart is pure before God, and filled with Christ's love, when the pressure comes, the only thing that will come out is His love. That's what I want.

Dr. Peeples helped me to understand that when I confessed my sin to Christ, He forgave me and cleansed my heart just as the Bible says, "If we confess our sins, he is faithful and just to forgive us our sins, and to cleanse us from all unrighteousness" (1 John 1:9, NKJV). At that point, I was pure before God. To stay that way, I need to avoid some things.

According to Psalm 1:1, "Blessed is the man Who walks not in the counsel of the ungodly, Nor stands in the path of sinners, Nor sits in the seat of the scornful" (NKJV). From this passage, I realized that I could not do things the way I had in the past. I could not walk in the counsel of the ungodly and do things the way "the world" handles them. Nor could I stand in the path of sinners, which to me meant that I could not hang around with people who are content to live their lives in disobedience to God, or even those who will allow me to be disobedient to Him. I want to be around people who will help keep me accountable to them, to my family, and most of all, to God.

The third part of Psalm 1:1, "don't sit in the seat of the scornful," spoke to me as well. I realized that I did not dare to be around angry, scornful people because their attitudes and actions could easily rub off on me. When I have to be around someone who is angry, I can try to challenge that person to deal with his or her anger; but if they refuse, I have no choice but to remove myself from their presence.

Positively, Dr. Peeples taught us that we should meditate on God's Word day and night (see Ps. 1:2). When I think on God's law and start applying it in my life, the Scripture says that I will be like a tree planted by rivers of water and shall produce His fruit in his time (Ps. 1:3). The fruit of God's Spirit is love, and His love never fails. Every day, God wants to replace my anger, bitterness, resentment, or other ugly characteristics with His holy love.

Another spiritual principle that has helped me overcome my anger is found in 2 Corinthians 10:5, "Take captive every thought" (NIV). Also, the Scripture says to think on "whatever things are true, whatever things are noble, whatever things are just, whatever things are pure, whatever things are lovely, whatever things are of good report, if there is any virtue and if there is anything praiseworthy—meditate on these things" (Phil. 4:8, KJV). To me, that means any thought that I have that does not line up with those Scriptures must be discarded. If I feel myself getting angry, I stop and think, *Do I have a right to be mad? Okay, maybe I do. Is this the appropriate time and manner to express that anger? Or do I need to realize that maybe Susie is just having a rough day and needs a hug to help her make it through?*

All of the things Susie and I were learning worked together to help revamp my heart, mind, and actions. It's difficult and probably unwise to place one incident above the others, since what was important for me might not be the most important for someone else. But God used all these things to bring me into the place with Him where He wanted me to be.

Why me? Why did I fly off the handle so easily when so many other men did not? Certainly, my personality traits and my psychological makeup have influenced my actions. In addition, the way I react to people and circumstances is a product of my environment. Obviously, my home life as I grew up has had an impact on the way I have behaved in my marriage. Ultimately, however, I have to take responsibility for my own actions. I can't and don't blame anyone else.I must own my sin

Thankfully, today I no longer have to be the kind of man I once was. I have been changed by the power of Jesus Christ. Yes, I still get angry, but my violent responses are gone. Interestingly, I have come to understand that anger itself is not always wrong. Quoting the Old Testament (Ps. 4:4), the apostle Paul wrote, "Be angry, and do not sin" (Eph. 4:26, NKJV). When I first considered that verse, it sounded like a contradiction to me. How could I possibly be angry and not sin? I was used to my anger leading to sin. The big issue, I came to realize, was: What am I angry about? Am I angry because God's name has been insulted? Or am I angry because somebody doesn't see things just the way I do, and I feel insulted? Much of my anger toward Susie fell into the second category. I'd get mad at her simply because she didn't agree with me on something.

As I studied the Bible, I discovered that when Jesus got angry it was because religious people were misusing God's name or His house, or they were taking advantage of someone. Jesus never defended His own person. He never lashed out at others with angry outbursts simply to protect His own ego or pride. His anger was holy. In contrast, I was defending myself, my ego, my pride, and that was sinful anger.

These days, I am learning how to deal with my anger on a day-by-day basis. The potential to explode is still with me, but I have learned to recognize the warning signs. Recently, for instance, Susie and I were at church on a Wednesday night and our children were in their classes in a separate building. At the close of the service, Hutch invited members of the congregation to the front of the sanctuary to pray. I wanted to respond, but Susie said, "We need to go get the kids." I told Susie that I wanted to go down front and pray. Susie grabbed my arm hard and said again, "I said we need to go get the kids, now." Her words and her tone of voice grated against me. I could feel anger sweep over me like a hot wax in a car wash.

I knew what time it was, and I also knew that we were always among the first parents to pick up our children after church every week. I didn't see the harm in taking time to pray, as our pastor had requested.

Susie and I were moving toward the front of the church. She scratched at my arm and said, "Give me the keys; I'll go get the kids."

I could see that she wasn't going to back down, so I replied angrily, "I'll go get the kids!" Susie stayed in the sanctuary, and I drove to the building where our kids were in class. When I got there, I had to wait about ten minutes because the kids' classes weren't over yet. That made me even madder.

On the way home, I was silent. We had a friend riding along with us, so Susie carried on a conversation with our friend while I stewed. When we got home, I went out immediately to feed the horses, still not saying a word. In the old days, I would have allowed the anger to continue to fester for days or weeks until the least little thing caused me to explode in violence. But that night, as we gathered in E. P. and Samuel's room to pray as a family, I was sitting on the bed, and I said to Susie, "I'm ticked."

Susie knew immediately what I was talking about and began to defend herself, but I stopped her short and said, "I don't want to hear any excuses. I just want you to know that I am angry about what happened tonight."

In years past, my words might have struck fear into the hearts of Susie and the kids. Not any more. My family knows that with the Holy Spirit's help, my anger stays under control. We went ahead and prayed, and then Susie and I went to our bedroom. We talked briefly about what had happened, and we apologized to each other for the way we had handled the situation, and then it was over. No broken furniture. No building steam. It was out on the table, we talked about it, and it was done.

Occasionally, the kids will remind me of my past actions, especially when I discipline them for some minor infraction. Once, not long ago, E. P. and Lucchese got into an argument and I told them I didn't want to hear any more talk like that. They continued to get at each other, until I finally got fed up with it. We were having company, so I warned them, "If I hear one cross word, from either one of you, E. P., I'm going to tie your right hand to Lucchese's left hand, and your right leg to her left leg. Then you will have to get along and work together."

E. P., now in his early teens and already as big as I am, turned around and challenged me, "Well, what about when you and Mom argue? Why don't you tie yourselves together?"

He had me cornered there for a while. He was right. Nevertheless, I told him, "Look, I am the authority here. You are to submit to that authority. We're not talking about your mom and me, we're talking about you and your sister." Still, deep down, I wished that I had a better answer. The next time I talked with Hutch, I mentioned E. P.'s point.

Hutch laughed and said, "Tell him that you're tied to Susie for life; he'd only be tied to his sister for a few hours."

Not long after that, E. P. raised the issue again: "What about when you and Mom argue?"

I told him, "E. P., your mom and I are tied to each other for life. We have to work out our differences. You and your sister are only here for a few more years—and you *will* work out your differences."

As in this situation, Hutch has been an invaluable source of practical wisdom and help to Susie and me. Although he does not sit down with us in a formal counseling situation, he gives us open access to his life, night and day. He has taught me by example how to deal with potential powder keg situations.

As Susie and I travel the country, sharing our story and the power of Jesus Christ to change lives, inevitably we meet men and women who are involved in domestic violence. Often, a man will come to me after one of our services and say something such as, "Paul, I can relate to what you said, and I have been allowing anger to get the best of me. But what can I do about it?"

Usually, I'll try to help the man see that much of his anger stems from a basic selfishness within us—that I want what I want and I want it now attitude. None of us can adequately deal a death blow to our own selfishness. To do so would go against our basic instincts of survival. We can, however, surrender to Jesus Christ, then day by day allow His Spirit to give us His character—the fruit of the Holy Spirit. Where the Spirit of the Lord is, there is liberty and true love. And as the Scripture says, "There is no fear in love; but perfect love casts out fear" (1 John 4:18, NKJV).

Chapter 26

A TENDER ROAD HOME

*O*ne of the questions that is often asked of me is why I never told anyone about the abuse that was going on in our home. During the worst times of our marriage, I never went for help. I did not call the police, nor did I tell a single soul that Paul was abusing me, until the night I told Marcie. If I had mustered the courage to do so, I honestly believe that we could have avoided a lot of emotional hurt and physical pain. As I said before, part of the reason I did not seek counseling or assistance of any sort was that Paul was always so sorry after the abusive incidents were over. He wasn't merely pretending to be sorry. He really was.

But he didn't change. That's where I was wrong to allow him to continue abusing me without going for help. It was a serious mistake on my part. I have repented of it, and I have publicly said that I was wrong to enable the abuse to go on. Now, when anyone tells me that they are in an abusive situation, I tell them to seek professional help immediately.

Call a pastor, or a close friend, or a professional counselor, but don't try to go it alone. Most cities and counties now have domestic violence agencies that offer free, confidential assistance. In the back of this book you will find toll-free telephone numbers of some national agencies that offer help to someone involved in abuse, both the abused person and the person who is doing the abusing.

I cannot overestimate the value of going for counseling if you are having troubles in your marriage. When Paul and I went to Elijah House in Idaho for a week of intense marriage counseling, it was one of the first steps toward getting our marriage back on track. The sessions were mostly common sense, but just hearing the suggestions and ideas from another source besides ourselves made it easier for Paul and me to first talk about the problems and then take some of the steps the counselors suggested.

The counselors at Elijah House told Paul that he was like a teakettle that would build up pressure and eventually blow, if he did not learn to let off steam in constructive ways. They told Paul, "You have to learn to diffuse yourself by expressing your feelings. Don't be afraid to say, 'Susie, it bothers me when you do this or that.' " They also gave us a lot of suggested words for Paul and me to use in expressing our feelings. We probably did not incorporate many of those words at first, but we have pulled them into our vocabulary over the years.

During our year-long sabbatical in the Seattle area, Paul was doing some part-time work building a house along with Matt Clay, one of our friends, and some other men. One day, I went to the job to take Paul his lunch. I noticed that Paul was nice to everybody else in the group, but he was cold toward me. That night, when Paul came home, I said to him, "You know, I feel like you have friendliness for everybody but me."

Paul looked at me and smiled. It had never dawned on him. Then he came over and gave me a big hug and said he was sorry.

In the past, my comment would have been a trigger for a big fight. Either that, or I simply would not have said anything and would have absorbed the hurt. That would have allowed it to fester into bitterness and resentment. I would have cowered someplace and nursed my self-pity, thinking, *He doesn't really like me.* Now, at least, we are able to place any such little irritations on the table and deal with them. And while that may not seem like much to some people, believe me, that is definitely progress for us!

In recent years, we have also received some great ideas from Jeff and Nancy Jernigan, counselors from the highly regarded Minirth-Meier Clinic. Their emphasis has dealt more with Paul's and my differences in personality and the need to realize that we do not respond to life in the same ways. For instance, Paul is an extreme extrovert, while I am an extreme introvert. Paul loves to be with people; they energize him and make him feel good about himself and life in general. I am just the opposite; I need time alone. Even though I enjoy ministering to crowds of people, when I am done, I need to allow myself quiet time to get recharged. Otherwise, I will be continually drained.

Jeff and Nancy taught us that we need to accept each other for who we are, and more importantly, that God accepts us and loves us for who we are. We do not have to constantly be proving that we are acceptable to God. This was especially helpful to Paul, who all his life has felt that he had to prove how tough he was in order to be accepted.

Whatever you do, if you are involved in an abusive situation, seek help. Please don't think that going for help is a sign of weakness, or that it is a poor reflection upon your Christian testimony. I suffered in silence for far too many years, as did Paul. Although he was the perpetrator, the abuse took a toll on both of us. Had we not broken that silence, we might still be entangled in abuse today. Either that, or one or both of us might be dead. Yes, it is that serious.

Another important suggestion for any wife who is a victim of abuse: pray for another man to come into your husband's life to whom he can be accountable. Paul and I thank God for sending to us two such men in Jim Bode Scott and Pastor Ken Hutcherson, men who were willing to get involved in our lives.

Certainly, the idea of being accountable to someone else is nothing new; twelve-step programs such as Alcoholics Anonymous have long used positive peer pressure to help keep their members on the straight and narrow. But there is something even more powerful about Christian men becoming accountable to one another to the point that they are willing to honestly admit their greatest fears, areas of vulnerability, and need for

God's supernatural help to overcome the temptations in their lives. Having one man in particular whom your husband respects and to whom he can be accountable concerning his actions will be a major step in stopping the abuse in your home.

A word to single women: If you are in an abusive relationship with a man, get out of that relationship. Run, don't walk; run as far as you must to get away from that man. You are not married. You are not legally or morally bound to stay with that person. Don't allow yourself to be emotionally intimidated into staying. If a man is beating on you, taunting you, demeaning you, or abusing you verbally or emotionally *before* you are married, you can be sure that the abusiveness is an ingrained facet of his personality. It will not get better once the two of you get married, but rather it will get much worse.

If you are the perpetrator of abuse of any kind, please, please, for your own good and for the good of those loved ones around you, seek help. Take some simple steps today to start on a tender road home. Call a Bible-believing pastor, call a domestic violence hotline, but please, do not ignore the problem. It will not simply go away by itself. Most of all, call out to Jesus Christ. His power is stronger than the power that is being manifested in your anger and violence. He can set you free. He has promised, "You shall know the truth, and the truth shall make you free. If therefore the Son shall make you free, you shall be free indeed" (John 8:32, 36, NASB).

Maybe you know somebody whom you suspect is being abused and you are wondering what you can do to help. First, keep your eyes open for telltale signs of abuse. Obviously, visible bruises and cuts on your friend or family member's body should set off the sirens in your mind. Keep in mind, though, that many abusers are devious and avoid marking the body of the person they are abusing, at least not in a readily visible location. I don't think Paul did it intentionally, but he was wary enough that he rarely hit me around the face where marks could be seen. Instead he kicked me, and although the bruises were not visible to the public, I hurt just as badly. *More importantly, the emotional pain was just as devastating, regardless of the location of the blows. Verbal abuse and demeaning remarks make a woman feel small, worthless, and useless.*

Does it ever all just go away? Not really. God has forgiven Paul and me, and we have forgiven each other for the mistakes we have made in our marriage, but we will always have a history of abuse in our past. We will continually be explaining our actions to our children as they grow older and more able to understand the nightmare we have all lived through. Our kids have already developed a healthy sense of humor about Paul's renewal. When Paul says or does something that reminds them of our past experiences, they will sometimes joke with Paul, saying, "Dad, do you remember when you hit that door and knocked a hole in it, or the time you kicked in the bottom of the door?" or "Do you remember when you tore up Mama's rocking chair?" In a way, being able to laugh about some of these things with our children causes Paul to be accountable to them as well as to Jim Bode, Hutch, himself, and to me.

Nevertheless, Paul and I do not feel that we have arrived, that we have learned everything we need to know in order to have a happy home. We don't feel that we have conquered every foe, and can now sit back and relax until we get to heaven.

No way. We continue to aggressively pursue those things that are going to make our marriage better—attending a marriage retreat, attending a marriage class at Sunday school, reading books about how we can improve our marriage, going to church together as a family, and having a time of Bible reading and prayer together as a family and as husband and wife. We also regularly re-evaluate our schedule and ask, "Does God really want us to be involved in this activity? doing this? going there? Is this something that will bring us closer together as a couple and as a family, or will it cause us to be driven apart?" Our goal is to do only those things that will draw us closer to the Lord and to each other.

Over the years, we've tried to establish some good, positive memories with our children, of special times that we hope will overshadow or at least balance the memories they carry from some of the things they have seen and heard in our home during their early childhood years. We believe so strongly in doing these things that we would do them even if the abuse had never happened. Establishing good memories develops our family relationships.

Mealtime is a special time around the Luchsinger household every day. As much as possible, we try to sit down and eat together as a family—with no television in the background and as few distractions as possible. Every so often we even have a "special night" during dinner. I cook one of the family favorites, and we put our best candles on the table. We get out the fancy wine glasses and fill them with sparkling apple cider. The telephone goes unanswered, and we concentrate on each other and what's going on in our lives. It is a relaxed, unhurried time together that takes priority over all other activities that night.

Another special time for us is playing hide-and-go-seek. Most people who play this favorite old game play it outside. The Luchsingers play it in the house . . . . at night . . . with all the lights turned off. We have discovered some unusual hiding places such as under the pillows at the head of the bed, or under the bean bags (that was a hard one for me!). Paul is the master at coming up with "secret" hiding places. Once he climbed on top of the upright freezer. The kids and I searched for fifteen minutes before we finally looked up and found Paul's perch. Another time, he slipped behind the clothes hanging in the closet. We almost never found him.

Playing hide-and-go-seek in the dark, of course, is a raucous time, with lots of yelling, pushing, and laughing. "I touched base!" "I got there first!" "You didn't get me!" Anyone going past our house at night during our game might really wonder about us. But that's okay; we're making special memories.

Do I ever fear that the "old Paul, the abusive, controlling Paul," will one day return to wreak havoc in our family again?

Sometimes.

One night Samuel was working on a little wooden car for a car race that our church was sponsoring for the children. The idea was for the children to get their family members to help them put the car together, sand it, and paint it. Lucchese and E. P. excitedly volunteered to help Samuel paint his model car. Paul too offered to help.

I watched as the family gathered in our den. The kids got out all the paints and started to work on Samuel's car. They were having a wonderful time ... until Paul got involved.

"Now, Samuel," Paul instructed, "you only paint in one direction. Only go in one direction. Did you hear me? One direction."

It was as though a lead balloon had suddenly descended upon our house. It was like, "Uh-oh, here we go again. Dad has to control the situation. What fun this is!" But this time, it was different. Paul had told us all to keep him accountable for his actions, so in their own way, the kids did so. They backed off and moved away from Paul and Samuel.

E. P. was the first to get up and leave. Although he was only thirteen, he was a big, strapping boy, almost as big as his dad now. As he walked past me, I winked at him to let him know that I understood what was happening. E. P. went over to our family computer and began playing one of the computer games.

I didn't say anything, but I began to pray silently, *Lord, please reveal to Paul what he's doing.*

Soon, Lucchese and I joined E. P. at the computer playing games. Lucchese looked at me and said in her inimitable way, "Mama, this makes me *so* nervous!" I laughed quietly and said, "I know, honey. It makes me nervous, too."

Meanwhile Paul was still scolding Samuel about how to paint his model car. "Samuel, I told you, only paint in one direction!"

A few minutes later, Paul looked around and suddenly realized that all of his excited painters had disappeared. He began to understand what he had done by taking control of the kids' fun. He lightened up on Samuel, then called to the rest of us, "Okay, well, maybe Lucchese and E. P. want to paint the hood. Come on, kids. I'll sit back, and you can take over helping Samuel." Lucchese and E. P. once again jumped at the chance to help paint the car.

Paul went over and sat down on the floor in front of the sofa. I went over to him, gave him a big hug, and said, "Yep, for a while I was thinking about writing a story about how to make family memories with the Luchsingers."

Paul and I both laughed. "Yeah, I was pretty demanding there for a while, wasn't I?"

"Yeah, you were certainly in control of the whole situation." We laughed again. Just being able to recognize Paul's controlling tendencies and being able to laugh about them was a major victory for us.

These days our family is doing wonderfully well. God has been so good to us. He has filled our home with a new love, a love far greater than we had ever known before.

Will Paul ever lose his temper again? Will he ever hit me again?

I don't believe he will. At least, not today—and by the grace of God, not tomorrow, or the next day, or ever again. Granted, we must be wise enough to take the steps to avoid conflict and to diffuse potential problems before they get out of hand. But even more important, Jesus is the Peace within us; He provides the peace for Paul and for our children and for me. And it is His peace that we depend upon.

His way truly is a tender road home.

SOURCES OF HELP

If you are either a victim or a perpetrator of domestic violence, here are some sources where you can receive confidential information and help. Please do not ignore a violent situation in your home. Take action. Start by talking things over with your local pastor or talking with a trusted friend. Pray and ask God to guide you to the right resources and people who can best address your situation.

God Bless You!

Susie and Paul Luchsinger

The National Organization for Victim Assistance	800-879-6682
The National Resource Center on Domestic Violence	800-537-2238
Office for Victims of Crime Resource Center	800-627-6872
Marriage Savers Resource Collection	815-987-3970

Be sure to look for Domestic Violence Agencies in your local area. They may be able to provide more immediate help.

Coming Soon:

A new exciting recording from Susie Luchsinger

A *Tender Road Home*

Enjoy these other Susie Luchsinger albums:

> *Come As You Are* (Integrity)
> *Real Love* (Integrity)
> *No Limit* (Psalms Ministries, Inc.)
> *Christmas Everyday* (Psalms Ministries, Inc.)
> *God's Still in Control* ((Psalms Ministries, Inc.)
> *First Things First* (MESA)
> *Lift Up the Name of Jesus* (Psalms Ministries, Inc.)
> *Come Bless the Lord* (Psalms Ministries, Inc.)
> *Susie McEntire Luchsinger* (Psalms Ministries, Inc.)

If you are interested in having Paul and Susie Luchsinger speak and sing at your church or other special event, contact Psalms Ministries at (405) 889-5219.